William Lyman Fawcett

Gold and debt

an American hand-book of finance, with over eighty tables and diagrams illustrative of the following subjects: the dollar and other units; paper money in the United States and Europe. Second Edition

William Lyman Fawcett

Gold and debt
an American hand-book of finance, with over eighty tables and diagrams illustrative of the following subjects: the dollar and other units; paper money in the United States and Europe. Second Edition

ISBN/EAN: 9783744741422

Printed in Europe, USA, Canada, Australia, Japan

Cover: Foto ©Suzi / pixelio.de

More available books at **www.hansebooks.com**

GOLD AND DEBT;

AN AMERICAN

HAND-BOOK OF FINANCE,

WITH OVER EIGHTY TABLES AND DIAGRAMS ILLUSTRATIVE
OF THE FOLLOWING SUBJECTS:

THE DOLLAR AND OTHER UNITS; PAPER MONEY IN THE UNITED STATES AND EUROPE; GOLD AND SILVER IN THE UNITED STATES AND EUROPE; SUSPENSIONS OF SPECIE PAYMENTS; THE ERA OF GOLD; VALUES OF THE PRECIOUS METALS; THE ERA OF DEBT; THE RISE AND FALL OF PRICES;

ALSO, A DIGEST OF THE

MONETARY LAWS OF THE UNITED STATES.

BY W. L. FAWCETT.

SECOND EDITION.

CHICAGO:
S. C. GRIGGS AND COMPANY.
1879.

KNIGHT & LEONARD, PRINTERS, CHICAGO.

A. ZEESE & CO., ELECTROTYPERS, CHI.

PREFACE.

THE author's first object in this book was the compilation, in a compact form, convenient for reference, of trustworthy statements and figures regarding the great factors in the financial problems of the day, and to which reference is continually made in financial discussions, viz.: the increase and decrease of the volume of paper money at various periods in the United States and in Europe during the last fifty years; the production of gold and silver, and the consumption of these metals in the arts since the beginning of the era of gold in 1849; the additions to the world's stock of gold and silver used as money, and the amounts now in use in all countries; and the increase of debts and traffic in this age of steam; also, in the compilation of monetary laws of the United States, to set forth in the language of the laws themselves the nature of the contract between the government as a borrower and the note and bond holders as creditors.

Whatever of a theoretic nature there is in the following pages has not been prompted by any preconceived notions, nor written in advocacy of any scheme for ameliorating the financial troubles of the times, but has in each case been incidental to the statement of the facts. If others, upon the basis of the same facts, should arrive at different conclusions, it should not render this compilation of facts any the less valuable as a book of reference, which it was the author's aim to make.

CHICAGO, Dec. 6, 1876.

TABLE OF CONTENTS.

THE DOLLAR AND OTHER UNITS.

Monetary units of all countries (Tables 4, 5 and 6), - - 259–264
In many cases only ideal coins, - - - - - 15
The pound sterling and the dollar as, - - - - - 17–19
The dollar — origin of the dollar symbol, - - - - 13
Origin of the name, - - - - - - - - - - - 22
American — of the Confederation, - - - - - 19, 170
American — of the United States, - - - - - 17, 171
Reduction in value of United States dollars in 1837, 21–175
Abolition of the American silver dollar, - - - - 180
The London Stock Exchange dollar, - - - - 25
The "dollar" in Frankfort and Paris, - - - - - 26
Ideal moneys, - - - - - - - - - - - - - 49
Of international exchange, - - - - - - - - 19
Of the mediæval banks, - - - - - - - - 38
Change from a silver to a gold currency in the United States in 1837, - - - - - - - - - - - 21
Similar changes in France in 1785 and Austria in 1857, - 21

PAPER MONEY AND COIN IN THE UNITED STATES.

Paper money and coin in the United States, - - - - 27
Table of the amounts of each in use each year from 1854 to 1876, - - - - - - - - - - - - 34, 35
Period of greatest contraction, - - - - - - - 32
Amount of coin in the United States, 1854 to 1876, - 35
The United States banks, - - - - - - - - - - 55
Estimated number of each class of banks in the United States in 1875, and the aggregate of their deposits, - 36

PAPER MONEY IN EUROPE.

Paper money in Europe, - - - - - - - - 38
Invention of, - - - - - - - - - - 40
First used in Sweden, - - - - - - - - 40
Table of amounts in Great Britain at various periods, - 43
France at various periods, - - - - - 44
Germany at various periods, - - - - - - 44
Austria, - - - - - - - - - - - 46
Russia, - - - - - - - - - - - - 48
Italy, - - - - - - - - - - - 49
Switzerland, - - - - - - - - - - 51
Table of aggregate in Europe, - - - - - - 52
Increase of in Europe, - - - - - - - - - 52
Great banks of Europe, - - - - - - - - - 49
Banks of Venice, Barcelona, Genoa, Amsterdam, etc., 38
Bank of England, - - - - - - - - - 40
Joint-stock banks in Great Britain, - - - - - 40
Bank of France, - - - - - - - - - 43–57
Specie in, - - - - - - - - - - 70, 85
Imperial Bank of Germany, - - - - - - 44
Bank of the Empire of Russia, - - - - - - 47
National Bank of Italy, - - - - - - - - 49–60
National Bank of Spain, - - - - - - - - 50
Banks in Switzerland, - - - - - - - - 51
Bank of Belgium, - - - - - - - - - 51
Banks in Sweden, - - - - - - - - - - 52

SUSPENSIONS OF SPECIE PAYMENTS IN ALL COUNTRIES.

Suspensions in the United States, - - - - - - - 54
The Bank of the United States, - - - - - 55
The suspension of 1862, - - - - - - - - 55
Depreciation in value of the currency each year, - 56
In Great Britain, 1791 to 1821, - - - - - - - 57
Of the Bank of France in 1848 and 1870, - - - - 57
Remarkably slight depreciation of the notes of the Bank of France (see note to page 557), - - - - - 58
Austria, - - - - - - - - - - - - - - 59
Italy, - - - - - - - - - - - - - - 60
Russia, - - - - - - - - - - - - - - 48, 61

Brazil, - - - - - - - - - - - - 61, 89
Various effects of on value of currency, - - - - 62
Inconvertible paper money—three causes affecting its value, 62
Its increase in value by reason of scarcity of any other medium of exchange, - - - - - - - - 63
Its stimulating effects on industry and trade, - - - 64

GOLD AND SILVER COIN IN EUROPE.

Estimated stock of gold and silver in Great Britain, - - 66
France, - - - - - - - - - - - - 67–72
Germany, - - - - - - - - - - - 72–75
The method adopted by the author of this book for approximating the amount of gold and silver in each country, 75–80
Table of approximate amount of coin in each country in Europe, - - - - - - - - - - 82
All estimates in regard to Asia entirely conjectural, - 95
Lavish use of both gold and silver in Asia for personal ornaments (foot notes), - - - - - - - 92, 93
The stock of gold and silver in Asia not a source of supply for Europe or America, - - - - - - 92, 93
Probable stock of gold and silver coin in the world, - - 95

AVERAGE RATIO OF NATIONAL REVENUE TO VOLUME OF MONEY IN USE IN ALL COUNTRIES.

The ratio of national revenue to the total volume of money in all countries, - - - - - - - - - 78
Table showing the uniformity in the proportions of money and national revenue per capita of the population in all countries, - - - - - - - - - - 78
The average amount of annual national revenue about 38 to 40 per cent of the total volume of money in use, - 79
Striking illustration of the above rule in the proportions of annual revenue to the volume of money in use in the United States each year from 1866 to 1876 (note to page 243), - - - - - - - - - - 79

COIN AND PAPER MONEY IN THE WORLD.

Total of paper money and coin in Europe, - - - - 83
United States, - - - - - - - - - - 34, 35

Canada, - - - - - - - - - - - - 87
Mexico, - - - - - - - - - - - - 88
Brazil, - - - - - - - - - - - - 88
South America, - - - - - - - - - - 90
Asia, - - - - - - - - - - - - - 95
The World, - - - - - - - - - - - 95
Diagram showing the approximate volume of paper money in the world each year from 1845 to 1875, and the *relative* decrease in the amount of gold and silver, - 128, 129

THE ERA OF GOLD.

The average annual product of gold prior to about 1825 was thirteen millions to fifteen millions dollars, - - 98
Increased to about forty-three millions dollars per annum between 1825 and 1848, - - - - - - 98
The great increase from the placers of California and Australia mark the beginning of the era of gold, - 99
Table of the product in the various quarters of the globe, - 101
Product of gold and silver in the United States, - - 102
Annual consumption of gold in the arts —Table of, - - 114
Jacob's estimate in 1830, - - - - - - - 108
McCulloch's estimate in 1857, - - - - - - 109
Author's estimate of total annual production, consumption and addition to stock in the world from 1840 to 1875, 110
Diagram showing estimated production and consumption of gold and silver, - - - - - - - - - 114, 115
Production, consumption and exports of silver for the United States, - - - - - - - - - - - - 112
Annual movement of silver to Asia, - - - - - 96–111
The end of the golden era about 1862, - - - - - 145

VALUES OF THE PRECIOUS METALS.

The values of gold and silver largely adventitious, - - 134, 139
Great changes in, - - - - - - - - - - 142
Depreciation in, from 1849 to 1854, - - - - - 129
Cause of the decline of silver with the decline of gold after 1849, - - - - - - - - - - - - 133
Relative values of gold and silver, in accordance with the experience of two hundred years, - - - - - 139

Tables of relative values of gold and silver, - - - 141, 142
Diagram showing the course of relative values from 1840 to 1876, - - - - - - - - - - 151, 152
Table of the relative legal values of gold and silver in various countries, - - - - - - - - 144
Relative values of gold and silver in the United States by the law of 1792, - - - - - - - 140, 171
The Latin Monetary Union, - - - - - - - - 144, 145
Demonetization of silver in Great Britain in 1816, - 145
Effects in 1872–3 of the British law of 1816, - - - 145
The exclusive gold standard of values impossible for all nations, - - - - - - - - - - 137
Exclusive standards of either metal in different countries inimical to the comity of nations, - - - - - 138
Report of the British Parliamentary Commission of 1876 on the depreciation of silver, - - - - - - 135

THE ERA OF DEBT.

Growth of national debts in the last twenty-five years, - 115
Railroad debts of the United States and of the world, 117
Municipal debts in the United States and Europe, - 118
American State and county debts, - - - - - - 121
Aggregate of funded debts in the world, - - - - - 122
Impossibility of liquidation, - - - - - - - 122
Aggregate annual interest, - - - - - - - 123
Lower rates of interest the necessary consequence of previous high rates, - - - - - - - - - - 122
Seven thousand millions of war debts created in eleven years, from 1860 to 1871, - - - - - - - 148
The difference between the burden of war debts and the debts of enterprise, - - - - - - - 133, 134
Narrow views of financiers and statesmen on the question of great debts, - - - - - - - - - 148

PRICES OF COMMODITIES IN GOLD.

Table of the rise in average prices from 1849 to 1854. The latter compared with 1875, - - - - - - 130, 131
Cause of the great rise of prices from 1862 to 1867, - - 131
Causes of the reaction in 1872–3, - - - - - - 134

Diagram showing the course of prices of commodities from 1840 to 1875, - - - - - - - - - 141, 142

PROGRESS OF THE AGE.

Traffic has nearly quadrupled in twenty-five years, - - 124
Increase in the value of railroad tonnage, - - - - 126
Table of the railroad mileage of each country in the world, 117
Increase of bank clearings in the United States and England, - - - - - - - - - - - 124, 125
Extent of the economization of currency by the clearing-house system, - - - - - - - - - 126
Agencies at work toward a new financial era, - - 147

MONETARY LAWS OF THE UNITED STATES.

Revision of the laws of the United States in 1873, - - 167
Coinage laws—all the clauses of all laws relating to the *weight, fineness* and *legal-tender value* of United States and foreign coins, from 1781 to 1876, chronologically arranged, - - - - - - - - - 170-182
The silver dollar the unit, - - - - - 170, 171, 175, 176
Half dollars, their legal weights and values, - - - 171, 175
Reduction in value of half dollars and other fractional coins. Fractional coins no longer legal-tender for more than five dollars, - - - - - - - - - - 177
Eagles, - - - - - - - - - - - - - 171, 175
Change in the value of, in 1837, - - - - - 171, 175
The gold dollar authorized, - - - - - - - 176
Made the unit of values, - - - - - - - 180
The trade dollar, - - - - - - - - - - 180, 181
Legal method of computing the value of the pound sterling, 182
Laws authorizing the issue and redemption of United States notes and bonds, chronologically arranged, from 1860 to 1876, - - - - - - - - - - - 183–202
United States notes made legal-tender for all debts, except duties on imports and interest on the public debt; Acts Feb. 25, 1862; July 11, 1862, and March 3, 1863. - - - - - - - - 186, 189, 190, 191
Made receivable the same as coin for all loans negotiated by the United States; Act Feb. 25, 1862, - 186

Made receivable in *payment of* all loans made to the United States; Act July 11, 1862, - - - - 188
Sinking Fund Act of Feb. 25, 1862, - - - - - - 187
Pacific railroad bonds, - - - - - - - - - 187
Amendment to Pacific Railroad Act of July 2, 1864, - - 194
Public Credit Act, - - - - - - - - - - - 197
Funding Act of July 14, 1870, - - - - - - - 197
Specie Resumption Act of Jan. 14, 1875, - - - 200
Subsidiary Silver Coin Law of July 13, 1876, - - - 201

PUBLIC DEBT AND FOREIGN TRADE.

Table of amount of each form of obligation of the United States outstanding, each year since 1860, - - - 152, 153
Total debt each year since 1791, - - - - - - 154
Foreign indebtedness of the United States, - - - 156
Imports and exports of merchandise and specie, each year since 1843, - - - - - - - - 159, 161
Foreign trade balances for and against the United States, each year since 1843, - - - - - - - 162
Authority of the Secretary to make interest-bearing treasury notes legal tender; Act March 3, 1863, - - - 190, 191
"Seven-thirty" treasury notes made a legal tender; Act June 30, 1864, - - - - - - - - - 193
Fractional currency, - - - - - - - - - - 192

NATIONAL BANKS AND BANK CURRENCY.

Organization and powers of national banks, - - - 203
Obtaining and issuing circulating notes, - - - - 214
Regulation of the banking business, - - - - 202
Dissolution and receivership, - - - - - - 235
Taxes on circulating notes, - - - - - - 244
Stamp tax on checks, - - - - - - - - - - 246
Crimes and misdemeanors, - - - - - - 248
Interest laws of the States, - - - - - - - 254

[In addition to the above captions there are marginal notes which furnish a complete index to all important clauses under each general head.]

REFERENCE TABLES.

Table 1.—National Banks in the United States each year since 1863, - - - - - - - - - 256
Tables 2 and 3.—Relative Values of Gold and United States Notes, with gold at any price not exceeding 285, - 257, 258
Tables 4 and 5.—Monetary Units of all Countries, with the declared values of their coins in United States money, January 1, 1874, - - - - - - - 259
Table 6.—Monetary Units of all Countries, and the declared values of their coins, January 1, 1876, - - - 264
Tables 7 and 8.—Prices of Leading Staple Commodities in New York for Fifty Years, - - - - - 265–267
Table of Population of each Country on the Globe in the period 1874–6, - - - - - - - - 268–270

THE MONEY SYMBOLS.

ON the cover of this book are grouped, in one design, the three emblems from which are derived the dollar symbol, $, and the pound-sterling symbol, £. The most prominent and interesting feature of the group is the two pillars, which were derived from the pillars of Hercules, one of the oldest symbols known to the human race. Their composition with the money symbols is due entirely to the emperor Charles the Fifth of Germany, who being also king of Spain adopted them as supporters on either side of his escutcheon, and also placed them in the device on the Spanish "pillar dollar" of the value of fifty-four pence sterling, which became the unit of Federal money in America, and upon the basis of which the pound sterling was valued at $4.44.44. Charles derived the idea from the poetic conceit which gave the name of "Pillars of Hercules" to the two mountains which stand on either side the Straits of Gibraltar, viz.: Calpe, or the Rock of Gibraltar, on the north, and Mount Abyla, in Africa, on the south. The scroll, which in the device on the dollar was twined about the pillars, has by long use been gradually modified, in making the symbol with the pen, so as to assume its present form in the dollar-mark. It is also presumed that in the pound-mark the £ was substituted for the scroll, thus still retaining the two pillars which had become what might be called the generic symbol of money in general, while the scroll and the *£* referred to the two monetary units most widely known to the world — the *£* being from *Libra*, a balance; or, in this connection, a standard of values. But before Charles adopted the pillars as supporters to his arms, they had been part of the metropolitan emblem of the city of Seville, and the scroll bore the device *Ne plus ultra*, referring to the ancient belief that westward of that coast of Spain there was nothing but sea and space. Charles elided the particle *ne*, and left the motto *Plus ultra*, in which form it appeared in the arms of the Empire and on the pillar dollar. Originally the pound-sterling symbol was made with two transverse bars. The custom of making it with only one horizontal bar, and the dollar-mark with only one upright bar, is an innovation of modern type makers.

THE DOLLAR AND OTHER UNITS.

ALL national governments assume the right to establish a *monetary unit*, viz.: to select a certain coin, either of gold or silver, in which accounts shall be kept within their territory. Also to coin money and regulate the legal tender value of their own coins and also of foreign coins, viz.: to declare at what proportion of the monetary unit the coins shall be received in payment of debts. But the declared or legal tender value of coins does not always agree with the bullion value of the coin selected as the monetary unit. In fact there have been, until within the last half century, very few instances in which the bullion value of the national coins of any country have corresponded to the bullion value of the coin selected as a monetary unit. This discrepancy has arisen from two causes. First, because — for their own purposes — national governments in the exercise of their right to coin money and regulate the value thereof, have frequently changed the bullion value of the coins struck at their national mints, while the monetary unit being in most cases an *ideal coin*, or at least a coin which had disappeared from circulation in any part of the world, could not be changed except by legislation to change the unit of values; an act which, in justice to all debtors and creditors in the country, would require that there should be a concurrent and corresponding change in the amount of all debts and accounts kept in accordance with the former unit of values. The second cause of the general discrepancy between the bullion value of the monetary unit of any country and the bullion value of the coins minted in the same country is the difference in the relative values of gold and silver. The monetary unit being *in all cases only one coin, of one metal*, the changes in the relative values of gold and silver would cause continual changes in the values of the coins of the respective metals.

There is reason for believing that the phrase "double standard," as popularly used with reference to countries where both gold and silver coins are a legal tender in any amount, is generally misunderstood. The standard in all countries must be the monetary unit established by law, and as a unit means *one* there cannot be "two units." The proper phrase with reference to the monetary systems of such countries would be "double legal tender," or legal option of payment of debts in either gold or silver coins at their declared legal (not bullion) value, proportionately to the established monetary unit.

But besides the monetary units established by different countries there are other ideal moneys or ideal quantities of pure gold or silver which have been selected, not by law, but by the custom of merchants, for the measurement of the coins of different countries in transactions of international exchange. These have, in most cases, been selected to correspond with the value of certain coins which have had at some time a wide international circulation. These are called "moneys of exchange," and do not necessarily agree with any of the monetary units established by different countries nor with the values of coins struck at the mints of any country.

In order to have a perfect idea of the function of moneys of exchange, or ideal moneys, which are with respect to coins as measures with respect to goods, it must be borne in mind that pure gold or silver is the only universal currency,—not gold nor silver coins, for the nominal values of all these are arbitrarily fixed by legislation, which is necessarily confined within local limits. The only true denomination of coins, to make them agree with the universal currency, would be by having the ounces, pennyweights and grains of pure metal which they contain stamped on them. If a sovereign was stamped "113.001 grains of pure gold," and a half eagle was stamped "116.100 grains of pure gold," their relative value would be patent to all people of other nations who understand the Arabic numerals, even though they might not be conversant with the domestic decimal system of the United States or the English system of sterling money. Indeed, such a nomenclature for coins seems to have been contemplated in the original divisions of British money into "pounds," "ounces" and "pence" or "pennies."

Originally the pound sterling represented a pound weight of silver, or about three times its present value, but it was being continually changed to suit the purposes of different monarchs, and through these changes in the coins the divisions of money were finally changed from pounds, ounces and pennies — or pennyweights — to pounds, shillings and pence. In 1266 an attempt was made to find a natural standard for the divisions of money, and it was enacted (3d Edw., 51) that "an English peny called a sterling, round and without clipping, shall weigh thirty-two wheat corns from the midst of the ear, and twenty pence to make an ounce, and twelve ounces one pound, and eight pounds one gallon of wine, and eight gallons of wine one London bushel," the money standards and the measures of capacity being originally parts of one series. The original grains of wheat were soon after the above period represented by metallic grains, which are supposed to be the origin of our modern troy grains, though the troy pound was afterward changed to twenty-four grains to the ounce, and the pound itself cut into twenty shillings for the money measure, instead of twelve ounces, the "penys" or "sterlings" becoming pence in money and penny-weights in troy weight. The origin of the farthings of sterling money was in the manner of minting the "peny," which was stamped with a deeply impressed cross, so that it could be broken in twain, or into fourths; hence *four*things, which was afterward corrupted into farthings.

The natural standard of wheat grains — which was found variable and altogether unreliable — having been abandoned, the alterations of the money standards continued the same as before: Elizabeth ordered the ounce cut into sixty pence instead of twenty. Henry VIII debased the fineness and altered the weights of the coins so much that at times none but experts knew their real value. The "nobles" and "rose nobles" and "angels" and "guineas" and "sovereigns" were only so many names given to disguise the changes in the value of the gold coins that were the nominal representatives of a pound of silver.

A historical table of the coinage of England shows that in the time of Edward III a pound troy weight of standard gold was coined into £14 0s. 10d. of sterling money. From that time down the value of the coinage was diminished under almost every monarch, until in 1717 a pound troy weight of the same standard gold was coined into £46 14s. 6d. During these five hundred years the gold coins were thus debased in the ratio of 3½ to 1, and the silver coins in the ratio of 99 to 32. During the same period the silver coins of France and Spain were debased in the ratio of 17 to 1. This trick of royalty, however, became stale in the latter part of the sixteenth century; and though it continued to be practiced to some extent its effects were nullified in a great measure by the clumsiness with which it was done. The people of Europe, too, began to get better acquainted with each other. Merchants of different countries mutually agreed on moneys of exchange as a measure of the value of coins; the ideal standards thus established were practically beyond the reach of legislation by single nations, and the ideal "dollar" or "pound" or "florin" of exchange always demanded and received its full quantity of pure gold and silver.

In 1786 the Congress of the Confederation of American States established the dollar of 4s. 6d. (54 pence sterling) as the money of account for government concerns and for foreign commerce (see Coinage Laws of the Confederation); but this dollar was never represented by any American coin. In 1792 the Congress of the United States established a national mint, and ordered "dollars or units" to be coined, to be each of the value of "a Spanish milled dollar." The coins minted under this law contained 371¼ grains of pure silver. Thus the monetary unit of the American States was changed from 54 pence sterling to 51¾ pence sterling. But the ideal dollar of exchange between Great Britain and the United States remained unchanged at

54 pence sterling, and formed the basis for the calculation of sterling exchange in the United States until such calculations were forbidden by the law of March 3, 1873 (see Coinage Laws).

There are 240 pence in a pound sterling, and to make it the equivalent of $4.44 4-9 (the old method of estimating the value of a pound in dollars) the dollar must contain 54 pence. But the American monetary unit—the silver dollar of the value of a "Spanish milled dollar"—was worth only 51¾ pence sterling, and was thus 4½ per cent below the standard of the ideal dollar of exchange; hence in all payments it was necessary to add 4½ per cent nominal premium. This continued until 1837, when the bullion value of all American gold coins was reduced. The eagle, which under the law of 1792 was to contain 247½ grains of pure gold, was reduced in value so as to contain only 232.200 grains of pure gold. (See Digest of Coinage Laws.)

But, while the monetary unit of the United States continued to be the silver dollar, both gold and silver coins were a legal tender, and the gold dollar being reduced in bullion value below the silver dollar, all debtors exercised their legal option of paying in gold instead of silver dollars. The bullion value of silver coins being greater than their legal tender value, as compared with the gold coins, the former passed out of circulation and were exported, leaving the gold coins as the principal part of the metallic currency in the United States. This was found so great an inconvenience that by the law of February 21, 1853, the silver fractional coins (but not the silver dollar) were reduced in weight, and though they were declared to be legal tender for no more than five dollars, their legal tender value was so much greater than their bullion value that they remained in the country until the issue of legal tender paper money in 1862.

The change from an almost exclusive silver metallic currency to one of gold in 1837 was not, as is frequently supposed, the result of a demonetization of silver, but only of the exercise of the legal option of all debtors to pay debts in the cheapest one of two legal tender metals. A similar change (except that it was from gold to silver) took place in France in 1785.*

In 1857–8 a somewhat similar change was made in Austria. By an imperial decree the value of the monetary unit, the silver florin, was reduced from 48½ cents in American silver dollars to 45$\frac{3}{10}$. Silver was established as the only legal metallic currency of the empire, though gold was also to be coined for commercial purposes.

But the American gold dollars measured by the silver dollar of exchange (54 pence) were 9½ per cent below par. Hence in foreign payments it was customary to add 9½ per cent nominal premium to the $4.44 4-9, which was presumed to be the equivalent of a pound sterling.

Seeing that none of our own coins nor those of other nations now in circulation agree with this standard of 4s. 6d., the query naturally arises as to how it came to be adopted. A complete answer to this requires a glance into history.

* In France a different valuation of the metals has had a different effect. Previously to the recoinage in 1785 the *louis d'or* was rated in the mint proportion at only 24 livres, when it was really worth 25 livres 10 sols. Those, therefore, who should have discharged the obligations they had contracted by payment of gold coin instead of silver, would plainly have lost 1 livre 10 sols on every sum of 24 livres. In consequence, very few such payments were made; gold was almost entirely banished from circulation, and silver became almost the only species of metallic money used in France.—SAY, *Traité d'Economie Politique*, tom. i, p. 393.

In a remote little valley in Bohemia in 1518, the Count of Schlick began to coin silver pieces of an ounce weight. These were not only of uniform weight and fineness, but they soon became very numerous. The traders of the time were in want of some international standard, fixed at least by common honesty as a measure of the value of other coins; and these coins soon became in good repute all over Europe under the names of Schlickten thalers or Joachim's thalers — the first from the name of the Count of Schlick, and the second from Joachims-*thal* or Joachim's valley, where they were coined. These names soon became synonyms for honest coins of full weight and value, but after a time the name was abbreviated, and the word *thaler* (literally, in this connection, "*valleyer*") was combined with other words to designate the established coins of various nations, which, though not of the same weight and fineness as the Schlickten thalers, were of uniform weight and fineness. Thus originated the German *thaler*, the Low German *dahler*, the Danish and Swedish *dalers*, the Italian *tollero*, and the more widely known *dollar*.

When the idea of a characteristic name for honest coins crept over into Britain it found a word there already coined for its adoption, viz.: the word "dollar," from the Gaelic *dol*, a valley, and *ard*, a hill, signifying in a valley shut in by hills, and there is yet in Scotland, near Clackmanan, a little valley parish and a village called Dollar.

Although there were no coins minted in England called dollars, there were many foreign coins of different values, from the various national mints of Europe, circulating there under the common name of dollars. Shakspeare uses the word twice (once in Measure for

Measure and once in Macbeth), and there is plenty of evidence that the term "dollars," as applied to coins, was in common use there previous to 1600. Some common measure or standard for these dollars was necessary as a matter of convenience, and Spain being then the leading country of Europe, her piasters of eight reals — called also "pieces of eight" — being in more general use than any other foreign coins, were adopted as the standard dollar. But previous to this, in 1519, when Charles V, king of Spain, became also emperor of Germany, he had adopted a new coat of imperial arms, in which those of Spain were quartered with those of the empire, and had stamped this new device on the coinage of Spain, the pillars in the device giving rise to the name of "pillar dollars" — this particular coin being then known in Spain as *colonato*. These dollars were from the mint of Seville, and in the table of "silver coins of the world," made by Sir Isaac Newton when assayer to the British mint, are set down at the exact value of 54 pence. This and the old French *ecu*, of about the same date, are the only coins of that exact value in the whole table. Thus that which was known in England as a dollar, and as our dollar of exchange, is the adaptation of an idea of German origin to a Gaelic word and a Spanish coin.

The dollar of 54 pence is an instance of that ideal money, or money of exchange, which has no existence in fact, but is used in calculating nearly all international exchanges.* With many nations, as with our own, it differs from the money used in domestic accounts, and

* Professor Sumner, in his *History of American Currency* (page 103), is mistaken in saying: "It is not known how this ratio ($1.44.44 to the £1) was determined." It is very plain that it was determined as I have described above.

almost universally differs from the coins in use. Coins being national, and in a great measure local, are subject to alterations and debasements by governments; but moneys of exchange, though rarely established by design, become widely established by the mutual consent of nations for convenience, and are in a measure beyond the reach of legislation. While we, through English custom, had taken our ideal dollar from the Spanish dollar of Charles V, custom has established in Spain itself a different ideal dollar. The "*peso duro*," or "hard dollar," was once a Spanish coin of eight reals, but was afterward altered to a greater value of ten reals. The first coinage of the "hard dollar," however, had been accepted by other nations as the standard of exchange with Spain, and though the value of the coin was altered so that eight hard dollars were worth ten and five-eighths dollars of exchange, the ideal dollar remained unchanged.

The ideal unit of values in the United States until 1873 was a dollar of 51¾ pence, and the ideal dollar of exchange adopted in London was 54 pence. Our coinage never agreed with either of these values. But in 1816 a new monetary system was adopted in Great Britain, and it was enacted *that gold coins only should be legal tender in all payments*, and that silver coins should be legal tender for only 40s.* The original pound of silver which previous to 1816 was coined into 62 shillings was then coined into 66 shillings, and the

* From 1664 down to 1717 the relation of gold to silver was not fixed by authority, and silver being then the only legal tender, the value of gold coins fluctuated according to the fluctuations in the relative worth of the metals in the market. In 1717 the ancient practice was again reverted to, and it was fixed that the guinea should be taken as the equivalent of 21 shillings, and conversely. —*McCulloch's Commercial Dictionary*, page 352.

sovereign was declared to be a pound. Thus the monetary unit of Great Britain agrees with its principal coin.

By the coinage law of February 12, 1873, the monetary unit of the United States was changed from a silver dollar of 412½ grains standard (371¼ grains pure) silver to a gold dollar of 25 8-10 grains standard gold, and the legal tender function of *all* silver coins was reduced to five dollars. But as far as the half dollars, quarters and dimes were concerned, this was only a reiteration of the law of February 21, 1853. By the law of July 13, 1876, the trade dollar was declared not to be a legal tender at all.

As shown in the preceding pages, the only "dollar" known in British finance was the dollar of 54 pence. This was distinctly defined by a proclamation of Queen Anne in 1704, to the effect that the Spanish and Mexican "pieces of eight," or dollars, were of the value of 4s. 6d. When, after 1860, the bonds of the United States payable in "dollars" were put upon the London market, though issued by a government whose nominal unit of values was a dollar of 51¾ pence, English brokers and bankers, still adhering to their old established idea of a dollar as the equivalent of 54 pence sterling, quoted the market prices of Unites States bonds in dollars of 54 pence. Thus when the bonds were really at par they were quoted in London at 91.33, this being the equivalent of a dollar of American gold expressed in the old dollar of 54 pence sterling. This custom was maintained in London until December 30, 1873, when a new "dollar" of *four shillings* having been adopted by the London Stock Exchange, United States bonds were, and are yet, quoted in that ideal standard. This new dollar is not represented by any coin of any nation, and is the equivalent of 96 cents and 96 hundredths of a cent in American gold. It will thus be seen that while the old London quotations made United States bonds appear to be nearly 8 per cent lower than they were in fact, the new Stock Exchange dollar makes them appear to be about 3 per cent higher (in London) than they are in fact. By this rule of the London Stock Exchange, and by the United States law in regard to the computations of sterling exchange, the old "dollar" of 54 pence appears to have passed entirely out of use as an ideal standard. This dollar, however, should not be confused with the American silver dollar established as the unit of values by the law of 1792, and which remained as such until abrogated by the law of February 12, 1873.

In Frankfort the quotations of the market prices of United States bonds are made in still another assumed "dollar," which is the equivalent of 4¼ marks. The gold mark being equivalent to 23 8-10 cents in American gold, makes the Frankfort stock exchange dollar, used for quoting United States bonds, equal to $103.05 in American gold. The Frankfort quotations, therefore, for United States bonds make them appear to be nearly 3 per cent lower than they would quoted in American gold dollars.

Still another fact complicates the foreign quotations for American bonds, viz.: In London the bonds are quoted "flat"; that is, including accrued interest to the date of quotation; while in Frankfort they are quoted exclusive of interest.*

* The following practical illustration of the various methods of quoting United States bonds in European markets is furnished by a banker for this publication:

"London assumes in the calculation of American bonds the gold dollar at 4

PAPER MONEY AND COIN IN THE UNITED STATES.

THERE has been no politico-economical question so much discussed in the United States during the last ten years as the amount of the outstanding volume of currency, and none which has been so much misrepresented. The public mind having been concentrated upon the "currency question," the opposing political parties have continually ascribed all changes and crises in commercial and industrial affairs to changes in the volume of the currency of the United States. They have started out in all cases with the erroneous assumption that the foundation of all the prosperity, or the cause of all the depression — as the case may have been — experienced in the last ten years, was to be found in

shillings including coupon. If, therefore, say, on the 28th of August a new 5 per cent bond is quoted in London 107 (while demand sterling in New York is 4.89) a $100 bond will cost:

107×4 shillings = £21 8s. @ 489 .... $104.65 gold.

"Frankfort assumes in the calculation of American bonds the gold dollar at 4¼ marks exclusive of coupon. The above bond quoted in Frankfort August 28 at 103¼ (while demand exchange on Germany in New York is 95¼ cents gold per 4 mark) will cost:

103¼×4¼ = mark 438.81 @ 95¼ .... $104.49 gold.
Accrued interest, August 1 to 28 41

$104.90 gold.

"On the same day new fives were quoted in New York 116⅛. Gold being then 111, made the bond worth $104.95 gold. This comparison, based on actual market reports, will show the quotations of 103¼ in Frankfort, 107 in London, and 116⅛ in New York to stand very near to each other. It may be added that Paris assumes the gold dollar at 5 francs including coupon, while Amsterdam assumes it at 2½ guilders excluding coupon. Berlin and the other German places figure exactly the same as Frankfort."

either the contraction or the inflation of the paper currency of the United States. In accordance with this narrow view of finance the partisans of one party or another have been continually printing in pamphlets and newspapers tables and estimates of the volume of currency in existence at one time as compared with another. The fault with all these estimates and tabulations has been that they have been made to sustain a preconceived theory of the causes of the changes in the financial situation at various times. The facts have in all cases been made secondary to the theories, and consequently only such facts as sustained the theories have been given, while all others — which in many cases, if fairly stated, would have completely upset the theories — have been omitted.

A great majority of the misstatements of the volume of currency in circulation have probably not been intentional; they are due simply to that proneness of all men to rest satisfied when they have found certain facts to sustain their preconceived notions. Indeed, the believers in theories founded upon a few indisputable facts, but ignoring others of equal importance, are always most thoroughly convinced of the truth of their own doctrines. Out of just such half-truths have arisen all the great errors of mankind on any subject. It is an error to presume that the apparent prosperity — the "flush times" experienced in this country from 1867 to 1872 — were due entirely, or even very largely, to a greater volume of currency then than now. A broader view of finance would show that the progress of financial affairs in the United States has been in accordance with the general situation throughout the commercial world, and as this little book is intended as a handbook of financial facts rather than of theories, the following table of the various kinds of paper currency in existence in the United States each year since 1853 has been compiled, in order, if possible, to remove the question of the exact amount of currency in circulation each year from the confusion to which it has heretofore been subject.

The propriety of including the 7 3-10 per cent notes, the compound interest notes, the 3 per cent certificates, and the various other forms of unfunded debt of the government among the forms of currency, will doubtless be questioned by some; but it is well known that all these did circulate to a large extent as money, though not so rapidly as the non-interest-bearing treasury notes. Reference to the law authorizing the 7 3-10 per cent notes will also show that they were intended to circulate as money; the Secretary was authorized to issue them as legal tender to all creditors for the amount of the principal, together with the interest accrued on any such note at the date of tender.* A large proportion of the $672,578,850 of 7.30 notes, and the $159,012,140 of compound interest notes, outstanding on July 1, 1865, were issued under authority of the law of June 30, 1864, which made them a legal tender for the face value of the notes and the accrued interest. The 3 per cent certificates, also authorized by the act of March 2, 1867, were intended as a substitute for $50,000,000 of United States notes, which were by that means released from the vaults of the national banks, where they had been held according to law as a reserve against circulation and deposits. These certificates were therefore practically an addition of $50,000,000 to the currency in 1867.

* See Digest of Laws, Act of June 30, 1864, and March 3, 1865.

While there may be some reasonable question as to the propriety of regarding the 7.30 notes and the compound interest notes as an addition to the volume of currency to the full amount of their issue, there can be no doubt that a just estimate of the volume of currency in use each year must take them into the account at some ratio of the total amount outstanding, even if it be not more than two-thirds their face value. As to the 3 per cent certificates, there can be no question that they were an addition to the volume of currency to the full amount of their issue. They were unlike the present non-interest-bearing certificates issued to the banks, because no special reserve of United States notes was held in the treasury for their redemption, whereas the United States notes received for the present certificates are held as a special deposit in the treasury, and are not used for any other purpose than the redemption of the certificates.*

Even if the practical effect of the 7.30 and compound interest notes to increase the volume of paper money be estimated at no more than one-half their nominal value, and if the total volume of bank notes and unfunded debt circulating as money in 1866 be estimated as equivalent to no more than $1,300,000,000, thus making a deduction of $500,000,000 for the amount of such notes that would not circulate to any considerable extent as money—even with this deduction, it will be seen that the period of greatest contraction in the paper money circulation of the United States was from 1866 to 1869.

But there is still another and even more important point to be considered in connection with the contrac-

* See Act June 8, 1872.

tion from 1866 to 1869. The war of the rebellion closed in 1865. Previous to that time there were twelve of the Southern States, viz.: Alabama, Arkansas, Florida, Georgia, Louisiana, Mississippi, North Carolina, South Carolina, Tennessee, Texas, Virginia and West Virginia, from which national bank notes and United States notes of any sort were practically excluded. These twelve States had a population in 1870 of 9,999,401. In the immediate vicinity of the armies of the United States in the border States, such as Tennessee and Virginia, there would of course be a large circulation of United States notes, but with the great bulk of the nearly 10,000,000 of population in these twelve Southern States United States notes and national bank notes were almost unknown until the close of the war. Until 1866 therefore, the entire amount of paper money included in the table was practically confined in its circulation to the population of the Northern and Atlantic States, a population which, from 1865 to 1866, probably did not exceed 23,000,000 to 24,000,000, and was only 27,000,000 in 1870. It was not until 1867 that the rehabilitation of the South began to draw much capital from the Northern States, and the amount of currency in the Southern States even in that year could not have been over one third as much *per capita* as in the Northern States. It is fair to presume, however, that by 1869 or 1870 the greatest effect of the new requirements of the people of the Southern States for currency had been experienced, and that from 8,000,000 to 10,000,000 more people were using United States and national bank notes as their only currency than in 1865–6. These facts will show the unreliability of any of the usual estimates of the amount of currency *per capita* in the United States based upon the entire population. There are so many elements to be considered that it is doubtful if any estimate of the amount of currency per capita of the population using it can be made that will not be open to criticism.

The table given on another page shows, however, conclusively that the period of greatest contraction of the paper money of the United States per capita of the population using it was from 1866 to 1869–70. It is therefore to be presumed that if the amount of paper money per capita of the population had been the controlling element in the stimulation or the depression of industry, improvements and trade, as is popularly believed, the most positive evidences of such depression from a scarcity of the currency per capita of the population would have been experienced from 1866 to 1870. But it is well known that this was popularly regarded as a period of unexampled prosperity in the United States. The increase of railroad mileage was greater each year during the whole period; beginning with an increase in 1866 of about 3 per cent on the mileage of 1865, the ratio of increase was greater each year afterward until, in 1871, it was over 12 per cent on the mileage of 1870; prices (in currency) of nearly all commodities advanced largely during the first half of the period and were maintained during the latter half, notwithstanding a decline in the average annual price of gold from 140 in 1866 to 123 in 1870. Values of real estate also, throughout the country, increased during the whole of the period in question. It is therefore plain that whatever would otherwise have been the effect of the great contraction of the currency from 1866 to 1870, it was neutralized and overcome by some more general and potent cause, which, it seems to the writer, is to be found in the increased production of gold and silver at the beginning of the period in question, and the effects of the three great wars of the preceding six years. Not only does the increased production of the precious metals at that period afford some explanation of the universal stimulus given to trade, enterprise and speculation from 1867 to 1872, but the decrease in the production of the same metals affords the clue to the causes which resulted in the crisis of 1873.

The following table gives the amount of each kind of treasury paper, as well as the amount of bank notes, in circulation each year, and also the aggregate of both each year, from 1854 to 1876:

NOTES TO TABLE ON FOLLOWING PAGE.

* The amounts given for the bank note circulation in the United States about the 1st of January each year for the years 1854-55-56-57-58 are taken from a report of the Secretary of the Treasury, and were published in a tabulated form in *Hunt's Commercial Magazine* for March, 1857.

† The circulation of the State banks in 1863 was given in the report of the Comptroller of the Currency for 1873, and the above amount was obtained for that publication from page 210 of the report of the Secretary of the Treasury on the condition of the banks at the commencement of the year 1863. The returns from Delaware, Maryland, Louisiana, Tennessee and Kentucky were not complete. The aggregate amount of State bank circulation reported at that time was much greater than at any previous period.

‡ The $45,449,155 of State bank circulation given for January 1, 1866, is the amount of State bank notes reported by the national banks, which at that time had recently been reorganized as such from State banks. But as there were still other State banks in existence, it is probable that the $45,449,155 was considerably below the aggregate of State bank notes in existence at that date.

AMOUNT OF EACH KIND OF PAPER CURRENCY IN THE UNITED STATES EACH YEAR FOR TWENTY-THREE YEARS.

	Demand and 1 and 2 year Treasury Notes (Acts March 2, 1861, Dec. 17, 1860, and Dec. 23, 1857,) outstanding July 1.	Temporary 10-Day Loans and One Year Certificates of Indebtedness, July 1 each year.	Treasury Notes, payable in 2 years and in 60 days (Act March 3, 1863), July 1 each year.	7.30 Three Year Notes, July 1 each year.	Compound Interest Notes, July 1 each year.	3 per cent Certificates, July 1 each year.	Non-Interest-Bearing, Demand and Legal Tender Notes (Acts July 17, 1861, Feb. 25, 1862, July 11, 1862, and March 3, 1863).	Fractional Currency.	Bank Note Circulation, January 1 each year. National Banks.	Bank Note Circulation, January 1 each year. State Banks.	Total of Bank Notes and of Unfunded Government Debt circulating to any extent as money each year.
1854...	....	....	....	....	....	....	....	....	....	* 204,689,000	204,689,000
1855...	....	....	....	....	....	....	....	....	....	* 186,952,000	186,952,000
1856...	....	....	....	....	....	....	....	....	....	* 195,748,000	195,748,000
1857...	....	....	....	....	....	....	....	....	....	* 214,779,000	214,799,000
1858...	....	....	....	....	....	....	....	....	....	* 155,208,000	155,208,000
1859...	....	....	....	....	....	....	....	....	....	193,306,000	193,306,000
1860...	....	....	....	....	....	....	....	....	....	207,102,000	207,102,000
1861...	20,153,455	....	....	....	....	....	....	....	....	202,205,000	222,358,455
1862...	2,849,112	107,628,696	....	122,836,550	....	....	150,560,000	....	....	183,794,000	444,786,208
1863...	897,912	259,168,327	....	139,970,500	....	....	381,997,589	20,192,456	....	† 238,671,210	1,043,610,415
1864...	278,512	233,059,191	153,471,450	109,356,150	15,000,000	....	431,959,670	22,904,877	30,155	....	968,059,995
1865...	118,912	205,489,061	42,338,710	672,578,850	193,756,080	....	433,160,569	24,915,829	66,769,375	....	1,639,127,386
1866...	117,512	147,567,196	3,454,200	806,900,750	159,012,140	....	400,891,367	27,070,876	213,239,530	‡ 45,449,155	1,803,702,726
1867...	110,712	20,261,070	1,123,930	488,647,140	122,394,480	....	371,992,029	27,830,723	291,093,294	6,961,499	1,330,414,677
1868...	110,512	13,815,029	555,492	37,717,650	28,161,810	50,000,000	356,141,723	32,627,952	294,377,390	3,792,013	817,199,773
1869...	108,212	198,310	347,772	1,166,500	2,871,410	52,120,000	356,123,739	32,114,637	294,476,702	2,734,669	750,025,989
1870...	94,825	186,310	248,272	641,000	2,152,910	45,545,000	356,106,250	39,878,684	292,833,935	2,351,993	740,039,179
1871...	94,850	85,370	213,348	475,900	768,500	31,863,000	356,096,506	40,582,874	302,028,626	2,035,800	734,244,774
1872...	94,750	83,500	206,817	352,150	583,520	12,220,000	358,188,206	40,855,835	318,043,841	1,886,538	736,349,912
1873...	94,675	83,500	142,105	293,450	479,400	30,000	356,079,967	44,799,365	336,289,287	1,511,396	738,291,749
1874...	94,575	83,500	127,565	247,650	415,210	5,000	382,076,732	45,961,295	350,020,062	(June 27)...	779,031,589
1875...	94,575	8,060	113,375	213,900	367,390	5,000	375,841,687	42,129,424	349,402,839	(June 26)...	778,176,250
1876...	94,525	8,060	104,705	199,850	328,760	5,000	369,839,201	34,446,595	330,809,136	(July 1)....	735,358,832

COIN IN THE UNITED STATES.

Estimate of the amount of coin in the country from 1854 to 1876:

	Coin in Banks.	Total in the Country.
1854	$59,410,000	$240,000,000
1855	55,945,000	....
1856	59,714,000	....
1857	59,272,000	....
1858	60,705,000	....
1859	....	275,000,000
1860	....	....
1861	....	....
1862	....	....
1863	....	....
1864	....	....
1865	....	....
1866	....	....
1869	....	....
1870 (October)	6,000,000	121,000,000
1871 (October)	6,000,000	116,000,000
1872 (October)	5,000,000	102,000,000
1873 (October)	5,000,000	109,000,000
1874 (October)	5,500,000	110,000,000
1875 (October)	5,000,000	100,000,000
1876 (June)	6,000,000	102,000,000

The estimates of the amounts of specie in circulation in the whole country at any period must of course always be open to criticism, for the reason that no exact statistics are possible. For the period from 1854 to 1859 the only trustworthy figures are those given in the annual reports of the Secretary of the Treasury, showing the amount of coin held by the banks on or about the 1st of January each year. These have been used as a basis of approximation to the whole amount in the country for that period.

For the period from 1870 to 1876 the data are more definite. There are only three items worthy of consideration in the estimation of the amount for each year, viz.: the amount in the national treasury, the amounts in the national and commercial banks of the entire country (including all commercial banks on the Pacific coast), and the amount in circulation in the Pacific States and Territories.* (The savings banks hold scarcely any coin.)

The actual amount of coin in the treasury of the United States each year, on October 1, was as follows, viz.: 1869, $108,800,000; 1870, $96,000,000; 1871, $90,500,000; 1872, $78,000,000; 1873, $80,300,000; 1875, $67,833,316; 1876 (June 3), $73,625,584.

According to the report of the Comptroller of the Currency for 1875, the total amount of nominal "coin" held by all the national banks of the United States on October 8, 1870, was $18,460,011. Of this amount $13,135,649 was held by banks in New York city. But of this $13,135,649 only $1,607,742 was actual coin, all the rest being United States coin certificates and checks on other banks payable in coin. Upon this basis the amount of actual coin held by all the sixteen hundred national banks of the United States in October, 1870, could not have exceeded $2,200,000 — this amount including all sorts of coin. Allowing $1,000,000 more

* The relative proportions of the banking business in the United States, transacted through the different classes of banking institutions, may be estimated by the following statement of the whole number of banks of each class, and the aggregate of deposits in each in the year 1875:

Class of Banks.	No. of Banks.	Aggregate of Deposits.
National Banks	2,087	$743,088,815
*State Chartered Commercial Banks	*1,000	*200,000,000
*Savings Banks	*800	*1,000,000,000
*Estimated.		$1,943,088,815

for the amount held by all other banks, not national (exclusive of the Pacific coast), and we have not to exceed $3,200,000. Estimating still $3,000,000 more for actual coin in the banks in California, it would leave a little over $6,000,000 as the aggregate of all coin in all banks in the United States and Territories in October, 1870. The amount of coin in the treasury of the United States October 1, 1870, was $96,000,000. If we make the very liberal estimate of $20 per capita for the 971,321 of the entire population of California, Nevada, Oregon, Arizona, Colorado, Idaho, Montana, New Mexico, Utah, Washington and Wyoming in 1870, it gives $18,426,420. Add this to the coin in the treasury and in the banks, and we have an aggregate of $120,-826,420, say $121,000,000, as the entire stock of coin in the United States and Territories on October 1, 1870.

On October 3, 1872, the amount of actual coin held by the national banks of New York city was only $920,767 (see report of comptroller for 1873, page 44), and on the same basis the total amount held by all the eighteen hundred and fifty national banks of the United States could not have exceeded $1,200,000, which would give a little over $4,000,000 for all banks in the United States and Territories. The "specie," as reported to the comptroller by the national banks of the United States on October 1, 1875, was classified as follows, viz.: actual coin, $3,364,569; United States coin certificates, $4,485,760; total, $8,050,329.

PAPER MONEY.

BANK NOTES.

BANK notes were not at first, as most people presume, an invention to increase the amount of money in circulation, but grew out of the necessity for some standard by which to regulate the value of coins. During the sixteenth and seventeenth centuries, as explained in the first chapter of this book, the debasements of the coins by different monarchs of Europe were so frequent and so great that merchants and traders had no safeguards against loss but continual resort to the assayers. These sometimes disagreed, and some authority of wider jurisdiction than the individual assayer was required. Banks had already been devised * as a means of assisting governments to secure the united co-operation of the people in the finances of the states, and in the exercise of this function it became necessary that each of the great banks should also fix the values of all home and foreign coins. The universal rule for this valuation was to receive all coins at the value of the pure gold or silver in them as compared with an ideal standard, viz., a specified number of grains of gold or silver, to be called a "ducat," a "florin," a "pound," or a "dollar." In most cases this ideal coin at first

* Bank of Venice, founded in 1157; Bank of Barcelona, in 1349; Bank of Genoa, in 1407; Bank of Amsterdam, in 1609; Bank of Hamburg, in 1619; Bank of Sweden, in 1656; Bank of England, in 1694.

corresponded to the principal national coin of the country in which the bank was located. But as the actual coins were debased from time to time, their value fell below that of the ideal coin accepted by the bank as its standard, and, in some cases, particularly that of the Bank of Venice, many of the foreign coins were received at valuations higher than warranted by the value of pure gold or silver in them. But these various coins once deposited with the bank the account was turned into "ducats" and the depositor credited with so many "ducats" of the ideal standard established by the bank. The amount thus credited, or any part of it, was transferable on the books of the bank, at the option of the depositor, to any other person to whom he might desire to pay money; but the money could not be withdrawn. The depositor thus got the benefit of a premium on many foreign coins which was not warranted by the value of the pure gold or silver in them. But this last mentioned inducement to deposit money in bank was peculiar to the Bank of Venice, and was one of the secrets of its popularity and good credit for so many years. The object was to secure the coin for the government, and the deposit was practically a subscription to a national loan. In the twelfth and thirteenth centuries, when the common rate of interest ranged from 15 to 25 per cent per annum, the loss on these coins, received at an overvaluation by the bank, was considered a small rate to pay for the use of the money for the state. But aside from this there was the consideration to the depositor in other banks as well as that of Venice, that he was at once assured of the value of the coin he received. The credits at the banks, instead of being only on the books and transferable by order, were soon made in the form of certificates of deposit, transferable by indorsement; and this suggested to a Swede named Palmstruck, who founded the Bank of Sweden, the idea of making the certificates in uniform amounts and the deposit payable to any holder, without indorsement. This conception was elaborated into the present bank note, the first note having been issued by the Bank of Sweden in 1658. "An *enquète* made by the French government, in 1729, recognizes the priority of Sweden in this matter, and declares the bank note to be an admirable Swedish invention, designed to facilitate commerce." *

BANKS IN GREAT BRITAIN AND IRELAND.

The Bank of England, founded in 1694, originated in the necessities of the government, then at war with France. William Paterson, a London merchant, conceived the scheme of organizing a bank to receive deposits and assist the government with money. The capital of £1,200,000 was raised by popular subscription, and it was provided that the whole of this should be permanently loaned to the government at 8 per cent per annum. The bank immediately issued notes of the denomination of £50 and upward. As there was no legal limit to the amount of issue, they soon depreciated, and in 1697 it was found necessary to increase the capital stock by £1,000,000. This was paid into the bank, and, for a short time, was not loaned to the government, and the effect was to cause the notes and the stock (which latter had fallen to 40 per cent discount)

* Palgrayes' *Notes on Banking*, page 87.

to appreciate to par. In 1844, an act was passed dividing the bank into two departments — the *issue* and the *banking* — the object of which was to prevent the issue of notes without a sufficient reserve of specie to redeem them. At the time of the division into the two departments the aggregate of permanent loans made by the bank to the government was £11,015,000. This debt was now declared to be due from the government to the issue department, which was authorized to issue notes to circulate as money to that amount. But some of the provincial banks had also been authorized to issue notes to a limited extent on the deposit of securities, and it was provided in the act of 1844 that whenever any of these provincial banks diminished their circulation permanently, from any cause, their right to issue notes on the deposit of government securities should accrue to the Bank of England, but that the latter bank should only issue two-thirds as much as the amount which the provincial banks should cease to issue. Under this arrangement the amount of "permanent issue" had increased to £14,475,000 in 1858. For the notes issued under the foregoing provisions no reserve of specie is required, but for every other note more than are issued as above, coin or bullion must be paid into the bank before the issue of the note. There is no distinction in the appearance of the two classes of issue; but when gold is wanted from the bank for any purpose, the notes are presented at the issue department, and, upon their redemption, are at once destroyed, and for every new deposit of bullion or coin, new notes are issued to the *banking* department.

Besides the Bank of England there were in England, in 1872, 116 joint stock banks with 1,007 branches.

In Scotland —

In 1825	there were	34	banks,	having	133	branches.
In 1850	"	18	"	"	382	"
In 1859	"	—	"	"	583	"
In 1872	"	11	"	"	801	"

In Ireland, in 1872, there were 9 joint stock banks with 305 branches.

The following shows the relative position, in 1874, of the Bank of England, the London joint stock banks and the Scotch joint stock banks:*

	Capital and Surplus.	Private Deposits.
Bank of England....................	£18,300,000	£19,630,000
London joint stock banks............	12,500,000	96,900,000
Scotch joint stock banks.............	14,000,000	77,500,000

* In an article by Mr. Charles Moran, in the New York *Bulletin*, in September, 1875, is the following succinct statement of the gradual development of the Bank of England:

The capital of the bank was increased —

In 1709 and 1710 to..	£5,560,000
In 1722 to..	8,960,000
In 1742 and 1746 to..	10,680,000
In 1782 to..	11,742,400
In 1816 to..	14,553,000

All the above accessions of capital were loaned to the government.

The following shows the gradual increase of the business of the bank:

	Circulation.	Deposits.	Securities.	Bullion.
1793........................	£10,865,000	£6,443,000	£14,810,000	£5,322,000
1800........................	15,047,000	8,355,000	22,138,000	5,150,000
1810........................	24,794,000	13,618,000	40,974.000	3,192,000
1815........................	27.249,000	12,696,000	44,854,000	3.409,000
1825........................	19,399.000	6,410.000	25.105,000	3,634,000
1840........................	17,170,000	6,254.000	22.075.000	4,299,000
1865........................	22,450,000	19 666.000	31.908.000	14.557,000
1875........................	27,280,000	24,840,000	32,720,000	22.390,000

The circulation, in 1875, is only equal to what it was in 1815. The deposits are about doubled, while the bullion has increased about seven-fold, and yet the securities held by the bank in 1875 are only £32,720,000, against £44,854,000 in 1815. These figures show clearly that the Bank of England has not kept pace in its operations with the vast increase of the production and commerce of Great Britain in the past sixty years.

But the Scotch banks are the most successful institutions of the kind that have ever existed. Until 1845 they were almost entirely exempt from legal

TABLE OF PAPER MONEY IN GREAT BRITAIN AND IRELAND.

Notes of the Bank of England, the Bank of Ireland, and of all joint stock and private banks in circulation at various periods:

Date.	B'k of England Notes.	All other Bank Notes.	Total in Circulation.
1854 Dec. 23	£20,298,000	£17,960,307	£38,258,307
1863 Dec. 13	20,607,000	17,447,513	38,054,513
1872 Dec. 28	25,162,000	18,225,892	43,387,872
1873 Dec. 23	25,787,168	....	... .
1874 April 1	27,014,407	....	....
1874 June 27	26,250,855	....	....
1874 Oct. 2	27,666,229	....	....
1874 Dec. 23	26,122,235	....	....
1875 April 1	26,929,025	....	....
1875 June 25	27,377,405	....	....
1875 Oct. 2	29,421,467	....	....
1875 Dec. 23	27,427,109	....	....
1876 Mch. 29	26,821,875	....	....
1876 July 5	28,408,850	....	....

FRANCE.

The Bank of France was organized under that name in 1803, but had previously existed as the Royal Bank. It is a government institution, the government having the appointment of the governor of the Bank and two of the directors. Its issues are not limited by law. There are, in all, sixty-two branches of the Bank of France in the various cities.

Amount of the notes of the Bank of France in circulation at various periods from 1854 to 1876, expressed in their equivalent in American gold dollars:

restrictions and governmental control. They were limited neither as to their capital, the number and location of the branches they established, the number of their shareholders, nor the amount of their issues and discounts. From 1800 to 1814, owing to the scarcity of coin, they issued notes as low as three shillings sterling. In 1826, out of a circulation of £3,300,000, £2,079,000 were notes under £5. In 1836, out of a circulation of £3,800,000, two-thirds were under £5.

1854	$122,908,040
1863	157,261,400
1865	168,000,000
1870 (January)	297,000,000
1871 (November)	460,000,000
1872 (January 31)	490,000,000
1872 (November 1)	503,982,000
1873 (January 1)	541,890,000
1873 (February 1)	551,124,000
1875 (January 28)	528,650,000
1876 (January 28)	499,600,000
1876 (June 1)	493,395,000

GERMANY.

The monetary system of the German Empire has been completely reorganized in the last few years, the laws previously passed for this purpose having gone into effect January 1, 1876. The changes made were, first, the adoption of the exclusive gold standard, with the gold mark of the value of $23\frac{8}{10}$ cents (in United States money) as the unit of values. Previous to this the unit was of silver, though both gold and silver were legal tender, the laws on these points being substantially the same as in the United States prior to 1873.

The main points in the re-organization of the banking system of the empire, and the regulation of the issues of paper money, the laws for which went into effect January 1, 1876, were as follows:

The imperial bank law decreed the formation of the "Empire Bank" at Berlin, with branches in all other important places in the empire. Besides all the ordinary business of a great commercial bank, the Empire Bank exercises, according to the imperial bank law, the function of "regulating the circulation of money in the whole of the German Empire." The Bank of Prussia was absorbed in the Empire Bank, and all the remaining thirty-two provincial banks were embraced in the regulations of the imperial bank law. The total of thirty-three banks (including the Empire Bank) are authorized to issue an aggregate of 385,000,000 marks (equal to $91,630,000) of what is called "uncovered circulation." Of this 385,000,000 marks of circulation, 250,000,000 (equal to $59,500,000) is apportioned to the Empire Bank, which may issue such portion of them as its business requires. The remaining 135,000,000 marks is apportioned to the thirty-two provincial banks according to their capital and business. The term "uncovered circulation," as currently used with reference to the above aggregate of circulation for the German banks, is liable to be misunderstood. The Empire Bank and the provincial banks are required to hold a reserve of 33⅓ per cent against all the circulation they issue. This 33⅓ per cent must be, according to the text of the imperial bank law, either "in German currency, in legal tender notes of the empire, in gold bars, or foreign coins valued at 1,392 marks for a pound of gold." This "uncovered circulation" is, therefore, unlike the £14,-750,000 of "permanent circulation" which the Bank of England may issue without any *legal* reserve. But the 385,000,000 marks is not the final limit of the volume of paper money in Germany. It is provided in the imperial bank law that "banks whose note circulation exceeds their 33⅓ per cent reserve and the respective amounts assigned to them (as their portion of the 385,-000,000 marks) shall pay yearly to the Exchequer on the excess a tax of 5 per cent, dating from the 1st of January, 1876. It will be seen, therefore, that the provincial banks have the privilege of issuing in excess of their prescribed amount, and in excess of their reserves, by the payment of 5 per cent tax on the excess. The Empire Bank and its branches, and the provincial banks and their branches, are required to accept at par all German bank notes, but the notes so accepted "can only be used either in presentation for redemption by the bank that issued them, or as payments in the town where the bank which has issued them has its seat." In addition to the bank notes, as above authorized, the state issues 120,000,000 marks ($28,500,000) of legal tender notes of the empire.

Amount of bank notes and government notes circulating in Germany at various periods from 1850 to 1876 expressed in their equivalents in American gold.

	Notes of Bank of Prussia.	Imperial Bank of Germany.	All other Bank and Govt. notes	Total Circulation.
1850.........	$15,120,000	$..........	$65,000,000	$80,120,000
1866.........	38,400,000	....	....	....
1870.........	102,398,400	....	79,876,182	182,274,582
1872.........	174,414,240	....	....	....
1873 (Feb. 1)	210,000,000	....	....	....
1876 (Jan. 1)	....	164,295,000	36,000,000	200,000,000
1876 (June 3)	....	166,575,000	....	....

AUSTRIA.

Amount of government notes and notes of the National Bank of Austria in circulation each year from 1852 to 1875, stated in florins, and their total approximate nominal equivalent in United States coin:

Year.	Government Notes, Florins.	Bank Notes, Florins.	Total Equivalent in United States Money.
1852	164,900,000	192,600,000	$165,000,000
1853	148,300,000	188,300,000	151,500,000
1854	....	383,500,000	....
1855	....	377,900,000	....
1856	....	380,200,000	....
1857	....	383,500,000	....
1858	150,000,000	385,000,000	241,000,000
1859	....	466,000,000	....
1860	....	....	....
1861	....	475,200,000	....
1862	112,900,000	....	....
1863	109,800,000	396,600,000	228,000,000
1864	102,000,000	375,800,000	215,000,000
1865	97,800,000	343,500,000	198,500,000
1866	325,500,000	....	....
1867	425,200,000	....	....
1868	424,300,000	....	....
1869	311,100,000	300,300,000	275,000,000
1870	373,600,000	....	....
1871	370,000,000	318,300,000	310,000,000
1872	344,000,000	352,100,000	313,000,000
1873	....	293,200,000	....
1874	....	302,100,000	....
1875 (Sept.)	340,000,000	302,000,000	288,900,000

RUSSIA.

Paper money in Russia is furnished almost exclusively by the government, and consists of treasury notes issued to the Bank of the Empire, for the debt of the government to that institution. The expenditures of the government have constantly exceeded the revenue since 1832. The aggregate debt thus accumulated amounted in 1869 to 1,375,385,000 roubles (a rouble is equal to $73\frac{4}{10}$ cents in United States money), and in 1873 to 2,277,081,364 roubles.

Specie payments have been suspended in Russia for nearly seventy years. There is no gold in circulation, and very little silver or other coin.

The following figures, compiled from an article in the *Bankers' Magazine*, will show the progress of paper money circulation in Russia:

RUSSIAN PAPER MONEY AND COIN IN CIRCULATION.

	Paper Money (roubles).	Silver and Copper Coins (roubles, estimated).
1788	100,000,000	100,000,000
1810	577,000,000	100,000,000
1817	836,000,000	....
1830	639,000,000	....
1858	755,297,000	....
1870 (January 1)	721,788,180	....
1873 (January 1)	797,313,480	....
1875	763,869,467	....

There is much confusion and error in the statements in cyclopedias and text-books in regard to the debt of Russia, and the proportion of it used as circulating money. The following will, however, explain some of the discrepancies in the statements as published in the various books.

The total debt of Russia on January 1, 1871, amounted in United States money to $1,241,750,000. This included about $575,000,000 (750,000,000 roubles) of paper money, or bills of credit issued by the government on the guarantee of all the banks and other credit establishments of the empire. These are called notes of the Bank of Russia, but are issued by the Imperial Treasury.

January 1, 1873, the total debt amounted to $1,684,-980,000 (2,277,081,564 roubles). In this amount is included $565,275,000 (763,869,467 roubles) of paper money, or bills of credit.

On January 1, 1875, the total debt had increased to $2,149,995,000 in United States money. Of this amount $580,000,000 (797,313,480 roubles) was bills of credit, or paper money. About $200,000,000 more of the total was treasury paper, which circulates to a considerable extent as money. The total paper circulation of Russia is therefore about $780,000,000, or over 1,000,000,000 roubles. While this shows an increase of about 250,000,000 roubles since 1858, it does not seem to warrant the assertion of the *Statesman's Year-Book* (London) for 1876, that "the paper money circulation of Russia has more than doubled in the last ten years."

Included in the above total debt there are about $200,000,000 of railway bonds, on which the interest is guaranteed by the government.

The *Scientific Review*, of Paris, for September 2, 1876, states the debt of Russia at 1,494,070,791 roubles ($1,097,047,960); but I presume this refers to the funded debt of the empire alone, and does not include either the treasury paper circulating as money or the railway loans on which the interest is guaranteed by the government.

ITALY.

Paper currency in Italy is furnished mainly by the National Bank of Italy, whose present position and relations to the national government have existed since 1863. Its present powers to issue legal tender notes, etc., were the result of the financial embarrassments of the new kingdom finally established in 1861 as a result of the Italian-French and Austrian war of 1859. The capital of the National Bank of Italy is 100,000,000 lire (a lire is of the same value as a franc, $19\frac{3}{10}$ cents), and in October, 1868, the outstanding circulation of the bank amounted to 775,879,712 lire, nominally equivalent to $147,417,145 in United States money, or at the rate of about $\$5\frac{40}{100}$ per capita of the nearly 27,000,000 of population in 1872. This does not comprise the entire paper currency of the country, but it is the greater part. There is but little specie in circulation, and the bulk of specie in the country is held in the National Bank, which, in October, 1868, held a metallic reserve of 178,000,000 lire, or equal to $83,800,000 in United States money. Silver being a legal tender for any amount in Italy, it is presumable that whatever metallic reserve may be in the bank now is mainly of silver, and also that whatever other coin there may be in the kingdom is almost exclusively silver.

SPAIN.

The National Bank of Spain has a capital of 120,000,000 reals vellon (equivalent to $6,000,000), and issues circulating notes to the amount of 60,000,000 reals vellon, or equivalent to $3,000,000 in United States money. Besides this a portion of the large public debt, which in May, 1872, amounted to $1,511,000,000, has circulated as money. The national government became bankrupt in 1873, the payment of interest on the public debt having ceased in July of that year.

SWITZERLAND.

In Switzerland there are twenty-eight banks, nearly all of which issue notes to circulate as money, the legal limit of such notes issued by each bank being double the amount of its capital. The reform in the banking system of Switzerland, adopted in 1875, requires each bank to receive the notes of all other banks at par, and also that each bank shall keep a metallic reserve on hand equal to one third the amount of its notes in circulation. There has been a large increase of paper money in Switzerland in the last few years, and a corresponding decrease of coin, gold having almost disappeared. The aggregate of paper money in circulation at various periods has been as follows, viz.:

1870	18,000,000 francs.
1873	47,000,000 "
1873 (October)	72,000,000 "

The 72,000,000 francs, equal to $13,800,000, gave a paper money circulation of $5.30 per capita of the 2,600,000 of population, and the legal limit to the aggregate circulation is 50 francs per capita, which would give at the utmost $26,000,000 of paper circulation. The coin circulation is mainly of silver.

BELGIUM.

The Bank of Belgium had a total of circulating notes outstanding June 1, 1872, equal to $44,712,000 in United States money, and against this held a specie reserve equal to $21,384,000. On February 1, 1873, the circulation had increased to $60,264,000 and the specie to $23,328,000.

SWEDEN.

In Sweden there is the National Bank of Sweden, with a circulation in June, 1872, equal to $14,924,870; also twenty-six private banks, with an aggregate circulation at the same date equal to $9,067,600. The notes, both of the national and private banks, are payable in silver. The above aggregate of notes is at the rate of about $5 per capita of the population. The coin circulation is almost entirely of silver.

TOTAL OF PAPER MONEY IN EUROPE.

We may now proceed to make an approximate estimate of the increase of paper money in Europe in twenty-two years by giving the amounts in millions of dollars (omitting six ciphers in each amount), giving the amount in each country for the year nearest to 1854 and again for the year nearest to 1876:

	Millions of Dollars.	Year.	Millions of Dollars.	Year.
Great Britain and Ireland	191	1854	235	1876
France	122	1854	493	1876
Germany	80	1850	200	1876
Austria	151	1853	289	1876
Italy	....	1854	300	1876
Russia	558	1858	750	1875
Spain	....	....	*3	....
Switzerland	3	1870	14	1873
Belgium	44	1872	60	1873
Sweden	20	1865	25	1872
	1,169		2,369	
Increase	1,200			

* This is only the notes of the Bank of Spain.

The average of the above periods is seventeen years, and the average increase of paper money something near $62,000,000 per annum. But a point of much significance is that of the total increase of say $1,200,000,000 of paper money in Europe, over $800,000,000 has been made since 1866, thus showing that the period of greatest contraction in the United States has been the period of greatest expansion in Europe.

SUSPENSIONS OF SPECIE PAYMENT IN ALL COUNTRIES.

THE UNITED STATES.

THERE have been four periods of suspension of specie payments in the United States in the last sixty-two years. Two were caused by the requirements of the government to carry on wars (1814 and 1861), and two (1839 and 1857) by the collapse of speculation induced by over-issues of bank notes under systems of banking not sufficiently guarded by law in regard to the security of an adequate specie reserve.

In 1814 the government was at war with Great Britain, and conducting extensive operations along the line between Canada and the United States. From 1812 to 1814 the government borrowed in all $45,000,000. Of the first $10,000,000, borrowed in 1812, $6,000,000 was taken by the banks in the middle States, as also a considerable portion of the other loans. The New England people were opposed to the war, and consequently the New England banks took scarcely any of the government loans.*

The result of these loans to the government was that in 1814 all the banks, except those in New England, suspended specie payments.

As a means of assisting the financial operations of the government, and also to encourage the banks to resume,

* Sumner's *History of American Currency*, page 65.

the Bank of the United States was organized in 1816–17. (This was the second institution under that name, the first one having been organized in 1791 and wound up at the expiration of its charter, March 4, 1811.) This second charter of the United States Bank extended to March 3, 1836, when there was a strong effort to have it renewed, and a bill for that purpose was passed by Congress but vetoed by President Jackson, July 4, 1832. The Bank of the United States, however, continued its business under a charter granted by the legislature of Pennsylvania. From 1834 to 1838 was a speculative era, not only in the United States but elsewhere, and owing to the absence of any legal restrictions on the issue of bank notes, or in regard to reserves, the volume of bank notes increased from $94,000,000 in 1834 to $149,000,000 in 1837. The result was a collapse of bubble speculations and banks. The Bank of the United States suspended October 9, 1839; it resumed again on January 15, 1841, but finally succumbed to the general tendency of affairs on February 4, 1841.

The next suspension was in 1857, from the same causes as in 1838–9. None of the three foregoing suspensions were legalized by any act of the national government. Legal tender paper money had been issued by some of the colonial governments prior to the war of Independence, but these were prohibited after 1750, and there was no legal tender paper currency from that time until 1862.

The act authorizing the suspension of specie payments and the issue of legal tender paper money will be found in the Digest of Monetary Laws in the act of February 25, 1862, and the amount of currency outstanding each year under this and subsequent laws will be found in the table of paper money in the United States each year. The value of the currency, measured in gold, fluctuated over a wider range in a shorter period in the United States than in any other country in which specie payments have been suspended. From 97 cents in January, 1862, it fell to 38.7 (the lowest point) in July, 1864, and rose again to 73.7 within ten months.* The fluctuation being entirely due to the aspects of the war.

* The following table is from the Report of the Comptroller of the Currency for 1875:

Table showing the gold-price in dollars of one hundred dollars in currency in the New York market, by months, quarter-years, half-years, calendar years, and fiscal years, from January 1, 1862, to August 31, 1875, both inclusive.

Periods.	1862	1863	1864	1865	1866	1867	1868	1869	1870	1871	1872	1873	1874	1875
January	97.6	68.9	64.3	46.3	71.4	74.3	72.2	73.7	82.4	90.3	91.7	88.7	89.7	88.9
February	96.6	62.3	63.1	48.7	72.3	72.8	70.7	74.4	83.7	89.7	90.7	87.6	89.1	87.3
March	98.2	64.7	61.4	57.5	76.6	74.1	71.7	76.2	88.8	90.1	90.8	86.6	89.2	86.6
April	98.5	66	57.9	67.3	78.6	73.7	72.1	75.2	88.4	90.4	90	84.9	88.2	87.1
May	96.8	67.2	56.7	73.7	75.9	73	71.6	71.8	87.2	89.7	88	85	89.9	86.3
June	93.9	69.2	47.5	71.4	67.2	72.7	71.4	72.4	88.6	89	87.8	85.8	90	85.4
July	86.6	76.6	38.7	70.4	66	71.7	70.1	73.5	85.6	89	87.5	86.4	91	87.2
August	87.3	79.5	39.4	69.7	67.2	71	68.7	74.5	84.8	89	87.4	86.7	91.2	88.1
September	84.4	74.5	44.9	69.5	68.7	69.7	69.6	73.1	87.1	87.3	88.1	88.7	91.2	86.4
October	77.8	67.7	48.3	68.7	67.4	69.7	72.9	76.8	88.7	88.3	88.3	91.8	91	....
November	76.3	67.6	42.8	68	69.5	71.6	74.4	79.2	89.8	89.9	88.6	92.1	90.2	....
December	75.6	66.2	44	68.4	73.2	74.2	74	82.3	90.3	91.5	89.1	90.9	89.6	....
First quarter-year	97.5	65.2	62.9	50.4	73.3	73.7	71.5	74.7	84.9	90	91	87.6	89.3	87.6
Second quarter-year	96.3	67.4	53.6	70.7	73.6	73.2	71.7	73.2	88	89.7	88.6	85.3	89	86.3
Third quarter-year	86.1	76.8	40.8	69.8	67.2	70.8	69.5	73.7	85.8	88.4	87.6	87.3	91.1	87.2
Fourth quarter-year	76.6	67.2	44.9	68.4	70	71.8	73.7	79.4	89.6	90	88.7	91.6	90.2	....
First half-year	96.9	66.3	57.9	58.9	73.5	73.4	71.6	73.9	86.4	89.8	89.8	86.4	89.2	86.9
Second half-year	81	71.6	42.8	69.1	68.6	71.3	71.5	76.5	87.7	89.2	88.2	89.4	90.7	....
Calendar year	88.3	68.9	49.2	63.6	71	72.4	71.6	75.2	87	89.5	89	87.9	89.9	....
Fiscal year ended June 30	....	72.9	64	49.5	71.2	70.9	71.5	72.7	81.1	88.7	89.4	87.3	89.3	88.8

GREAT BRITAIN.

The Bank of England suspended specie payments on February 26, 1797, in consequence of a drain of specie and the increase of public expenditures resulting from the war with the French.

Bank of England notes were declared legal tender; but their issues were so much restricted by law that they remained at par until 1800, when the issues were increased, and they fell to a discount of 8 per cent for gold. In 1810 the discount was 13½ per cent, and at another period, in 1815, 25 per cent, at about which depreciation they continued until 1816. In 1817 they had risen to 2½ per cent, and in 1819 declined to 4½ per cent. In May, 1821, the bank resumed specie payments.

FRANCE.

The Bank of France first suspended specie payments in 1848; the cause being the revolution of that year, which obliged the bank to make large advances to the provisional government and the city of Paris. But in order to prevent too great depreciation of the paper money the issues of the bank were restricted by law to 350,000,000 francs. In 1851 the bank resumed specie payments.

In August, 1870, the Bank of France again suspended specie payments in consequence of the war with Germany. The effects of this upon the notes of the Bank of France are thus described by M. Victor Bonnet, in an article in the *Revue Des Deux Mondes:*

"The movements of the paper-money circulation inflicted on France by the war are destined to surprise a multitude of people. There is," he says, "in those movements a complete overturning of the economic and financial ideas which the best authorities had endeavored to establish in the previous history of monetary science. These authorities have always raised their warning voice against paper money and legal tender laws. They tell us with one accord that if the quantity of paper money be not strictly limited, and excessive issues prevented, the public confidence will fail, and depreciation will soon follow. In apparent defiance of these sound principles, we find that in the midst of the war troubles of France, paper money to the amount of 1,800,000,000 of francs was issued, and has been kept at par by means of a coin reserve of 600,000,000 francs, or 33 per cent. This paper money never for a single moment lost its value, or fell to a discount until the first payments were made to Prussia. At that crisis the premium on gold rose to 2½ per cent, and, strange to say, this premium fell immediately when the law was passed to expand the circulation, and to increase the issues beyond 1,400,000,000 francs, which was the limit at first assigned to the maximum of the note issues. In November, 1871, these issues were 2,300,000,000 francs, and the depreciation was 2½ per cent. At the end of January, 1872, the issues were 2,450,000,000 francs, and the depreciation had fallen to 1 per cent.

"At length, after the lapse of a certain period, when new issues had been authorized, and the legal limit had been fixed at 3,200,000,000 francs, the premium on gold was merely nominal, and nobody paid any attention to it, except those concerned in the foreign exchanges.

The singularity of this was the more noteworthy because these large emissions of notes took place amidst grave incertitude. For, in the first place, France was paying her immense indemnity to the Prussians, and was seeking in every possible way to augment her specie resources; and, secondly, she seemed likely, in spite of all she could do, to lose her whole aggregate of coin circulation. Never before had such dangers been surmounted with so much success."

AUSTRIA.

In March, 1848, in consequence of the revolution in Vienna, there was a run upon the National Bank, which suspended specie payment. In May, 1851, the premium on silver florins over bank notes was 30 per cent. At the beginning of 1854 it had declined to 22 per cent. On November 1, 1858, the National Bank of Austria resumed specie payments. In 1859 the war of Italian liberation, in which Italy and France were combined against Austria, compelled the National Bank of Austria to again suspend specie payment. In June, 1859, the depreciation of the notes of the National Bank was 42 per cent, in September of the same year 16 per cent, and at the end of January, 1860, was 33 per cent. In January, 1861, the depreciation was 32 per cent, and at the beginning of 1862 was about 27 per cent. In December, 1862, an act was passed peremptorily requiring the bank to resume specie payments on January 1, 1867. Under the influence of this the discount on national bank notes for silver decreased to 6 per cent in 1863. But in 1866 the war with Prussia obliged an increase of paper money, and the discount on national bank notes and government notes increased to 19 per cent in July, 1866, and 21 per cent in January, 1867, and was reduced again to 15 per cent by the end of that year. During the years 1874 and 1875 the premium on silver over bank or government notes averaged about 5 per cent.

ITALY.

In Italy there was scarcely any paper money in circulation previous to 1859, but the war of Italian liberation, which caused the Bank of Austria to suspend in 1859, also obliged great expenditures on the part of the new Italian government, and the National Bank of Italy, which had been founded under a royal decree in 1863, by the consolidation of the National Bank of Turin with that of Tuscany, had already made large advances to the new government. The latter, finding that it could no longer raise money by popular loans (the price of its "rentes" having fallen to 45 per cent), and requiring still further aid from the bank, authorized it, in 1866, to issue inconvertible legal tender paper money. The total of government and bank notes in circulation in April, 1865, had been stated at 247,000,000 francs, or $49,000,000, but the result of the new law was that by 1874 the total paper money amounted to 1,500,000,000 francs, or $300,000,000. In 1866 the depreciation of the paper money was 19 to 20 per cent, but with a largely increased amount in 1874 the depreciation was only 3 per cent, and at the beginning of 1876 about 7 per cent.

RUSSIA.

Specie payments have been suspended in Russia for more than 60 years. During the period from the suspension to 1870 the depreciation of the paper money fluctuated over a range from 17 to 29 per cent. According to the reports of the last few years the range of depreciation has been from 10 to 15 per cent.

BRAZIL.

Specie payments have been suspended in Brazil for nearly 50 years. During that time there have been various unsuccessful attempts to resume. One plan upon which these attempts were made was to reduce the value of the metallic monetary unit. Thus the *millreis*, which is the monetary unit, and is now established at the equivalent of 54½ cents in United States money, was originally established at $136.35. The other method, upon which there have been several attempts to resume —the last one in 1858—was by contracting the currency. In 1848, incident to the cessation of the slave trade,* there was a large importation of gold bullion. This was coined and put into circulation by the government, and for a time it was claimed specie payments were resumed, but the gold soon went out again in the adjustment of balances created against Brazil in her foreign trade. On this occasion it was thought that the specie once put into circulation at par with paper would maintain the latter at par. But after the specie had

* *Bankers' Magazine* for April, 1875.

disappeared the theory was that the temporary equality of the two was caused by a depreciation of gold, which was recovered when the metal disappeared.

EFFECTS ON THE VALUE OF PAPER MONEY.

The foregoing summary of the effects of the suspension of specie payments in various countries to depress the value of the currency affords the following facts:

First. That the depreciation by no means corresponds to the volume of the currency. This is illustrated by the experience in France and Italy, where the value of the currency increased concurrent with an increase of its volume.

Second. That coin put forcibly into circulation at par with an inconvertible currency, as was the case in Brazil, will immediately flow out of the country. Not being used to redeem the currency, it is only a commodity for which there is no use, and like other commodities is temporarily depressed in value to an extent which, though slight, is sufficient to cause its exportation.

The causes which operate upon the value of an inconvertible currency, as compared with gold and silver, may be specified as follows, viz.:

First. The prospect of redemption. This is, of course, the most potent, producing much the greatest effect and in much shorter periods of time. This prospect may be diminished by the unfavorable aspect of a war, as was frequently the case in the United States, or by a decrease of revenue or a decrease of the stock of coin in the treasury, or by a failure of important crops, which would show the probability of a larger export movement of coin. The prospect of redemption would, however, be increased by the opposite of any of the above circumstances. In the case of France, which M. Victor Bonnet considers so remarkable, there was an increase of coin in the Bank of France concurrent with the increase of paper money, and though it was not near so large as the increase of bank notes, it was sufficient to inspire the public with confidence in the ability of the French financiers to borrow the whole amount for the indemnity to Germany, and also to redeem the notes of the bank. In short, this was "confidence"—confidence in the redemption of the paper money in coin.

Second. The demand for currency to use in the usual payments in trade—this demand, of course, fluctuating with the increase or decrease of the general volume of trade—and causing an increase in the coin value of the currency. Thus, if we assume that the prospect of redemption of the currency in coin would fix its value for the time being at say 75 cents on the dollar, an increase of internal traffic might cause a premium on this price. The inconvertible paper money having expelled coin from the channels of circulation might be inadequate to supply the requirements for money, and yet the prospect of redemption be so remote that the premium paid for the paper money as the only instrument of exchange would not be sufficient to raise it to par with coin. The operation of this was, I think, visible to some extent in Italy. Previous to the establishment of the new kingdom, in 1860, there had been but little progress of any kind in Italy; the habits and ideas of its people seemed fossilized in the forms of the seventeenth century. But with the new kingdom a new era began in economic and industrial affairs. Bank notes were scarcely known in Italy before 1860, but between 1866 and 1874 the six banks of issue in the kingdom had increased their branches from fifty-two to ninety-five, and productive and manufacturing industries were greatly stimulated. From 1869 to 1872 the imports of foreign goods increased 25 per cent, and the value of the total annual exports increased 50 per cent. But with all this increase of traffic and industry the annual expenditures of the government exceeded the revenue by nearly $50,000,000 each year, and the aggregate of these deficits from 1861 to 1873 was about $500,000,000. Notwithstanding this continued increase of debt and the increase of the inconvertible paper money from $49,-000,000 in 1865 to $300,000,000 in 1874, the value of the paper money, as compared with gold and silver, advanced from an average of about 80 cents in 1865–6 to about 93 to 95 cents in 1874–6. There were, of course, many concurrent features in the political and industrial affairs of the country which exercised their influence to cause fluctuations in the prospect of redemption; but coin had been practically expelled from the country, and the volume of paper money being limited, the premium paid for it over its real value, though not sufficient to raise it to par, was, I think, largely the cause of the advance of 12 to 15 per cent from 1866 to 1876.

Third. The temporary depreciation in the value of gold and silver, either brought from abroad and forced into the market by coinage and issue by the government, as in the instance in Brazil, or by production, as in our own country. The inconvertible paper currency having deprived the gold and silver of their function as money, the latter become only commodities, and as such, being cheaper than in countries where they are used both as a commodity and as money, they are immediately exported. I am aware that some political economists deem it almost a heresy to say that the value of gold can be less in one country than in another. But to me it seems plain that gold, like wheat or cotton, flows to the market where it bears the highest value relatively to other things. The precious metals have always been selected as standards of valuation, not because their value was unchangeable, but because they changed *less* than those of other commodities. Paper money has no intrinsic value, but only a prospective one, viz., the prospect of redemption. It is, therefore, impossible for paper money to be a standard of values. It may appear to be so, but in reality the values that seem to be measured by a "paper money standard," are measured by the gold and silver standards modified by the prospect of redemption of the paper money. The paper money price of anything is only the gold or silver price with an allowance made for the uncertainty of ever getting the gold and silver promised in the paper money. But this temporary depreciation of gold or silver, in any country, is concealed by the use of paper money; consequently the prices of other commodities do not immediately decline, buyers and sellers are slow to adjust prices to a change in the value of the precious metals, and in nearly all cases the accumulation of cheapened precious metals flows out in exportation before any change is made in the currency prices of commodities; but, in the meantime, the inconvertible paper money has been overvalued.

GOLD AND SILVER COIN IN EUROPE.

IN 1800, the total amount of gold coin in the United Kingdom was estimated at only £8,000,000.

In 1844, the total of gold coin in the kingdom was estimated by Newmarch at £36,000,000, this amount including the coin in the bank. The same authority also estimated the total of gold and silver coin in the kingdom, at the close of 1856, at £70,000,000.

In 1868, Professor W. Stanley Jevons made a partial census of the gold and silver coins in the United Kingdom, and, upon this as a basis, made an estimate of the whole amount. His conclusion was that the total amount of gold coin in the kingdom in March, 1868, was not to exceed £80,000,000, and that it was possibly £3,000,000 to £5,000,000 less than that aggregate. The result of his estimate, which included the gold in bank, was as follows:

Sovereigns in circulation	£64,500,000
Sovereigns undistributed, in bank	3,500,000
Half sovereigns (24,000,000)	12,000,000
Total gold circulation	£80,000,000

The amount of silver coin in the kingdom was at the same time estimated at £14,000,000.

The London *Economist* of March 15, 1873, estimated that the amount of gold coin in the kingdom had been increasing at the rate of about £2,000,000 per annum for several years. This estimate of increase was based upon the annual movements of coin to and from the Bank of England and the interior at the seasons of the spring and fall settlements and crop movements.

Assuming this ratio of increase to be correct, Dr. Edward Young, of the Bureau of Statistics, at Washington, made an estimate of the amount of gold and silver coin in the United Kingdom at the close of 1872, with the following result, viz.:

Total amount of gold coin circulating in the United Kingdom at the close of 1872	£84,551,000
Total amount of silver coin circulating in the United Kingdom at the close of 1872.....................	15,000,000
Total amount of bronze coin circulating in the United Kingdom at the close of 1872......................	1,148,000

Assuming that silver coin constituted about the same proportion of the whole in 1856 as in 1868, we have the following approximate statement of the amounts of gold and silver coin in Great Britain and Ireland at the periods stated, viz.:

	Gold Coin.	Silver Coin.
1856................................	£60,000,000	£10,000,000
1868................................	80,000,000	14,000,000
1872................................	84,551,000	15,000,000
1876................................	88,500,000	16,000,000

Owing to the fact that previous to 1795 the gold coins of France were very much undervalued as a legal tender, gold was almost entirely banished from France, and even after there was a modification of this, in 1795, silver continued almost the exclusive metallic currency of France until a comparatively recent period. In 1848, also, the Bank of France suspended specie payments in consequence of the revolution, and its notes to the amount of 350,000,000 francs were made a legal tender, which condition of things lasted until 1851. It may therefore be presumed that what coin was not driven out of the country by the suspension of specie payments was at least three-fourths silver. The population of France in 1848 was not to exceed 35,000,000, and allowing eighty francs per capita as an estimate of the probable amount of coin and notes in use at that time, we have an aggregate of 2,800,000,000 francs, from which deduct 350,000,000 francs of notes, and it leaves an approximate estimate of 2,450,000,000 francs of coin, which, if one-fourth gold, would leave silver coin to the amount of 1,840,000,000 francs.

Roswag estimated the amount of coined money in France in 1856 at 4,000,000,000 francs, and expressed the belief that in the nine years to 1865 the aggregate had declined to 3,000,000,000.

M. Louvet, minister of agriculture and commerce, and also M. Charles le Touze, estimated the amount of coined money in France in 1870 at from 5,000,000,000 to 6,000,000,000 francs.

The French indemnity to Germany, in accordance with the treaty signed at Paris February 26, 1871, was 5,000,000,000 francs, of which 1,000,000,000 was to be paid in 1871, and the rest within three years.* Not-

* M. Wolowski, a member of the Institute and a deputy to the National Assembly, printed an article in the *Journal des Economists*, in December, 1874, in which he summed up the French payments to Germany as follows, viz.:

To sum up the totals of remittances made to Germany, we delivered:

	Francs.	C.
In notes on the Bank of France	125,000,000	00
In French gold	273,003,058	10
In French silver	239,291,875	75
In German specie and bank notes	105,039,145	18
In thalers	2,185,313,721	04
In Frankfort florins	235,128,152	79
In marks banco of Hamburg	265,260,990	29
In marks of the Empire	72,072,309	62
In florins of Holland	250,540,821	46
In Belgian francs	295,704,546	40
In pounds sterling	637,349,832	28
Total	4,990,060,453	29

withstanding the remarkable financial ability of the French ministers, by which a system of gigantic borrowing in foreign countries was inaugurated, there was a considerable drain of specie from France, though nothing like so large as was generally anticipated. This movement of coin was, however, in all probability, sufficient to cause an important decrease in the stock of coined money in France from 1870 to 1874. If even the lower estimate made by Louvet of the amount of coin in France in 1870 was not too large, it must be remembered that there was an increase of over $250,000,000 of paper money in France from 1870 to 1875, and that the premium of even 2½ per cent on gold over paper would cause a large export of gold. A very liberal estimate of the aggregate of coin in France — including the metallic reserve of the bank — in 1875 could not exceed 5,000,000,000 francs, or say from $1,000,000,000 to $900,000,000. This amount of coin, together with nearly $500,000,000 of bank circulation in 1875, would give the population of France an aggregate circulation so much larger per capita than any other country in the world that, in view of the fact that *all figures of the amounts of coin are only estimates*, I should be inclined to estimate the amount of coin in France in 1875 even lower than $900,000,000. But as it seems very difficult to discover where and how the presumed aggregate of gold in the world is distributed, I take the higher estimate. As arguments against any important increase in the amount of coin in circulation in France from 1870 to 1875, we have the following facts: first, the note circulation of the Bank of France was increased nearly 1,250,000,000 francs, or $250,000,000, from January, 1870 to January, 1875. This was intended to, and probably did, substitute an equal amount of coin paid to Germany; second, France borrowed nearly 4,000,000,000 francs, or $800,000,000, of the money to pay the indemnity, in Great Britain, Holland, Belgium and Germany; and though the foreign holding of this French loan had undoubtedly been considerably reduced by 1875, the average annual interest to be paid by France to foreign creditors during the four years to 1875 could not have been less than $50,000,000, or an aggregate of $200,000,000, in gold in the four years from 1871 to 1875.

If the constitution of the metallic reserve in the Bank of France at different periods may be accepted as an index of the relative proportions of gold and silver coins in circulation, it would show that even down to 1869 the coin in circulation in France was about three fourths silver, viz.:

In 1860, of the total of about 425,000,000 francs, average metallic reserve of the Bank of France, only 100,000,000 was gold. But in 1871 there was a great change in the policy of the bank in this respect. It sought to dispose of its silver and hoard gold. During the year 1875 the bank paid out a total of 1,127,500,000 francs in coin, of which 630,000,000 francs was gold and 495,000,000 francs was silver. The change in the proportions of gold and silver in the reserve of the bank is thus stated in an article in the *Bankers' Magazine* for December, 1874:

Maximum of the Years.	In Gold. Francs.	In Silver. Francs.	Total in Francs.	Total in Dollars.
1869 (Dec. 23)..	704,000,000	501.000.000	1,266,000,000	253,200,000
1871 (Aug. 25)..	591,000,000	98.000,000	691,000,000	138.200,000
1872 (Dec. 18)..	657,000,000	133.000.000	792.000.000	158,400,000
1873 (June 5)...	690,000,000	125,000.000	820.000.000	164,000,000
1874 (Mar. 31)..	729,000,000	311.000.000	1.040.000.000	208,000.000
1874 (June 17)..	884,000,000	318.000.000	1.163,000.000	232,600.000

Since the above dates the relative amount of silver in the bank reserve has remained at about one quarter of the whole.*

The proportions of gold and silver paid out by the Bank of France during 1875 afford ground for the presumption that the proportion of silver in circulation among the people is much larger than in the reserve of the bank. It is not probable that those who received metallic money from the bank would have accepted four ninths of it in silver coin if that was not about the proportion of silver in the general circulation of the country. But there is another fact which indicates the use of a large amount of silver coin in France, viz.: that the Bank of France issues very few notes of small denominations. Of the notes in circulation in 1875 the total value of those of denominations as small as 5 francs was only $1,342,000, and the total value (expressed in

* In reply to an inquiry of the Cincinnati *Commercial* on this point, the following letter was received by the editor of that paper from the banking house of Marcuard, Andre & Co. at Paris, viz.:

PARIS, *June 23, 1876.*

Sir,—We can reply as follows to the several inquiries conveyed by your letter of the 2d inst.: The 5-franc piece is an unlimited legal tender, and may, therefore, be employed to any extent for payments; the smaller silver coins are of inferior fineness, and acceptance of the same cannot be enforced beyond an amount of 50 francs per each payment. The Bank of France issues no more 5-franc notes, and destroys those which return to the bank in course of circulation. The bank has at present on hand 581,258,000 francs in silver coin and bullion, 1 468,340,000 francs in gold coin and bullion. In March, 1875, the bank held 495,000,000 francs in silver, and 1,325,000,000 francs in gold, which shows that the respective increase of the silver and gold paid in have taken place in proportions which do not differ so widely as might be anticipated from the great abundance of silver. From our previous remarks on 5-franc pieces it follows that, in case the bank resumes specie payments, these could be legally effected in silver coin, using the pieces inferior to 5 francs, to the maximum extent of 50 francs per payment. We will add, for your guidance, that ¼-franc pieces have been withdrawn from circulation, and are replaced by 20-centime pieces (one fifth franc). The commercial value of gold and silver is as follows, viz.: Silver of 1,000-1,000 fineness, 218.89 francs per kilogramme; gold of 1,000-1,000 fineness, 3,431.41 francs per kilogramme. The kilogramme is equivalent to 32 1,543-10,000 ounces. It is on the above basis that silver and gold are quoted with so much per cent loss or premium. The mint receives, however, these two metals on the following footing: Gold, 3,437 francs per kilogramme; silver, 220.56 francs per kilogramme. In consequence of the international treaties, the mint, being provided with silver for its coinage till December, 1878, does not, for the present, receive any more of this metal.

MARCUARD, ANDRE & CO.

United States money) of notes as low as 25 francs and including all those of smaller denominations was only $62,238,280. Now in the United States, with a population just about equal to that of France, the total amount of notes of denominations as small as one dollar and under, including the fractional currency, is about $75,000,000, or nearly sixty times as much as the 5 franc notes of the Bank of France. Comparing the amount of notes in the United States of the denomination of $5 and under with the amount of French notes of the denomination of 25 francs and under, we find $224,500,000 of the former in the United States against only $62,238,000 of the latter in France. This deficiency of small notes in France is undoubtedly supplied by silver coin. Still another fact, which has a bearing on this question, is that the total coinage of France in the four years from 1869 to 1872 inclusive was, of gold, 330,000,000 francs, and of silver 114,000,000 francs. The export of coin from France is probably more largely of gold than of silver.

Upon the above facts as a basis we may estimate the amounts of gold and silver coin in France at various periods approximately as follows, expressed in their equivalent in United States money:

	Gold Coin.	Silver Coin.
1848	$122.000,000	$368,000,000
1856	200,000,000	600,000,000
1870	250.000,000	750,000,000
1875	650,000,000	350,000,000

There are no statistics, nor even any estimates, that are of any value in regard to the amount of coin in Germany. The entire lack of anything like uniformity in the official reports of the different German States previous to their consolidation into the present empire makes it worse than useless to rely on them as a basis for estimating the amount of coin in the country.

In 1868, with a view to ascertaining the condition and amount of the monetary circulation of the North German Confederation, Bismarck, then chancellor, addressed circulars of inquiry to all the states of the confederation, which were the same as those in the present German Empire with the exception of Bavaria, Wurtemburg and Baden, which were not in the confederation. In response to these circulars a large mass of statistics of coinage was obtained, and upon these an estimate was made that the total amount of coin in the hands of the people and as reserves in the banks, in 1869, was 632,435,362 thalers, composed of 442,147,371 thalers of silver and 173,219,850 thalers of gold.

The utter unreliability of this estimate will be seen from the following facts: First, that the aggregate of 632,435,362 thalers is obtained by simply giving the coinage of eight different German mints for all sorts of periods, varying from thirty-three years to over one hundred years. From these sums were deducted the recoinages of their own coins by the same mints, and from the *disjecta membra* thus obtained, without making any allowance for either import or export of coin or bullion, was drawn the conclusion that in 1869 there was the above mentioned amounts of gold and silver coin in circulation and in banks in Germany. This estimate of coin in Germany has been used in Congress and in many political discussions in the United States, but the basis on which it was made was so incomplete as to be utterly worthless, and there is nothing to even give countenance to the estimate except that it corresponded to the popular belief that there was not so much coin in Germany as in France. The estimate of $900,000,000 of coin in France in 1870 would give an average of about $18 per capita of the population (38,000,000 in 1866 and 36,000,000 in 1872), whereas the estimate of coin in Germany would give about $15 per capita of the estimated population of 30,000,000 in Germany in 1870. It is in view of these latter facts alone that the estimate of a coin circulation in Germany in 1869–70, equal to $455,000,000 in coin of the United States, is worthy of any consideration.

The reports of German coinage made to Bismarck in 1869 are, however, of some value in determining the proportion of silver to gold coins in circulation at about 40 per cent of gold coins to 60 per cent of silver.

If, therefore, we accept the estimate of $450,000,000 of coin in Germany in 1869–70, we must make a large addition for the effect of the payment of the French indemnity of 5,000,000,000 francs from 1870 to 1874.

France paid her indemnity to Germany somewhat as follows: 20 to 25 per cent of the whole in the actual transmission of coin from France to Germany; about 35 per cent of the whole amount was borrowed in England, Belgium and Holland, and bills on those countries remitted to Berlin for the amounts borrowed, thus giving Germany the power to draw an aggregate of about $350,000,000 of coin. About 30 to 35 per cent more of the total indemnity was borrowed in Germany. This latter item would not cause any influx of coin into Germany except for the interest on the loans. It is also well known that the coin was not drawn very rapidly by Germany on the French bills on England,

Belgium and Holland, and much of the coin thus drawn would soon gravitate back to the countries from whence it came, so that it is probable that the greatest addition to the aggregate of coin in Germany at any time from the payment of the war indemnity did not exceed $400,000,000, about the close of 1873.* We may, therefore, make the following estimate in United States money of the amount of gold and silver coin in Germany:

	Gold Coin.	Silver Coin.
1869	$180,000,000	$270,000,000
1874	380,000,000	370,000,000

The foregoing estimates of the amounts of each gold and silver coins in Great Britain, France and Germany have been made after taking into consideration not only all previous estimates made by various acknowledged authorities, but also all official reports and documents that seem to have any important bearing on the question. But for the remaining countries of Europe even an approximate estimate of the total amount of coin in circulation and in banks is much more difficult, because there are no official data that give any trustworthy information on the subject. In proceeding, therefore,

* The London *Economist* of September 13, 1873, remarks that the indemnity has been paid with but slight use of bullion and without a drain of specie from France. This result has been achieved to a very great extent by a gigantic borrowing on the part of the French government and individuals abroad. A large part of the loan is still held out of France by the syndicates of bankers and other capitalists whose bills received in payment of installments have been handed over to the German government. Another part of the loan is held by individuals, who have, either directly or indirectly, exported securities which they held, and invested the proceeds in the loan.

France has thus avoided a large export of specie, but has permanently increased her foreign indebtedness. The suspension of specie payments has not in France had the same effect which was produced by suspension in this country, namely, that of driving the precious metals out of circulation.—*Report U. S. Bureau of Statistics, September, 1873.*

to the inquiry as to what may be the amounts of gold and silver coin in the other countries of Europe, there seems almost no method except to establish approximately the following premises, viz.:

First. The financial condition of the people in each country, and their consequent ability to possess money of any kind. This may be estimated, perhaps, as well by their ability to pay taxes as by any other general fact that can be made to apply to all nations; and though the pressure of taxation undoubtedly varies very much in different countries, the average annual revenue raised by the governments will indicate in some degree the ability of the people to have money.

Second. The extent to which coin may have been displaced by the use of paper money and suspensions of specie payments.

Third. The effect which the decline in the price of silver may have had to cause a substitution of silver coins for gold in countries where silver is the exclusive standard of values, as in Austria and Russia.

The table on page 78 of the populations and revenue of each country for some one of the last four or five years will aid in showing the ability of the people to pay taxes, though of course there are qualifying features in each case that will somewhat change this relative ability as presented at first glance. There is, however, a reasonable degree of correspondence between the pressure of taxation in France in 1873 and Austria and Russia in 1871 and 1874. It is true that the two latter countries have not so recently been engaged in great and expensive wars, but in both countries the annual expenditures of the governments have largely exceeded the revenue each year for about thirty years, and the aggregate of annual deficits has piled up a great debt in each case. In Italy and Spain the financial affairs of the governments have been in even worse plight, but the government machinery for collecting taxes has not been so well organized and the amount of revenue raised has probably been no greater in proportion to the ability of the people to pay than it has been in Russia and Austria. If we find that in Sweden, for instance, where the government finances are in fair condition, the people pay nearly twice as much revenue per capita as in Russia, where there has always been a pressure to increase the revenue, we must conclude that the ability of the people of Sweden to pay taxes and possess money is at least double that of the people of Russia. Upon the same basis we may reasonably conclude that if the amount of revenue raised in Great Britain and France is about three times as great per capita as in Russia and Austria, the amount of money of any kind per capita in the latter countries is only one-third as great as in the former. These would be reasonable propositions even if there were no statistics by which they could be proven. But the definite knowledge of the amount of currency in use in the United States affords facts of great value in verifying the proportions of revenue to money in all countries.

No such facts have been at the command of economic science until within the last few years. Strenuous endeavors have been made in Great Britain and France to estimate the amount of money per capita; but it is only when corroborated by the experience of the United States that the law of the proportions can be eliminated from all the facts.

The following table of population in each country and the amount of national revenue per capita will serve as a measure of the amount of money in circulation and in banks, per capita of the whole population:

POPULATION AND ANNUAL REVENUE.

	Population.		Revenue.		Revenue per Capita.
United States......	42,000,000	1875–6	$287,482,090	1875	$6 87
Canada...........	4,000,000	1875–6	24,205,000	1874	6 05
Gt. Britain & Irel'nd	31,000,000	1875–6	377,000,000	1870	12 16
France............	36,000,000	1872	547,000,000	1873	15 19
Prussia...........	24,600,000	1874	167,500,000	1874	6 40
Austria-Hungary...	35,912,000	1874	*200,000,000	1871–2	5 55
Russian Empire....	82,000,000	1874	393,000,000	1874	4 79
Sweden...........	4,297,972	1874	38,707,476	1875	9 00
Belgium...........	5,087,000	1874	39,300,000	1873	7 72
Switzerland.......	2,669,000	1874	7,152,704	1873	2 69
Italy..............	26,800,000	1872	†178,000,000	1870	6 65
Spain.............	16,835,000	1870	113,500,000	1871–2	6 73

The analogy between the proportions of revenue and estimated volume of money in the United States, Great Britain and France are very striking. Thus, taking the whole amount of paper money and coin in the United States in 1875 at $850,000,000 it gives $20 per capita, or just about three times the amount of annual revenue per capita. In the United Kingdom of Great Britain and Ireland the total of paper money and coin is $765,-000,000, which gives $24.70 per capita, or a little more than double the ratio of revenue per capita. In France the total of paper money and coin was equivalent to $1,500,000,000, or $45 per capita, or just three times the ratio of average annual revenue per capita. Putting

* The official annual budget, or estimate of the revenue in Austria, is made under two different heads, one for the ordinary expenses of the empire at large and another for the separate countries—Austria and Hungary. The amount given above is an estimate made from both.

† Besides the $178,000,000 of ordinary revenue, the Italian government raised an extraordinary revenue in 1870 of $190,000,000 from taxation of church property.

these figures into the form of a table, we have the following result, viz.:

	Coin and Paper Per Capita.	Annual Revenue Per Capita.	Percentage of Revenue to Money.
United States	$20 00	$ 6 87	34.35
United Kingdom	24 70	12 16	49.23
France	45 00	15 19	33.53

Thus we find that in the three countries where the estimate of the volume of paper money and coin in existence is presumed to be more nearly correct than in any other countries of the world, there is a remarkable correspondence in the ratio of annual revenue to the total volume of money, which I have ventured to assume as the law governing the proportion of revenue to money in all countries.* The average of the percentage of revenue to money in the above table is 39, and in view

* The reliability of this rule for estimating the amount of money in use in any country is strikingly illustrated by the case of the United States for a series of fiscal years.

	Volume of Paper Money Alone.	Total Net Revenue.	Per Cent.
1866	$1,803,702,726	$558,632,620	31
1867	1,330,414,677	490,634,010	37
1868	817,199,773	405,638,083	49
1869	750,025,987	370,943,747	49
1870	740,039,179	411,255,477	55
1871	734,244,774	382,323,944	52
1872	736,349,912	374,106,867	50
1873	738,291,749	333,738,204	45
1874	779,031,589	289,478,755	37
1875	778,176,250	288,000,000	37
1876	735,358,832	287,482,039	39
Average			44

The foregoing shows that for a period of eleven years the annual revenue of the government has been an average ratio of 44 per cent of the paper money in use. But if now we estimate an average of $120,000,000 of coin in use in the United States and Territories each year, it makes the average annual revenue 37 per cent of the total of coin and paper money.

of the impossibility of even approximate statistics of the amount of coin in any countries but the United States, Great Britain and France, this seems the most satisfactory rule of estimation. There are, of course, exceptions to all rules; but in the cases of exception to this the causes are pretty well known. Switzerland, for instance, is known to have a much larger percentage of money to revenue; but the cause is plainly in the fact that she has no public debt of any consequence. But in the case of nearly all the remaining countries in the table the exceptions are in the opposite direction. They all have great public debts. The pressure of taxation to pay the interest on these, as in Russia, Austria, Italy and Spain, has resulted in a revenue larger in proportion to the amount of money in the countries than in England and France, until, as in the cases of Italy and Spain, it has impoverished the people and, in the case of Spain, bankrupted the government. Therefore, taking the remainder of Europe (exclusive of Great Britain, France and Germany), the amount of annual taxation and revenue is larger in proportion to the amount of money in the countries, and we should assume at least 40 per cent as the ratio of the former to the latter.

Under this rule the total annual revenue of Austria-Hungary, being $200,000,000, would represent a total monetary circulation of $500,000,000, or about $14 per capita. Of this amount $300,000,000 is paper money, thus leaving $200,000,000 of coin, which is known to be almost exclusively silver and token coinage.*

Upon the same basis there should be in Russia an aggregate of $982,000,000 of monetary circulating me-

* See article on Suspensions of Specie Payments in all Countries.

dium. By reference to the table of paper money it will be seen that the aggregate of paper money in Russia in 1873 was equal to $780,000,000, in United States money, thus leaving an aggregate of $200,000,000 of coin, which is known to be, as in Austria, almost exclusively silver and base metal.

The total ordinary revenue of Italy, stated in the foregoing table at $178,000,000 for 1870, if accepted as representing 40 per cent of the total monetary circulation of the kingdom, would indicate the total of money to be $445,000,000, or $16.60 per capita. The total of paper money in Italy in 1874 was 1,500,000,000 francs, equal to $300,000,000 in United States money. Deducting this latter amount from the whole, it leaves $145,000,000 to be represented by coin. Silver is a legal tender in any sum in Italy, and even if gold was not driven out by the suspension of specie payments, the recent decline in the value of silver would have the effect to leave nothing but silver and copper in circulation.

The disorganization of finances in Spain is so complete that it is impossible to estimate the amount of government paper that has recently been used as money. But the government being hopelessly bankrupt, its paper has lost all value.

The countries most critically examined in the foregoing pages, viz.: Great Britain, France, Austria, Italy and Russia, contain 70 per cent of the population of Europe, and the conclusions to be drawn from the premises sustain the popular opinion that the wealth of Europe — in gold and silver as well as other things — is concentrated mainly in Great Britain and France.

In view of all the foregoing facts, the estimates of the total value of gold and silver coin and bullion in banks and in circulation in the respective countries of Europe would stand about as follows, viz.:

GOLD, SILVER AND BASE METAL COIN AND GOLD AND SILVER BULLION IN CIRCULATION AND IN BANKS IN ALL EUROPE.

	Gold.	Silver and Base Metal.
Great Britain	$442,500,000	$80,000,000
France	650,000,000	350,000,000
Germany	380,000,000	370,000,000
Austria		200,000,000
Russia		250,000,000
Italy		145,000,000
Spain		200,000,000
Sweden	300,000,000	70,000,000
Belgium		38,000,000
Switzerland		5,000,000
All other States of Europe		360,000,000
	$1,872,500,000	$2,060,000,000

The only countries of Europe not named in the above list are: Netherlands, population, 3,674,400; Luxembourg, population 197,500; Norway, population 1,741,000; Greece, population 1,457,000; Turkey in Europe, including Montenegro, Servia and Roumania, with a total population of 15,747,000, and Portugal, population 4,249,000, making an aggregate population of 25,600,000, not embraced in the table. In the Netherlands there is great wealth, but in all the other countries great poverty. If, therefore, we make an estimate of $18 per capita as the average coin in circulation and in banks in these countries, it would give an aggregate of $460,000,000. In the Netherlands and in Greece silver is the standard, and it would be a liberal estimate to say that $100,000,000 of the whole was gold coin and bullion in banks and in circulation. With these additions we should have the total of each kind of money in Europe about as follows, viz.:

Gold coin and bullion	$1,900,000,000
Silver and base metal	2,000,000,000
Paper money	2,300,000,000
Grand total	$6,200,000,000

The figures for the metallic circulation, and especially for the gold, fall so immensely short of the commonly received estimates of the amounts in use as money in Europe, that it is only after several careful reviews of all the premises that I venture to commit them to paper; and though the rule I have adopted, of assuming the annual revenue of each country to be the measure of from 38 to 40 per cent of its entire monetary circulation, may not produce results corresponding to some popular notions, it is at least logical, and seems the only one available for application in all countries.

But when we come to sum up the whole matter we find that the total monetary circulation of Europe, including the paper money (of which I think the total volume has heretofore always been underestimated), gives for the 300,500,000 total population of Europe an average of $21.40 per capita, or $1.40 more per capita than the total of paper and coin per capita in the United States.

In Austria, Russia and Italy, with an aggregate population of 145,000,000, or nearly one half of all Europe, specie payments have been suspended for many years, and the depreciation of the legal tender paper money would have a tendency to drive gold and silver out of circulation. In the other countries, as in Belgium, Sweden and the Netherlands, where there has been no suspension of specie payments, but where silver is a legal tender in any amount, the decline in the value of silver as compared to gold in the last year would have the effect to displace gold with silver. In Russia and Austria silver is the only standard, and the only legal metallic money of account, and under any circumstances, whether specie payments were suspended or not, silver would be the only coin in circulation to any considerable extent, except the token coinage. The operation of all these causes (and particularly the change in the relative values of gold and silver in the last year) has been to drive the gold out of other countries of Europe and concentrate it in Great Britain, France and Germany. In Germany this influx of gold has gone largely into general circulation in place of silver, which was demonetized under the new monetary system of the empire. In France the monetary circulation being already very large, it was not wanted in popular use and it went into the Bank of France. In Great Britain it went partly into circulation, but also accumulated to a considerable extent in the Bank of England.* The increase of specie in these banks has, I think, led to exaggerated estimates of the increase of gold and silver in use in Europe as money, whereas this was, to a large extent, merely the effect of the displacement of specie in general circulation by the increase of paper money throughout Europe.

Chevalier estimated the total of gold, in its various forms of coin bullion and personal ornaments, in the world, in 1848, at about $2,830,000,000, and various other accepted authorities estimated the amount of gold

*The effect of the movement of specie from all other parts of Europe to Germany, France and Great Britain, has, I think, contributed more than anything else to increase the specie reserve of the national banks of these three countries. This increase of specie in the banks of England, France and Germany, which has been ascribed to the increased production of gold and silver,

coin and bullion in Europe, in 1847, at about $1,250,-000,000. Albert Gallatin, after a careful consideration of the production and consumption, estimated the total of gold coin, bullion and ornaments in the world, in 1834, at only $1,800,000,000. In May, 1876, also, before a select committee of parliament, Mr. Seyd estimated the total stock of gold in circulation in the current year at the enormous figure of $3,750,000,000, of which he appor-

has been greatest since the production of gold has diminished, as will be seen by the following table of the amounts of specie in each of the three great banks at different periods in the eighteen months to July, 1876, (the amounts are given in their equivalents in United States money).

	Bank of France.	Bank of Germany.	Bank of England.
Dec. 26, 1874	$266,200,000	$..........	$105,120,125
Dec. 24, 1895	333,700,000	....	113,138,775
Jan. 31, 1876	....	112,780,000	....
Feb. 7	....	115,095,000	....
Feb. 10	347,153,000	....	....
Feb. 15	....	116,335,000	....
Feb. 17	350,853,000	....	....
Feb. 23	....	119,115,000	....
Feb. 24	355,348,000	....	....
Feb. 29	....	121,250,000	....
March 2	360,602,000	....	116,398,100
March 7	....	121,250,000	....
March 9	366,144,000	....	....
March 14	....	121,250,000	....
March 16	869,130,000	....	....
March 23	374,900,000	126,745,000	....
March 30	377,126,000	....	125,004,940
March 31	....	124,650,600	....
April 6	378,367,000	....	....
April 7	....	123,615,000	....
April 13	378,883,000	....	....
April 15	....	126,525,000	....
April 20	381,775,000	....	....
April 22	....	128,990,000	....
April 27	385,588,000	....	....
April 29	....	130,355,000	....
May 4	390,697,000	....	131,294,455
May 9	....	133,626,000	....
May 11	393,759,000	....	....
May 22	....	139,555,000	....
June 1	402,351,000	....	138,005,000
June 7	....	140,228,000	....
June 15	406,862,000	....	....
June 15	....	140,945,000	....
June 22	409,660,000	....	....
June 22	....	137,965,000	....
June 29	412,363,000	....	....
July 18	....	132,110,000	150,953,150
July 20	415,210,000	....	....

tioned $1,300,000,000 to France, $650,000,000 to Great Britain and 150,000,000 to the United States. Mr. Seyd's estimate of the gold in the United States is based on the estimate of the director of the United States Mint for June 30, 1875, which was $167,000,000 for the total amount of gold *and silver coin and bullion* in the United States at that date; but even in this estimate the director of the Mint stated that no deduction had been made for the amount of gold consumed in the arts for two years. This estimate also allowed $10,000,000 of actual gold coin and bullion as being held by the national banks, which is unquestionably too large an estimate. It is therefore apparent that Mr. Seyd's estimate of $150,000,000 of gold in the United States is about $50,000,000 too large, and I think his allowances to Great Britain and France are overestimates in about the same ratio. Seyd estimated the stock of gold coin alone in the commercial world, in 1872, at $2,600,000,000, and before 1848 at $2,000,000,000. Ruggles estimated the world's stock of gold coin in 1867, at $2,600,000,000. These estimates seem to be the merest conjectures, without any thorough investigation, and the method by which Mr. Seyd and others have arrived at their present estimates of the amount of gold in circulation is to add 75 per cent of the presumed production of gold in the world since the dates mentioned. Thus we have Gallatin's estimate of the total of gold coin, bullion and ornaments, in 1834, at $1,800,000,000. Chevalier's of $2,830,000,000, in 1848, and Seyd's of $3,750,000,000 of gold coin alone in 1876. If Gallatin was right Chevalier was wrong, and if Chevalier was right Seyd is wrong.

All these estimates are, however, open to the criticism that, first, they were made without any investigation of the financial condition of different countries of the world, or even of Europe; second, that they were not made upon the basis of any rule of wealth in each of the countries; that each later estimate has been made upon the presumption that the earlier ones were correct and that the only thing to be done was to add the 75 per cent of the estimated product of the mines. It is by this method of conjecture piled upon conjecture that men have contrived to arrive at the estimate of $3,750,000,000 of gold in use as money in the world at the present time. But it is in vain that they attempt to apportion it out to the respective countries,— the sum is too large to admit of apportionment.

If in the inquiry as to where this presumed immense sum of gold used as money is distributed we turn to our own part of the world, we find on the continent of North America a total population of about 56,000,000 in 1875. Of this total there was in the United States say 42,000,000, in Canada 4,000,000 and in Mexico 9,000,000. We know that the total of gold coin and gold bullion in the United States at the close of that year did not much exceed $100,000,000.

The population of Canada, in 1875, was estimated at a little over 4,000,000. The total revenue raised in 1874 was $24,205,000, or at the rate of $6.05 per capita. Assuming this to be in accordance with the rules applied to other countries, viz., 33⅓ per cent of the money in circulation and in banks, it would give an aggregate of $72,600,000 of all kinds of money, or at the rate of $18.15 per capita. The circulation of the Canadian banks on December 31, 1875, was $25,412,321, leaving a presumed aggregate of $47,200,000 in all sorts of coin.

There is a mint in each of the eight States of Mexico, and the aggregate coinage of these in the fiscal year 1872–3 was $20,374,554, of which $19,686,434 was silver coins, leaving only $668,120 of gold. The total coinage of 1869–70 was $20,677,021, with the same ratio of gold and silver, and in that year the total export of coin from Mexico was $17,479,014. Comparing these facts with similar ones for the various States of Europe, we should not expect to find in the whole of Mexico an aggregate of more than $40,000,000 of all kinds of coin, of which at least $35,000,000 would be silver.

According to the latest statistics the total population of South America and the West Indies aggregates about 29,000,000, of which 10,000,000 are in Brazil, 4,000,000 in the West Indies, and nearly 5,000,000 in Peru.

Of the 10,000,000 population of Brazil nearly or about one third are either savage nomadic tribes or persons recently manumitted from slavery under the act for gradual emancipation passed in 1871, and the proportion of the population using any kind of money to any considerable extent is not above 7,000,000 or 8,000,000. But the fact in connection with Brazil most pertinent to our present inquiry is that coin of any kind has for many years been almost entirely banished by the use of inconvertible paper money. Shortly after the first great increase of paper money in 1856–7 the entire monetary circulation of the empire was made the subject of careful investigation, the result of which was the following statement of all kinds of money in circulation in the empire at the close of 1857, viz.:

Government notes	43,000,000 millreis.*
Notes of Bank of Brazil	49,667,450
Gold, silver and copper coins	5,000,000
	97,667,450 millreis.

In 1858 the Bank of Brazil made an ineffectual attempt to resume specie payments, and by 1865 the total of bank and government notes was reduced to an aggregate of 75,000,000 millreis. But in consequence of the Paraguayan war, which ended in 1870, the Brazilian government increased its issues of inconvertible paper money 122,000,000 millreis, and in 1875 the monetary circulation of the empire was stated as follows, viz.:

Government notes	159,000,000 millreis.
Notes of the Banks of Brazil, Maranham, Pernambuco and Bahia	38,000,000
Gold, silver and copper, estimated	7,000,000
Total	204,000,000 millreis.

The total paper money circulation of Brazil was therefore equal to $52,204,230 in United States money in 1857, and increased to $106,380,000 by 1871, while the total coin circulation amounted to the insignificant sums of $2,700,000 in 1857 and $3,500,000 in 1871, at about which it has remained since.

The State of Paraguay was rendered totally bankrupt by the war with Brazil, and there can be but little coin of any kind in circulation.

The Argentine Republic resorted in 1866 to the issue of government treasury notes in denominations of $5, $10, $20, $50 and $100, and these have largely displaced coin of any kind.

* This word is the plural of *real*, and one *real* in Brazilian money is about half a mill. In Portuguese coin, however, it is about one mill. The modern Brazilian *milréis* (written 1$000, one thousand reis) is equal to 54½ cents in gold. The Portuguese millreis is worth about double that of Brazil.

In the republic of Peru the revenue of $23,499,653, collected from its population of 4,500,000 in 1873 ($5.22 per capita), would indicate an aggregate monetary circulation of about $76,000,000 to $80,000,000 (from $16 to $18 per capita); but there are banks of issue and also some issues of government money. The standard of values is exclusively silver, and whatever coin there is would be almost entirely of silver.

In the republic of Chili the revenue in 1871 was $11,788,500, or $5.89 per capita of the 2,000,000 of population, thus indicating an aggregate monetary circulation of from $18 to $20 per capita. Gold is the exclusive standard in Chili, and what circulation is not of paper or subsidiary coin would probably be of gold.

The revenue of $3,400,000 collected in the republic of Colombia for the year 1873 would indicate an aggregate monetary circulation of probably $12,000,000 to $15,000,000, but here the exclusive standard of values is silver, and whatever of the monetary circulation was not either paper or subsidiary coins would be almost exclusively of silver.

We have thus glanced at the probable volume of money and the materials of which it is presumably composed in the six principal states of South America, the population in these comprising 18,000,000 of the 25,500,000 on the whole continent; and the conclusion seems unavoidable that there is not above $60,000,000 of gold in use as money on the whole continent of South America. There remains yet but the West Indies, with an aggregate population of 4,200,000, among whom there may be $15,000,000 of gold in circulation, thus making say $75,000,000 for South America and the West Indies. If now we add the very liberal estimate of $175,000,000 for the whole of North America, we have a grand total of $250,000,000, which, added to the $1,872,500,000 estimated in the tables for Europe, gives a grand total of say $2,047,000,000 as the amount of gold coin and bullion in use as money in Europe and North and South America. Where then shall we look for the other $1,700,000,000 presumed by some to exist in the world as coin or bullion at the present time, or even for the remaining $600,000,000 estimated by Seyd to exist in 1872, and by Ruggles in 1867? If statistics are worth anything at all they prove beyond a doubt that no such sum of gold coin or bullion as even the smaller of these exists in Asia as money, though a much larger amount probably exists as ornaments. In India and China, whose populations compose 80 per cent of the entire 798,000,000 of population in Asia, silver is the exclusive standard of values, and gold does not circulate to any great extent as money. In Japan, the next largest state of Asia, gold is the exclusive standard of values, but Japan also has a system of national banks modeled after that of the United States, and a large part of the circulating medium is paper. The coin circulation is also composed largely of silver and copper coins.

Where then shall we look for the remaining $1,700,000,000 of gold presumed to exist in the world as money ere we are forced to the conclusion that it is, to a great extent, only a myth?

For all practical purposes, as a stock of gold coin upon which the commercial world may rely as a circulating medium or a reserve for the redemption of paper money, or for the payment of interest or principal of national or corporate debts, the entire amount is in

Europe and the United States. The total of what there is in South America is too small to be of any importance. As for what may have been produced in Asia or exported there in the last quarter of a century, it has been to a large extent, if not wholly, absorbed in the arts and in the manufacture of the personal ornaments of which the inhabitants of India and more particularly the semi-barbaric races of Asia Minor wear such a profusion—a characteristic which has in all ages imparted the glitter of romance to all oriental countries.*

* A whole volume might be filled with instances showing with how much greater profusion even the masses of the people in India, Afghanistan and Persia use the precious metals as personal ornaments than in the more highly civilized countries. Indeed the highest type of civilized man has almost abandoned personal adornment with gold as a relic of barbarism.

In the account of the embassy of Lord Mountstuart Elphinstone from the British Government of India to the King of Cabul in 1808, he describes the ornaments of the *common people* of Afghanistan as exhibiting this semi-civilized characteristic. "The ornaments of the women are strings of Venetian sequins worn round their heads, and chains of gold or silver, which are hooked up over the forehead. Ear-rings and rings on the fingers are also worn, as are pendants in the middle cartilages of the nose, which was formerly the custom in Persia, and still is in India and Arabia."

In an enumeration of the trades and occupations of the city of Cabul, Lord Elphinstone begins his list of seventy trades with "jewelers and goldsmiths," not as the most numerous, but as the most important.

It will perhaps be said that this was the condition of things seventy years ago, and that in the progress of the age all this has been changed. But the following synopsis of the testimony of Mr. J. T. Mackenzie, given in May, 1876, before a British parliamentary committee appointed to inquire into the causes of the decline in value of silver, will show that the customs of the people of India, and in all probability of those of Afghanistan and all Asia Minor, in the lavish use of gold and silver as personal ornaments, have not changed.

Mr. J. T. Mackenzie, of Kintail, said he was, when in India, a proprietor and merchant, and had been a merchant in Great Britain in the India trade. As a zemindar, or landowner, he had had considerable experience on this subject in Bengal. In every village there were a number of agents who acted as bankers for the farmers. Practically, a very small amount of silver passed in the transactions. The retail business in the villages was transacted by means of cowries, of which 200 were equivalent to 1 pice. A large quantity of the silver coined in India had been used for purposes of ornament. There was a silversmith in every village, who took his tools to the house of the man who wished the ornaments made. Among the peasantry the business was so small that gold did not enter into the settlement of the transactions. If gold

Whatever gold there may be in either Asia or Africa is practically almost as unavailable as any source of supply to Europe and the United States, as if it had not yet been dug out of the mines.

But there is another source of error in the commonly received estimates of the stock of gold and silver money

was procurable, probably it would also be turned into ornaments, as a gold ornament enhanced a man's importance. As a planter, witness received remittances of silver every month from Calcutta. If the amount received as rents had not been supplemented by remittances from the mint, the price of silver would have decreased and the value of commodities would have increased. In many districts the circulation was still totally inadequate to the wants of the people. The public works had not greatly affected the circulation. The only large amounts introduced in this way were in connection with the railways, but of the cost of the railways only 40 per cent was expended in India, and 60 per cent in England. The existing coinage, when introduced in 1835, was received with universal distrust, as the natives were extremely cautious in respect to any changes in the coinage. He believed but a small amount of silver left India for the interior of Asia, inasmuch as such a movement depended upon the excess of purchases over sales. He had heard the amount estimated at 5 per cent of the annual importation of silver. The balance of trade between India and Europe had been nearly always in favor of India. From 1834 to 1838 the export trade averaged £10,000,000 sterling a year, and from 1854 to 1858 it averaged £22,750,000; but from 1865 to 1874 the average increased to £56,000,000 per annum. The excess of imports over exports of bullion was £1,750,000 per annum from 1834 to 1838, £8,625,000 from 1854 to 1858, and £11,250,000 from 1865 to 1874. For the first five years, 1865-9, the average was £16,000,000; and for the last five years, 1870-4, £6,500,000, or an annual decrease of £9,500,000. The exports from India between the years 1865 and 1869 amounted to £279,000,000; from 1871 to 1874, £281,000,000, showing an increase of £2,000,000. The imports into India from 1865 to 1869 were £158,000,000, and from 1871 to 1874, £161,000,000, an increase of £3,000,000. The amount of bullion imported into India from 1865 to 1869 was £79,000,000, and from 1871 to 1874, £33,000,000, showing a decrease of £46,000,000; and the home requirements had increased between the two periods just named from £37,000,000 to £52,000,000, showing an increase of £15,000,000. The difference between the exports and imports for the ten years 1865-74 showed an excess of exports from India amounting to £240,000,000. The excess of treasure imports over exports in the same ten years was £112,000,000, and the home requirements were £89,000,000; and this total of £201,000,000 deducted from the £240,000,000 named above showed a difference in the adjustment of £39,000,000. The rapid increase in the home requirements was shown, the witness said, by the fact that prior to 1858 (when the Crown took over the government of India) they were about £4,500,000 yearly, while last year the amount was £10,000,000, exclusive of the £4,500,000 interest on the railway loans, or a total of £15,000,000. In other words, in the last five years the home requirements were £25,000,000 more than in the preceding five years.

in the commercial world, viz., the assumption that previous estimates were correct. I have shown that the estimate made in 1868–69 of the amounts of gold and silver coin in Germany were made upon premises that were worse than worthless. They were made from statements of the coinage of nine different states of Germany, but there was no correspondence whatever in the periods; they varied from 33 to 103 years, and no allowance was made for the recoinage of the coins of other states, so that the same metal may have been coined three or four times by different governments of Europe; neither was any allowance made for the import or export of specie. Mr. Ernest Seyd, in his estimate of $3,750,000,000 of gold in circulation in the commercial world at present, arrives at it by assuming that there was $2,000,000,000 in circulation before 1848, and that up to 1875 $1,750,000,000 had been added; and yet there is not the slightest ground for the assumption of $2,000,000,000 in circulation before 1848 except conjecture. Indeed, so much do these authorities differ in their guessing that we find even the more moderate ones differing by amounts that make the whole matter seem ridiculous. Thus Professor Jevons estimated the amount of coin in the United Kingdom, in 1868, at £94,000,000, while in *McCulloch's Commercial Dictionary*, in the article on Coins, page 332, we find the following in regard to coin in Great Britain, viz.:

"On the whole, however, we shall not be far wrong if we estimate the stock of coin at present (1868) in possession of the public and of the different joint stock banks (exclusive of Bank of England) at £30,000,000."

The coin and bullion in the Bank of England at the time referred to by McCulloch was probably about

£15,000,000, thus making an aggregate of £45,000,000 against Professor Jevons' £94,000,000. There is reason to think that Professor Jevons' estimate is much the nearest to correct, though he acknowledged at the time of the estimate that the amount of gold coin might not be above £70,000,000, instead of £80,000,000, which latter estimate I have used in the table of coin in the United Kingdom. These facts serve to show how unsubstantial is the foundation for the estimate of $2,000,000,000 in circulation in the commercial world before 1848. It is, of course, probable that in my own estimates of the coin and paper money in different countries of Europe and America, based largely on the ability of the people to hold or have money, I have made some erroneous estimates, but none, I think, which would change the total amount of gold, silver or paper money in either Europe or America over 15 per cent. As regards Asia and Africa, there is absolutely nothing to assist the statistician — it is all conjecture. With these reservations I should state the amount of each kind of money in the different quarters of the globe about as follows in millions of dollars of United States money:

	Gold.	Silver and Base Metal.*	Paper.
Europe	1,900	2,000	2,300
North America	175	100	780
South America	75	250	125
Asia	300	4,000	...
Africa	250	350	...
	2,700	6,700	

* The proportion of subsidiary silver and base metal coins is probably one-tenth of the amount under the head of silver and base metal.

The largest amount in the foregoing table is the $4,000,000,000 set down as an estimate of the aggregate of silver and base metal coins, bars, ingots, and even ornaments, used as mediums of exchange in Asia. Unfortunately for economic science this largest amount is the very one about which the least is known, and I have arrived at the above estimate only upon the following hypothesis, viz.:

The total production of silver in the world in the last one hundred years has, according to the best information attainable, been about $5,000,000,000. The value of silver consumed in the arts is very small compared to the value of gold consumed (in the last quarter of a century it has not been more than one fifth as much per annum). If, therefore, we assume that $1,000,000,000 of silver was consumed in the arts in Europe and America in the last hundred years, it would leave $4,000,000,000 for other purposes. The aggregate of silver coin in Europe has probably increased $500,000,000 in a hundred years, thus leaving, say $3,500,000,000 for distribution to the rest of the world. Of this latter amount probably not less than $3,000,000,000 has gone to Asia, and if we estimate only $1,000,000,000 of silver in use as a medium of exchange in Asia one hundred years ago, it would give the aggregate of $4,000,000,000 estimated in the table. It is probable that the amount in use there at that period was very much larger than $1,000,000,000, but in semi-barbaric countries a much larger estimate must be made for loss by abrasion of coins and for loss in wars and by casualties; and in view of these features the amount of silver in use by the nearly 800,000,000 of people in Asia cannot be estimated below $4,000,000,000, and is probably larger than that.

THE ERA OF GOLD.

IT will be seen that at the close of the preceding article the total stock of gold, silver and base metal coin in the world is estimated at $9,400,000,000. Deducting from this, say, $400,000,000 for coins composed wholly of other metals than gold and silver, and we have a total of $9,000,000,000, of which, say, $6,300,000,000 are silver, and $2,700,000,000 are gold. This estimate, it must be remembered, has been arrived at by a totally different method from any ever used before, and without the slightest thought of making the result correspond with any of the numerous estimates of the stock of coin made by the usual method of adding the production of the mines (less the amount presumed to be used in the arts) to some estimated amount presumed to have been in existence at some previous period.

But as the increase or decrease of the annual production of gold and silver have an important bearing on finances and prices generally, we may now proceed to the questions of the production, consumption and remaining stock of the precious metals from the beginning of the present century down to 1875.

Singularly enough, there seems to be much more harmony among the acknowledged authorities in regard to the annual production of gold in the remotest part of the period in question than there is with reference to the last fifty years, or even twenty-five years.

Birkmyre estimated the amount of pure gold produced in America, Europe and Asia (exclusive of China and Japan) in 1801 at $13,060,000.

Professor W. P. Blake, one of the United States commissioners to the Paris Exposition in 1867, made an elaborate and very valuable report on the precious metals, in which, after reviewing the essays of Chevalier, Humboldt, Jacob, Danson and others, he says (page 207): "It will thus be seen that all these authorities concur in estimating the annual product of gold at the commencement of the present century at about $13,000,000 per annum, in round numbers."

Mr. R. W. Raymond, United States Commissioner of Mining Statistics, in his report for 1875, estimates (though without citing any previous authority) the product of gold (pages 477, 478) at the beginning of the present century at $15,000,000 per annum, and the product of silver at $40,000,000 per annum.

The entire gold product of the world was constant at about this average annual rate of $13,000,000 to $14,000,000 per year until the development of the Russian and Siberian mines, about 1825. From an annual product of less than $4,000,000, from the Russian and Siberian mines, between 1825 and 1830, there was an increase in the amount to about $15,000,000 annually between 1840 and 1850. This, together with some revival of the gold product of South America, contributed to increase the total annual gold product of the world to about $30,000,000 in 1846, and $93,000,000 in 1850.* But now we come to the period in which it is well known there was an increase in the production of gold so vast as to well

* The last two amounts are the estimates of Birkmyre, who made a table (reproduced in Blake's Report, page 358) of the gold and silver product of all

warrant the title of the *golden era of the world.* The product of $93,000,000 per annum in 1850 shows the first effects of the discovery of gold in California in 1848. While the supplies from these new mines were increasing a gold-hunting fever prevailed all over the world, resulting in the discoveries in Australia in 1852. In 1853 the product of gold from the Australian mines alone was $60,000,000, or double the product of the whole world six years before, and nearly five times the annual product of the world for many years prior to 1830. "The annual product of gold," says Blake, "continued to increase until 1853, when it reached its maximum of $193,500,000. From that to the present time (1867) it has been decreasing." * The amount of gold produced in the first twenty years of this era was probably as great as the whole product of the preceding century.

A table made by Mr. Newmarch,† in response to an

countries in the world, exclusive of China and Japan, for those years, with the following results (omitting 00,000 in each amount):

	1846.		1850.	
	Gold.	Silver.	Gold.	Silver.
North and South America	6,5	26,0	66.5	36,0
Europe, Asia and Africa	22,5	6,0	26,5	7,5
Totals, in millions of dollars	29,0	32,0	93,0	43,5

* See Blake's Report, page 211.

† The table prepared by Mr. Newmarch presented the following results:

Total average annual product of gold and silver in the fifteen years from 1849 to 1863, inclusive:

GOLD.	Average	Total.
1849 to 1851, three years	$119.000.000	$357.000,000
1852 to 1856, five years	193.500.000	967.500.000
1857 to 1859, three years	182.500.000	347.500.000
1860 to 1863, four years	167,500,000	670 500.000
		$2.342.500,000

In the same table Mr. Newmarch estimated the product of silver for the same fifteen years at £251,000,000, or an average of $83,500,000 per annum.

inquiry of a French government commission, estimates the product of gold, in the fifteen years from 1849 to 1863, inclusive, at an aggregate of $2,342,500,000, or an average of $156,000,000 per annum.

The net result of Blake's inquiries on this point (which occupy a large part of his report) is that the total product of gold in the twenty years from 1848 to 1868, was $2,757,600,000, or an average of $137,880,000 per annum. The difference of $22,000,000 per annum in the annual averages, according to Newmarch and Blake, does not necessarily imply a disagreement, as the estimate of Newmarch is for the fifteen years of largest production, while Blake's includes five years more of diminished production.

The decrease in the production of gold noted by Blake in 1867, and which he predicted must soon cause a rise in its value,* has continued since at even a much greater rate than contemplated by him. At the time Blake made this prediction (1867) the annual production of gold had only fallen to $130,000,000. Since then the annual product has fallen until it touched its minimum, somewhere about $90,000,000, in 1874. It

* With this continued decrease in the annual production, it seems probable that gold will soon begin to sensibly appreciate in value, unless some new and unlooked for discovery of placers shall be made, of which, however, there does not appear to be much probability.

It was argued by Chevalier and others soon after the great discoveries in Australia and California, that gold would necessarily depreciate in value; that its purchasing power was destined to be much lessened by the great influx of the metal from these new sources. But the relative value of gold has not changed as much as was expected, and it would now seem that the supply did not more than keep pace with the ever increasing demands of commerce and industry, stimulated as they have been by an increasing supply of gold. The wonderful increase of the industrial activity of the world, resulting chiefly from the varied developments and application of the physical sciences, has been sufficient to appropriate all the excessive production of the past twenty years.—*Blake's Report on the Precious Metals*, page 235.

is mainly to point out the great decrease of $40,000,000 per annum in the gold product of Australia and New Zealand from 1857 to 1874, and the decrease of the same amount ($40,000,000) in the annual gold product of the United States and Territories in the same years, that I have compiled the following table, viz.:

ANNUAL GOLD PRODUCT OF THE VARIOUS QUARTERS OF THE GLOBE AT VARIOUS PERIODS FROM 1850 TO 1874.

	United States and Territories.	Australia and New Zealand.	Russia and Asia.	All the rest of the World.	Total Production.
1850	(McCulloch's Commercial Dictionary, estimate)				$ 94.000,000
1853 ...	$65,000.000	$60,000,000	$25.000,000	$10,500.000	160,500,000
1857	55.000,000	65,000,000	25.000,000	10,000.000	150,000,000
1867	56,725.000	37,500.000	25,500,000	11,130,000	130,855.000
1872	36,000.000	37,000,000	24.000,000	10.000 000	107,000,000
1874	26,358,776	26,500,000	24,000,000	10,000,000	86,858,776

The amount of $26,358,776, for the total production of gold in the United States and Territories, is taken from the report of R. W. Raymond, United States Commissioner of Mining Statistics, for 1875, page 488. This table, showing such a great decrease, was not made by Raymond, but by Mr. J. J. Valentine, superintendent of Wells, Fargo & Co.'s Express. Commissioner Raymond's report for 1875 was not given to the public until about July, 1876, and even then it contains no later estimate of the annual product of gold in the United States and Territories than the one above mentioned for 1874, and even for that year Commissioner Raymond does not himself venture to make any estimate of the amount of gold distinct from silver produced either in 1874 or 1875, though he corroborates Mr. Valentine's estimate by stating the *total product of both gold and silver in 1874 at* $72,428,206, whereas

Mr. Valentine makes the total of both gold and silver $74,461,055. The cause of the difference, however, is easily seen in the fact that Mr. Valentine includes $1,636,200 of gold and $357 of silver from British Columbia, and $84,635 of gold and $714,223 of silver from Mexico, none of which are included in Raymond's aggregate. It will be seen, therefore, that the known product of gold in the United States and Territories in 1874 was in fact only $24,637,941,* but as the silver

* The following are the tables from United States Commissioner Raymond's Report for 1875, page 488, viz.:

J. J. VALENTINE'S STATEMENT OF THE AMOUNT OF PRECIOUS METALS PRODUCED IN THE STATES AND TERRITORIES WEST OF THE MISSOURI RIVER DURING THE YEAR 1874.

States and Territories.	Gold dust and bullion by express.	Gold dust and Bullion by other conveyances.	Silver bullion by express.	Ores and base Bullion by freight.	Totals.
California........	$16,015 568	$1.601.556	$967.857	$1,715,550	$20,300.531
Nevada	345,394	34.539	30,954.602	4.117.698	35,452,233
Oregon	553.564	55.356	150	... .	609.070
Washington	141.396	14.139	....	....	155,535
Idaho	1,207.667	120,765	551.572	....	1,880,001
Montana.........	2.581.362	258.136	....	600,000	3,439.498
Utah.............	83,721	8,372	746,565	5.072.620	5.911.278
Arizona..........	23.333	2.333	400	....	26,066
Colorado.........	1,590,700	....	1.745,705	855,000	4,191,405
Mexico	84.655	....	714.223	....	798,878
British Columbia.	1,487,473	148.747	357	....	1,636.557
Grand total..	$24,114.833	$2 243.943	$35.681 411	$12,360.868	$74,401,055

R. W. RAYMOND'S STATEMENT OF THE AGGREGATE PRODUCT OF GOLD AND SILVER IN THE UNITED STATES AND TERRITORIES IN THE YEAR 1874.

Arizona..		$ 487.000
California		20.300.531
Colorado		5.188.510
Idaho...		1,880,004
Montana..		3.844,722
Nevada...		35,452,233
New Mexico		500,000
Oregon	$609.070	
Washington	154,535—	763.605
Utah..		3,911.601
Wyoming and other sources.........................		100.000
		$72,428,206

bullion in Valentine's table was presumed to contain a considerable amount of gold, I have accepted the larger figure as representing the gold product of the United States and Territories in 1874.

The gold product of Australia and New Zealand for 1853 I have derived from an official report to the French government. The product for 1867 is from United States Commissioner W. P. Blake's Report in 1868; the amounts for 1857 and 1872 are approximate estimates made by me from the official colonial reports of the exports of gold coin and bullion from Melbourne and Sidney in those years; the amount for 1874 is based upon a statement in the Melbourne *Argus* of the product of 1,102,614 ounces of gold in all Australia in 1874, and to which I have made an addition of 20 per cent for the product of New Zealand.

The amounts set down in the table made by me as the annual products of Asia, Africa and South America, are, like all other estimates ever made for those countries, merely conjectural. If, in regard to them, I have erred, I think it has been in setting them too high, so as to avoid the possibility of exaggerating the vast decrease in the world's product of gold in the period from 1857 to 1874, and it will be found that the amounts set down for Russia, Asia and the rest of the world, exclusive of Australia and North America, agree with the highest estimates made by others who have examined the subject.

Within the past year, since public attention has been drawn to the great decrease in the production of gold, several tables have been made and published, purporting to give the amount of gold and the amount of silver produced each year since the beginning of the era of great production of gold. One of the most elaborate of these was printed in the *Journal des Economists* for March, 1876, and has been much referred to as an authority.* But had there been any data upon which a table of the annual product of the precious metals could be made in such detail for each year, United States Commissioner Blake, who made such an elaborate and valuable report for the time down to 1867, would probably have found them. In fact, all the "authorities" on the product of both gold and silver are extremely vague and discordant in their estimates for particular years, and I should be inclined to make a large allowance from the apparent exactness for each year in the *Journal des Economists* table. Reference to the table of Mr. Newmarch will show how much even "authorities" differ on this point.

* The following is the *Journal des Economists* table of the production of gold and silver each year since 1852:

	Gold, millions.	Silver, millions.	Total Gold and Silver, millions.
1852	$182½	$40½	$223
1853	155	40½	195½
1854	127	40½	167½
1855	135	40½	175½
1856	147½	40½	188
1857	133	40½	173½
1858	124½	40½	165
1859	124½	40½	165
1860	119	40½	159½
1861	114	42½	156½
1862	107½	45	152½
1863	107	49	156
1864	113	51½	164½
1865	120	52	172
1866	121	50½	171½
1867	116	54	170
1868	120	50	170
1869	121	47½	168½
1870	116	51½	167½
1871	116½	61	177½
1872	101½	65	166½
1873	103½	70	173½
1874	90½	71½	162
1875	97½	62	159½

But in order to make an approximate estimate of the amount of gold produced in the world from 1850 to 1875, it is necessary to harmonize, as near as possible, the conflicting estimates. For this purpose I have taken Blake's estimates, or the authorities cited by him, whenever they were for specified years, with the following result:

TOTAL PRODUCT OF GOLD IN THE WORLD FROM 1840 TO 1874 (INCLUSIVE) BY PERIODS OF FIVE YEARS EACH.

1840 to 1844	$150,000,000
1845 to 1849	196,000,000
1850 to 1854	660,000,000
1855 to 1859	680,000,000
1860 to 1864	560,000,000
1865 to 1869	615,000,000
1869 to 1874	530,000,000
Total for thirty-five years	$3,391,000,000

In the foregoing table the total product of gold in the world in the 35 years to 1874 inclusive, is estimated at $3,391,000,000. But in the preceding chapter on Gold and Silver Coin in Europe, the total stock of gold coin and of bullion used as bank reserves in the world was estimated not to exceed $2,700,000,000. What then has become of the $639,000,000 difference, and of all the stock of gold coin existing at the beginning of the period in question?

All estimates of the consumption of gold in the arts and of loss by wear, by casualties, etc., have been only guesses without method, and yet it is only by adopting some method or rule of general application for the consumption of gold that any approximation can be made to the amount of gold coin in existence at any previous period.

Undoubtedly the largest item in the consumption of gold is the manufacture of jewelry and personal ornaments, and though the jewelry is not consumed, it is pretty well understood that very little ever comes back into the market as "old gold." Articles of jewelry are as a rule kept as souvenirs even after they are no longer worn by the owners, and there is good reason for the belief in a continually increasing stock of jewelry and gold ornaments in the world. In the endeavor to estimate the amount of gold thus annually withdrawn from circulation as coin, we must first approximate to the amount of jewelry manufactured and sold.

The United States census for 1870 shows that 681 jewelry manufacturing establishments in the United States produced goods annually to the amount of $22,000,000, and that the value of the materials used in the manufacture of this amount of goods was $9,187,000. Besides this the manufacture of watch-cases amounted to $2,333,340, in which the value of the materials was $1,152,979. The declared value of the net imports of foreign jewelry into the United States was $1,020,000 in 1871, $1,040,000 in 1872, $866,000 in 1873, and $275,000 in 1874. This includes neither watches nor watch movements, though the value of the import of both these aggregates from $2,000,000 to $3,000,000 annually. The amount of jewelry smuggled is believed to be larger than the amount reported to the customs officers. With these data we may estimate an annual supply of something near $27,000,000 of jewelry per annum for a population of say 40,000,000 in 1873. It would also be a moderate estimate to say that the total value of gold used in the manufacture of the $27,000,000 worth of jewelry is one fourth of the whole, say $7,000,000. But the jewelry manufactured as above mentioned is only the product of large establishments;

an addition of at least $500,000 more gold per annum must be made for articles manufactured by individual working jewelers. The amount of gold leaf and gold foil manufactured in the United States is between $2,000,000 and $3,000,000 annually, all of which is consumed here by dentists, gilders, photographers, etc. These items make an aggregate of at least $10,000,000 of gold per annum used in the arts in the United States. This amounts only to the apparently insignificant sum of 25 cents to each individual of the presumed population of 40,000,000 in 1873. But if we extend this ratio to 3,500,000 of population in Canada and 4,500,000 (half the population) of Mexico, it gives a total of $12,000,000 per annum, and if we extend it to the 300,500,000 population of Europe, it aggregates $87,-100,000 per annum. It is, however, not to be presumed that the people of Europe and North America are the only consumers of gold in the 1,300,000,000 population of the globe, and we must reckon at least 150,000,000 more in Asia Minor, the northern coasts of Africa, the coasts of South America, the West Indies and Australia, thus giving at least 500,000,000, and omitting entirely 800,000,000 of the people of the world as either too poor or too barbarous to use gold either as ornaments or in the arts. Extending the ratio of 25 cents per capita per annum to this 500,000,000 it gives an aggregate of $125,000,000 per annum.

But something must be estimated for the abrasion of coins and for the loss of coin in fires, shipwrecks and other casualties. Dr. Farr, the English actuary for life insurance computation, made an elaborate calculation, based on experiments as to the loss from abrasion of coins, and arrived at the conclusion that the wear on

British gold coins was $\frac{4}{100}$ of 1 per cent per annum, or 1 per cent in 25 years. This is sustained also by the testimony of Mr. J. Miller, of the weighing room of the Bank of England, given before a royal commission in 1868. The loss by fires, wrecks and other casualties can scarcely be computed, but it is probably larger than the loss by abrasion.

McCulloch estimated in 1857 that the value of gold and silver in Great Britain at that time in the form of plate and jewelry was about $20 to each individual. He also estimated that the annual consumption of gold and silver in the arts in Europe, North America and Australia was at least $80,000,000 per annum, but that of this $80,000,000 about 20 per cent was obtained by the fusion of old plate, the burning of lace, picture frames, etc.

With these data we may proceed to estimate the consumption of gold in the arts about 1873 as follows, viz.:

Total gold used in the arts, and in the loss, wear and accumulation of jewelry	$125,000,000
Deduct 20 per cent of the amount used in jewelry, returned as old gold, say	18,000,000
	107,000,000
Add, for loss and abrasion of gold coins	3,000,000
Total consumed and absorbed annually	$110,000,000

Jacob estimated the amount of gold and silver consumed in the arts in 1830 at about $30,000,000. This has been thought by all other authorities as too low. But at the same time he estimated so large an amount for the loss and abrasion of coins that he concluded the whole supply of precious metals between the years 800 and 1492 had been only about sufficient to keep the stock on hand equal to what it was in 800. From the discovery of America in 1492 to the beginning of the eighteenth century there was an increase, but mainly of silver, which became the money of the world, gold being used as the material for personal ornament, and regarded much in the same light as precious stones. There was, however, an increase in the production of gold between 1810 and 1825, and with this and the advance in the arts the presumption is warranted that by 1839 the consumption of gold in the arts, together with the loss and abrasion of gold coins, was at least $25,000,000 annually of gold alone.

McCulloch's estimate of $80,000,000 (net $64,000,000) for the annual consumption of gold and silver by the 322,000,000 of population in Europe, North America and Australia in 1857, would be at the rate of about 20 cents per capita, and if this ratio were extended to 150,000,000 more of the world's population, it would aggregate $94,000,000 per annum. As the vast increase in the use of the precious metals, indicated by the difference between the estimates of Jacob and McCulloch, was evidently due to the great production of gold, it is to be presumed that the increased use of the metals was largely of gold; and though there are no data by which to estimate the proportions of each, I have assumed the net total consumption of gold in the arts, and the absorption in the loss, wear and accumulation of jewelry in the world in 1857 at about $60,000,000. We have thus three points in the consumption of gold by which to estimate the aggregate since 1839, viz.: $25,000,000 in 1839, $60,000,000 in 1857, and $110,000,000 in 1873.

In accordance with the foregoing premises, the production of gold, the consumption in the arts and in the accumulation of jewelry, with the surplus added to the stock of gold coin, may be stated for periods of five years each about as follows:

Periods of 5 years.	Production.	Consumption.	Additions to stock of gold coin.	Decrease of stock of gold coin.
1840–1844	$150,000,000	$132,000,000	$18,000,000	
1845–1849	196,000,000	149,000,000	47,000,000	
1850–1854	660,000,000	180,000,000	480,000,000	
1855–1859	680,000,000	295,000,000	385,000,000	
1860–1864	560,000,000	398,000,000	162,000,000	
1865–1869	615,000,000	475,000,000	140,000,000	
1870–1874	530,000,000	539,000,000	....	$9,000,000
	$3,391,000,000	$2,168,000,000	$1,232,000,000	
			9,000,000	
Net addition to stock of gold coin in 35 years			$1,223,000,000	

The above table shows a presumed addition to the world's stock of gold coin and bullion, of $1,223,000,000 in the thirty-five years ending with 1874. In the article on gold and silver coin in Europe it was estimated that the world's stock of gold coin and bullion was not above $2,700,000,000 in 1875. If, therefore, there was an addition of $1,223,000,000 in the preceding thirty-five years, it would show the total stock of coin and bullion in the world in 1839 to have been $1,477,000,000. This nearly agrees with estimates made by various writers, and should, I think, be regarded as sustaining the correctness of the methods by which I have attempted to arrive at the production, consumption and stock of gold and gold coin in the world.

The total product of silver in the world during the last twenty-five years is estimated at about $1,250,000,-000, or at the average rate of $50,000,000 per annum. But while the annual silver product of Mexico (the former chief source of supply) has been decreasing, there has been an enormous increase in the United States and Territories, the total product having increased from $2,000,000 in 1861,* to $50,000,000 in 1874, thus bringing the total product of the world up to $70,000,000 in 1874. The total consumption of silver in the arts in Europe and North America is probably from $18,000,000 to $20,000,000 per annum. If there is $2,500,000,000 of silver coin in circulation in the world, exclusive of Asia, the annual loss by abrasion and by casualties would average at least the fourth of one per cent per annum, and thus make an aggregate of $6,000,000 per annum. According to the statistics of silver exports given in the testimony of Sir Hector Hay and Mr. S. Pixley before the Parliamentary Commission in May, 1876, the movement of silver from Great Britain to India and China for eleven years to the end of 1875, had been $174,281,000, or at the average rate of $15,740,000 per annum. Add to this an average movement in the last few years of about $8,000,000 per annum from the United States to China, and it makes an aggregate of say $24,000,000 per annum. But from this must be deducted an average export back from all Asia to Europe of about $5,000,000 to $6,000,000 per annum, leaving the net movement of silver to Asia from Great Britain and the United States say $18,000,000 per annum. Considerable silver also goes to Asia from the Mediterranean and South America, and the total net annual absorption of silver in Asia has probably been $25,000,000 per annum for the last five or six years.

* Raymond's Report, page 480.

PRODUCTION, CONSUMPTION AND EXPORTS OF SILVER FOR THE UNITED STATES AND TERRITORIES.

Year.	Produced in the U. S. and Territories.	Imports of coin and bullion.	Total supplies.	Total exports of silver coin and bullion.
1871	$22,000,000	$13,120,000	$35,120,000	$20,330,000
1872	25,750,000	4,838,000	30,406,000	27,580,000
1873	36,500,000	12,800,000	49,300,000	40,392,000
1874	50,000,000	9,000,000	59,000,000	32,587,000
	$134,250,000	$39,758,000	$173,826,000	$120,890,000

The above shows a difference between the total supplies and the total exports for the four years of $43,680,000. The statements of the production of silver in the above four years are from the report of W. R. Raymond, United States Commissioner of mining statistics for 1875, page 480. But these, like all other statistics of the production of the precious metals, are only approximations, and may vary from the real amounts at least five per cent. It is quite certain that there was no such accumulation of silver coin in the United States in four years to 1874 as $43,680,000. The total silver coinage of the United States Mint for the four years ending June 30, 1875, was $32,416,000. This, however, throws but little light on the question of disposal of the $43,680,000. In the report of the Secretary of the Treasury for 1875 he states that in accordance with the resumption act of January, 1875, the treasury had purchased and coined and held in the treasury on June 30, 1875, subsidiary silver coins to the amount of $10,000,000. Deducting this, and estimating $10,000,000 consumed in the arts in the United States in four years, and it still leaves a presumed accumulation of $23,680,000. Part of this has probably gone to supply the monetary circulation of the

Pacific States and the new territories west of the Missouri river, leaving a stock of bullion and ores on hand to the extent of probably $15,000,000 to $18,000,000 from the product of the four years to the end of 1874.

EXPLANATION OF DIAGRAM No. 1,

Showing the relative product of gold and silver each year, and the consumption of gold each year since 1825:

The feather line which begins in the lower left hand corner and ascending through the years 1847 to 1853 to the point marked 193 indicates the increase in the production of gold to its culmination about 1853. The figures given at intervals along the line indicate the amount in millions of dollars and the year for which various writers have estimated the product of gold, the names of the authorities being given in the upper margin of the diagram.

The descending of the feather line from the figures 160 in the year 1853 to 87 in the year 1874 indicates the decline in the production of gold in accordance with the table made by me.

The dotted line represents the table of the *Journal des Economists*.

The double line (═) indicates the progress of the product of silver since 1825, and has been made after examining the authorities cited by Blake, and also with reference to the reports of the United States Commissioner of Mining Statistics.

ASSUMED PROGRESS OF THE ANNUAL CONSUMPTION OF GOLD IN THE ARTS, BY THE LOSS AND ABRASION OF COINS, AND BY THE LOSS, WEAR AND ACCUMULATION OF JEWELRY:

Year.	Millions.	Year.	Millions.
1839	25	1857	55
1840	25.5	1858	59
1841	26	1859	63
1842	26.5	1860	67
1843	27	1861	71
1844	27.5	1862	74
1845	28	1863	77
1846	28.5	1864	81
1847	29	1865	85
1848	29.5	1866	89
1849	30	1867	92
1850	32	1868	93
1851	34	1869	97
1852	37	1870	101
1853	40	1871	105
1854	43	1872	109
1855	47	1873	110
1856	51	1874	108

DIAGI

Showing the Annual Production of Gold, the Annual Producti

Fifty

Explanation.—The names on the upper margin of the diagram are the autho gold in particular years. The names stand directly over the amounts and the yea to 1875, is drawn after the figures in the table of the *Journal des Economists* give

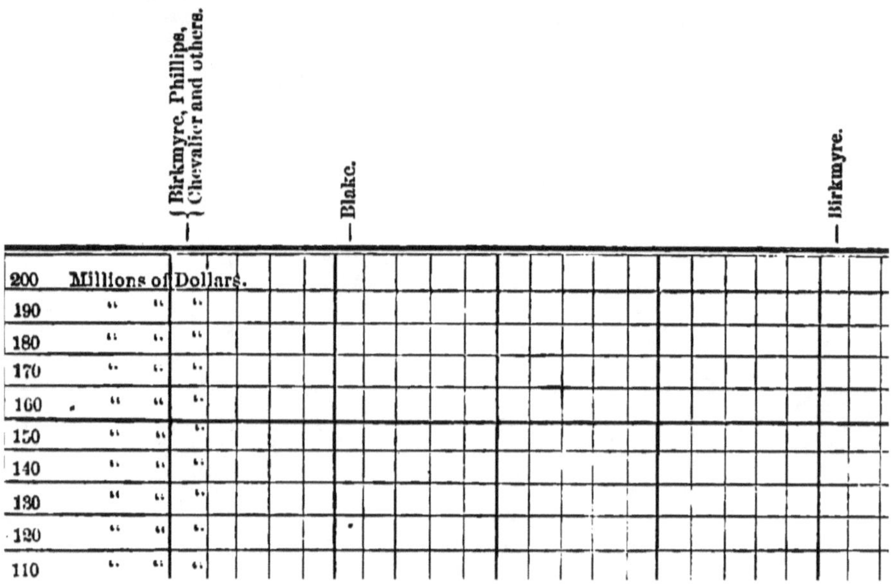

I No. 1.

OF SILVER, AND THE ANNUAL CONSUMPTION OF GOLD IN THE ARTS FOR

EARS.

s for the amounts given at irregular intervals in the line showing the production of
› which they refer. The dotted line beginning in the year line 1852, and extending
ı page 104. For full explanation see page 113.

—Birkmyre.

—*Journal des Economists.*

—Blake and Newmarch.

—Author's estimate.

—Blake.

—Author's estimate.

THE ERA OF DEBT.

THE following compilation of the national debts of all countries was made mainly to show the general increase of that class of indebtedness in the last twenty-five years. It is, however, impossible to ascertain in all cases the amounts for 1850. In most of the instances where no amount is given at as early a date as that there was no debt, and the amounts given for years subsequent to that are intended only to show the increase in the latter part of the period. The amounts are given in each case in their equivalent in United States money:

	Amount.	Year.	Amount.	Year.
Austria-Hungary	$625,000,000	1848	$1,655,964,500	1875 Dec.
Belgium	123,798,281	1844	185,909,802	1873
Denmark	74,312,325	1866	55,769,055	1875
France	*1,000,000,000	1850	3,750,337,006	1875 Jan.
Prussia	....	....	246,000,000	1875 Jan.
Bavaria	86,006,000	1855	156,685,000	1874
Wurtemburg	*30,000,000	1850	73,500,000	1874 May.
Saxony	....	....	3,000,000	1874
Great Britain and Ireland	3,928,000,000	1836	3,876,000,000	1875 Mch.
Greece	25,000,000	1850	75,000,000	1875
Italy	586,000,000	1860	1,951,500,000	1873
Netherlands	....	....	386,300,000	1874
Portugal	105,000,000	1856	364,000,000	1873
Russia	625,000,000	1850	2,149,900,000	1875 Jan.
Spain	*1,075,000,000	1869	2,650,000,000	1875 June.
Sweden	....	....	43,000,000	1875
Norway	....	....	8,000,000	
Switzerland	....	....	6,000,000	
Turkey	None.	1850	900,000,000	1874
United States	63,452,773	1850	†2,245,018,579	1876 Jun. 30
Canada	70,000,000	1868	116,092,917	1875 July.
Mexico	317,357,250	1865	395,500,000	1874

* Estimated.

† This includes all the non-interest-bearing debt and the Pacific Railroad bonds.

	Amount.	Year.	Amount.	Year.
Brazil.................. ..	....	....	369,294,430	1875 June.
Argentine Republic.......	....	1850	67,700,000	1875 June.
Bolivia	....	1850	17,000,000	1875
Chili......................	....	1850	63,400,000	1875 Sept.
Colombia	....	1850	75,000,000	1873
Ecuador....................	....	1850	16,400,000	1855
Guatemala..................	....	1850	4,400.000	1875
Hayti......................	....	1850	16,000,000	1875
Honduras....	....	1850	29,700,000	1875
India......................	299,700,000	1859	537,675.000	1874 April.
Egypt........	....	1850	350.000.000	1875
Japan......................	....	1850	16,500 000	1875
Colony of Good Hope.....	....	1850	8,615,000	1874
Ceylon	... .	1850	3,200.000	1874
New South Wales........	....	1850	54,500,000	1874
New Zealand	.. ..	1850	50.000.000	1873
Queensland	....	1850	15 000.000	1873
South Australia...........	....	1850	17.000 000	1875
Victoria...................	....	1850	60,000,000	1875
Nicaragua	....	1850	9.500,000	1874
Paraguay	....	1850	24.000.000	1875
Peru.......................	....	1850	25.750.000	1875
San Domingo.............	....	1850	3.750.000	1875
Uruguay	....	1850	211.785,000	1875 Mch.
Venezuela	....	1850	100,000,000	1875
Totals	$9.032,626.023		$23,439,471,926	

The next most important class of funded debts is that created in the construction of railways, nearly the whole of which has been the growth of the last twenty-five years. It was only as far back as 1814 that George Stephenson constructed his first locomotive, and the first railroad ever constructed with a view to carrying passengers was the Stockton and Darlington road, opened September 27, 1825. The Liverpool and Manchester was opened in 1830. The first road opened in the United States was from Quincy, Mass., to tide-water, four miles, in 1826. The first important road begun in the United States was the Baltimore and Ohio, in 1828. In 1829-30 roads were begun in nearly all the Atlantic States. So great was the activity that in 1836-7 the railroad mileage of the United States exceeded that of any other country in the world, a position which the United States continues to hold, as will be seen by the fact that her railroad mileage is about 40 per cent of the whole amount in the world. In 1850 the total mileage of the United States was 9,021. By 1860 it had increased 300 per cent; by 1870, 500 per cent, and at the close of 1875, 800 per cent. This may be taken as the general measure of the advance of that agency which has revolutionized the commerce of the world in the brief space of twenty-five or thirty years.

Poor's Railroad Manual states the aggregate of funded and floating debts of railroads in the United States at the close of 1875 at $2,459,607,349, or at the average rate of $31,600 per mile of the 74,658 miles of road. If $30,000 per mile were taken as the average indebtedness of the 182,699 miles of railways in the world at the close of 1875, it would give an aggregate of, say, $5,481,000,000.* But in Belgium, Germany, Denmark, Holland and Sweden the governments have constructed an aggregate of about 9,500 miles. In Rus-

* The following table of the railroad mileage of the world at the close of 1875 is condensed from *Poor's Railroad Manual:*

	Miles.		Miles.
United States	74,658	France	12,376
Canada	4,486	Germany	17,372
Mexico	327	Russia	12,074
Cuba	427	Italy	4.787
Central America	144	Austria	6.366
Jamaica	34	Hungary	3,966
Brazil	837	Spain	3,818
Argentine Republic	994	Sweden	2,478
Peru	972	Belgium	2,249
Chili	629	Switzerland	1,098
Uruguay	197	Holland	1,062
Guiana	68	Denmark	789
Paraguay	47	Portugal	643
Colombia	43	Norway	325
Venezuela	39	Turkey	1.116
Australia	2 148	Roumania	766
India	6,172	Egypt	1,013
Ceylon and Java	291	Algeria	333
Japan	41	Tunis	37
Great Britain and Ireland	16,696	Mauritius and Cape Colony	155

sia, also, the government has aided the construction of railways something after the plan upon which government aid was extended to the Pacific railways in the United States. In these cases the railroad debt has been counted as part of the national debt, and included in the debts of that class in the table of national debts. We must, therefore, deduct about $500,000,000 for these and the floating debts, thus leaving the aggregate of funded railroad debts in 1875 about $5,000,000,000. Measured by the mileage, the aggregate of these debts was probably about as follows, in round numbers, viz.: $3,500,000,000 in 1870; $2,000,000,000 in 1860, and $700,000,000 in 1850.

Municipal debts come next in point of magnitude, and in these as they relate to American cities we find an increase exceeding that of any other class of funded debts, except those of the railroads, the aggregate at the close of 1875, as indicated in various compilations, was about $700,000,000.* As regards a similar class of debts

* The most comprehensive summary I have seen of these was printed in the *Public* (New York), as follows:

	(*b*) 1870.	1875–76.
New York	$54.436.180	$161.165,299
Philadelphia (*a*)	42,103,866	69,616,523
Boston	22.598.361	43.933,165
Brooklyn	20,000	38.494,000
Baltimore	13,568,431	32.943,425
New Orleans	26,500,000	22,699,438
Washington	2,363.885	22,000,000
St. Louis	13,613 000	17,423,000
Cincinnati	5,020,000	17.235.500
Chicago	14,103,000	16.996,387
Jersey City	5,133,414	14.247,500
Pittsburgh	4,042.619	13,533,819
Louisville	5.006.000	10,795.000
Newark	3,100,000	9.465,750
Providence	1,795,870	8,843.800
Cleveland	2.101,255	8,086.900
Buffalo	2.031.530	7.264.291
Portland	2,706,011	6.462,800
Memphis	5.271,892	5,851,786
Rochester	634.567	5.579.000
Charleston, S. C	5,137,208	5,514.814
Elizabeth	2,678,700	5,400,000

in Europe, there is no satisfactory source of information. In some of the capitals the debts properly chargeable to

	(*b*) 1870.	1875-76.
Richmond	2,111,431	4.632,708
Cambridge	6,028,559	4 280,400
Toledo	401,962	3,782,280
Savannah	2,099,592	3,726,917
Albany	2,800,000	3,683.000
San Francisco (*a*)	7,458,647	3,431,000
Worcester	2.774,429	3 099,732
Mobile	2,195,458	2,864,100
Fall River	1,462,033	2,569,157
Milwaukee	118,000	2,544.963
Bangor	448,493	2,484.000
Powell, with Cambridge in Middlesex Co.	... .	2,289,000
Detroit	723,600	2,282.900
Norfolk	1,855.741	2,150,014
Augusta	1,395,250	2,100.000
Lynn	4,424,465	2,030,500
Nashville	2,050,000	1,737.282
Alleghany, with Pittsburgh in Alleghany Co.	....	1,667,000
Chelsea, with Boston in Suffolk Co.	....	1,661,840
Lawrence, with Lynn in Essex Co	....	1.594.346
Springfield	646,439	1,562,805
Salem, with Lynn in Essex Co	....	1,483,725
Somerville, with Cambridge in Middlesex Co.	....	1,472,854
Indianapolis	155,000	1,455.000
St. Joseph	500.000	1,380,900
Brookline.	648,794	1,311,350
Columbus, Ohio	none..	1,261.392
St. Paul	812,014	1,230,262
New Bedford, with Fall River in Bristol Co.	....	1,195,000
Beverly, with Lynn in Essex Co	....	1.041,800
Lynchburg	720,895	921.509
Galveston	250,000	873,000
Holyoke, with Springfield in Hampton Co.	....	836,500
Fitchburg, with Worcester in Worcester Co.	....	698.027
Northampton	357,778	663.779
Columbus, Ga	400,000	582,500
Zanesville	none..	548,059
Newburyport, with Lynn in Essex Co..	....	535,613
Peabody, with Lynn in Essex Co.	....	523,577
Medford, with Cambridge in Middlesex Co.	....	519,500
Total	$276,804.299	$618,205.488
Massachusetts (other towns)	1,292.676	14,161.991
Ohio (other towns)	549,150	8,424.388
Total	$278.646.125	$640,791.867

(*a*) Census statement of county debt given for 1870.

(*b*) In this table, under 1870 are placed, not the debts of cities at that date, but the debts of all municipalities in the counties in which those cities are located, as given in the census report. When there are several cities in the same county, the name of the county is given against each city after the first named, in place of repeating the total indebtedness of municipalities in that county. Thus the first column gives an indebtedness larger than was reported to the census marshals for the cities named, and as no city debt was then reported for Philadelphia or San Francisco, the amounts then reported as county debt are inserted.

the municipalities are complicated with the national debts, though, on the whole, municipal debts are believed to be much smaller in proportion to population than in the United States.* It would seem, however, that a very moderate estimate of the aggregate of public debt, not national, in Europe in 1875 at say $3,000,000,000, and also to assume that the rate of growth of these since 1850 had corresponded with the growth of railroad and national debts. The primary object of this compilation of debts is to show the aggregate amount of funded debts negotiable in the financial centers of Europe and America, thus showing the increased demand for coin to pay interest, and this even without the details of railroad and municipal debts in Europe, the aggregate given for Europe must be about correct.

* The annual interest on the debt of Paris, together with the amount appropriated to the sinking fund for the year 1873 was 46,170,825 francs, or about $9,230,000, thus indicating a debt (at four per cent) of about $183,000,000. The following statement of the debts of English cities is also said to have been called out by some discussions in Parliament in 1875.

Cities.	Population, 1871.	Debt.
London	3,266,987	$25,918,000
Liverpool	493,405	19,552,000
Manchester	379,374	16,300,000
Leeds	259,212	11,800,000
Bradford	145.830	8,950,000
Bristol	182,552	5,508,000
Halifax	65.510	5,080,000
Bolton	92.658	3.600,000
Brighton	103.858	2.950.000
Birmingham	343.787	2,865.000
Oldham	113,100	2.600,000
Salford	124,801	2,430,000
Rochdale	63.485	2.150.000
Huddersfield	74,358	2,014,000
Wolverhampton	156.878	1,873,000
Preston	85,426	1,730.000
Newcastle	128,443	1.654.650
Blackburn	82.928	1,300,000
Ashton	37,389	1,187,000
Sunderland	104.409	1.112.000
Swansea (Wales)	80,782	1,090,000
Total		$121,663,650

Of American State debts the aggregate in 1875 was about $370,000,000,* and of county debts about $180,000,000. These two classes having increased much less rapidly than city or railroad debts.

We have, therefore, the following as the approximate statement of the aggregate of funded national, railroad, municipal and corporate debts in 1875, intended to be

* The following statement of the debts of the respective States in 1875, as compared with 1860, is compiled from an elaborate table printed in the New York *Bulletin* of February 8, 1876 showing the relative increase of population, taxation and debt in the several States, viz.:

	1860.	1875.
Maine	$1,162,727	$5,272,688
New Hampshire	82.148	3,849,000
Vermont	175,000	312,000
Massachusetts	7,175,978	29,465.204
Rhode Island	....	2,563,506
Connecticut	50,000	5,014,500
New York	34,192,975	28,828.686
New Jersey	95.000	2,496,300
Pennsylvania	38,638,961	23,233,137
Delaware	....	1,231.000
Maryland	14,885,167	11,372,077
District of Columbia	....	18.792.563
Ohio	14,250,234	7,949,920
Indiana	9,597,741	5,003.538
Michigan	2,649.335	1,588,136
Illinois	11,329.747	1.480,972
Wisconsin	100,000	2.252.000
Minnesota	2.563,653	2,755,000
Iowa	322,296	543.056
Nebraska	....	458,228
Missouri	23,903,000	20.839.000
Kansas	....	1,385,775
Virginia	22.003.441	33.548.309
West Virginia	11,001,720	17.068,094
Kentucky	5,579.244	2.159.517
North Carolina	9,558.935	28.952.345
Tennessee	16,643,667	25.031,000
South Carolina	6,691.574	7,674.702
Georgia	3,170.750	10,986.500
Florida	158,000	1,433.767
Alabama	6,027,000	12,132,000
Mississippi	7.271,707	6,383.087
Louisiana	10,023.903	10,061.645
Arkansas	3,592.622	16,483,780
Texas	....	5,321,914
California	3.885,000	3,472,000
Nevada	....	960,000
Oregon	....	290,477
	$266,781,525	$367,146,023

negotiable in the financial centers of Europe and North America, viz.:

National debts	$23,400,000,000
Railroad debts	5,000,000,000
State and municipal debts	4,250,000,000
	$32,650,000,000

The actual liquidation of this vast sum, amounting to just about eight times the total of all the gold and silver used as money in Europe and America, is of course not to be contemplated—it is impossible. In countries where the revenue is sufficient to pay the interest on the public debts and all other expenses, without leaving a deficit to be added to the principal each year, the national debts will in most cases become permanent institutions, the principal payable never, as in Great Britain; and in a few cases, as in Great Britain and the United States, the burden of annual interest may be reduced from year to year, unless the process of reduction is interrupted—as in most cases it has been—by expensive wars. But in many countries whose governments are infirm, and whose revenues are fluctuating and uncertain, the high rates of interest they are obliged to pay insures the ultimate bankruptcy of the national treasuries, and the final repudiation of the debts, as in the cases of Mexico and Spain. The very magnitude of the volume of funded debts in Europe and America is now compelling a reduction in the general rates of interest for money, a decline which it seems must become permanent as one of the characteristic features of this *era of debt*, and affecting all the employments of capital. Until the aggregate volume of annual interest on the funded debts of Europe and America is reduced to a point where it can be paid without distress to the commercial and industrial interests from which the interest is drawn, there will be frequent defaults and repudiations on large debts. This would of itself divert capital to the securities of the best credit, and by its concentration on them establish lower rates of interest for money throughout the world.

At say 5 per cent (which is probably about the average of the stipulated rates in the various classes of funded debts referred to in the preceding pages), the total annual interest amounts to about $1,600,000,000. Payment of the principal being left entirely out of the question as impossible for any considerable portion of it, this item of the aggregate annual interest is one of the three great factors in the financial problems of the time, the other two factors being the amount of non-interest-bearing debt, or paper money, and the amount of gold and silver in the commercial world available for use as money.

In endeavoring to give the relative proportions of these for Europe and America, there seems no way but to include a great portion or nearly the whole of the debts of South America, Egypt and India. Portions of these are, of course, held in the countries where they were created; but it is well known that the great bulk of the South American loans, as well as those of Egypt, Turkey and India, were negotiated in London, and though the interest on these debts would be paid by the industries of the countries whence they came, the products of those industries would first have to be sold for the money of Europe.

For Europe and North America, with their aggregate of 357,000,000 of population, of which say 340,000,000 are civilized and commercial people, I should therefore estimate the three above mentioned factors at about the following proportions in 1875, viz.:

Paper money	$3,100,000,000
Annual interest on funded debts	1,000,000,000
Stock of gold and silver used as money	4,000,000,000

The next item having an important bearing on the use of money, and consequently on the demand for gold and silver, either for circulation or as bank reserves held for the redemption of paper money, is the increase of traffic. On this point there can of course be no statistics that will not be largely conjectural. As an index of the volume of traffic at any time in the past twenty years, I have assumed that the aggregate of bank clearings in the ten largest commercial cities of the United States represents about one third of the total volume of payments of money in the traffic of the country. In New York the daily average clearings of the banks, exclusive of the stock exchange transactions, is stated by the manager of the clearing house as averaging $40,000,000 per day in 1874. The average daily clearings in Philadelphia in 1874 were about $7,500,000; in Chicago, $3,500,000; in Baltimore, Pittsburgh, Cincinnati, St. Louis and New Orleans together, $5,000,000. The aggregate transactions of the clearing houses of the ten largest cities of the United States, exclusive of the stock exchange business in New York, in 1874 was about $64,000,000 daily, of which about 62 per cent was transacted through the New York clearing house. If this aggregate of $64,000,000 daily comprises, as I have assumed, one third of the total payments of money in commercial transactions, exclusive of the stock exchange business in New York, it would imply payments of currency to the extent of $128,000,000 daily, thus giving an aggregate of $192,000,000 paid daily in commercial transactions. This would imply that nearly 18 per cent of the total of $750,000,000 of paper currency was paid out each day, thus using the whole volume of currency in every week, but leaving an average of say 78 per cent of it resting temporarily in the national treasury, in the banks, and in the pockets of the people.

Upon the presumption that the New York bank clearings, exclusive of the stock exchange business, represent over 30 per cent of the total volume of payments in commercial transactions in the United States, we may estimate the increase of traffic in the United States by the increase of bank clearings in that city, and in Europe by the increase of the London clearings (given in dollars), as shown in the following table, viz.:

NEW YORK CLEARINGS.			LONDON CLEARINGS.
Year ending Sept. 30.	Currency Exchanges.	Cash Balances Paid.	Years ending Apl.
1854	$5,750,455,987	$297,411,493	....
1855	5,362,912,098	289,694,137	....
1856	6,906,213,328	334,714,489	....
1857	8,333,226,718	365,313,901	....
1858	4,756,664,386	314,238,910	....
1859	6,448,005,956	363,984,682	....
1860	7,231,143,056	380,693,438	....
1861	5,915,742,758	353,383,944	....
1862	6,871,443,591	415,530,331	....
1863	14,867,597,848	677,626,482	....
1864	24,097,196,655	885,719,204	....
1865	26,032,384,341	1,035,765,107	....
1866	28,717,146,914	1,066,135,106	....
1867	28,675,159,472	1,144,963,451	....
1868	28,484,288,636	1,125,455,236	$15,278,055,000
1869	37,407,028,986	1,120,318,307	17,670,195,000
1870	27,804,539,405	1,036,484,821	18,603,116,500
1871	29,300,986,682	1,209,721,029	20,092,315,000
1872	32,636,997,403	1,428,582,707	26,748,610,000
1873	33,972,773,942	1,152,372,108	30,016,675,000
1874	20,850,681,962	971,231,280	29,970,000,000

These figures for the New York clearings include the stock exchange business, which in 1874 comprised about 40 per cent of the whole. But even deducting this, the increase since 1854 is about 150 per cent. The London clearings are, I believe, given exclusive of the stock exchange business, and these show an increase of nearly 100 per cent in the six years. From these facts, together with the vast increase of railroads, which have stimulated internal traffic in all countries to a much greater extent than is shown in their export or import trades, it seems reasonable to conclude that the total volume of traffic nearly quadrupled in the twenty-five years from 1850 to 1875.* Further evidence in support of this estimate of the increase of traffic is to be found in the *value* of the tonnage and in the gross earnings of the railroads as compared with twenty-five years ago. These items for the United States are given in *Poor's Railroad Manual* as follows:

	Railroad Mileage.	Value of Railroad Tonnage.	Gross Earnings from Freight and Passengers.
1851................	10,982	$810,725,200	$39,406,358
1870................	53,399	10,875,750,000	....
1875................	72,623	(say) 15,000,000,000	503,065,505

* Much has been said of the diminished use for either paper currency or coin by reason of the economizing expedient of the clearing house system. The extent of this I estimate as follows, viz.: The total daily bank clearings in Europe and North America do not exceed $300,000,000; deducting say 3⅓ per cent for "balances" paid in money, it would leave the total economy of paper money and coin say $290,000,000. This is the total extent of the economy for one year as well as one day.

EXPLANATION OF DIAGRAM No. 2.

Gold and Silver. The upper double line is intended to show the probable aggregate of gold and silver used as money in Europe and North America, the presumption being that nearly the whole increase was of gold, the continuous movement of silver to Asia having prevented any considerable increase of that kind of money in Europe or North America, the effects of the increase in the production of silver from 1863 to 1874 having been neutralized in this respect by the demonetization of silver in Germany.

Stock of Gold as Money. The line of dashes (— —) is intended to represent the stock of gold used as money in Europe and North America, it being assumed that about 80 per cent of the average annual increase of gold in the world from 1848 to 1870 was added to the stock in these countries.

Volume of Paper Money. The great fluctuations in the dotted line, representing the volume of paper money, are explained by the following facts: First, an increase in Austria from 1854 to 1858 of about $100,000,000. Second, an increase in the United States from 1862 to 1866 of nearly $1,600,000,000, about $1,000,000,000 of this being composed of the 7-30 and compound interest notes and the various issues of certificates of indebtedness issued by the treasury, which, though not of the same class of paper as the other treasury notes and bank notes, did circulate to a very large extent as money. The great bulk of this had, however, been retired by 1869, leaving the stock of paper money in the United States about $600,000,000 greater than in 1861. Third, an increase of nearly $400,000,000 in France from 1869 to 1873. Fourth, an increase in Italy of $300,000,000 from 1861 to 1876. Fifth, an increase of probably $200,000,000 in Russia in the last ten years. Besides these greatest additions, there was an increase of about $120,000,000 in Germany, and about $45,000,000 in Great Britain, in the whole period, and an increase in Switzerland of $11,000,000 to $12,000,000 from 1870 to 1873; $12,000,000 in Belgium from 1872 to 1873, etc.

Annual Interest. This line has been drawn with reference to such events as the civil war in the United States and the Franco-Prussian war, concurrent with the increase of railroad and municipal debts.

The courses of the lines in the diagram show the following changes in the percentage of money to debts, or promises to pay money, comparing 1845 with 1875, viz.:

	1845.	1875.
Percentage of gold and silver to paper money	200	140
Percentage of gold to paper money	75	68
Percentage of aggregate of gold and silver to annual interest	600	260
Percentage of gold to annual interest	225	131
Percentage of gold and silver to all obligations to pay interest and redeem paper money	160	90
Percentage of gold to all obligations to pay interest and redeem paper money	56	45

DIAGR

SHOWING THE APPROXIMATE AMOUNTS OF GOLD AND OF GOLD AND S
THE TOTAL VOLUME OF PAPER MONEY IN EUR

For full explan

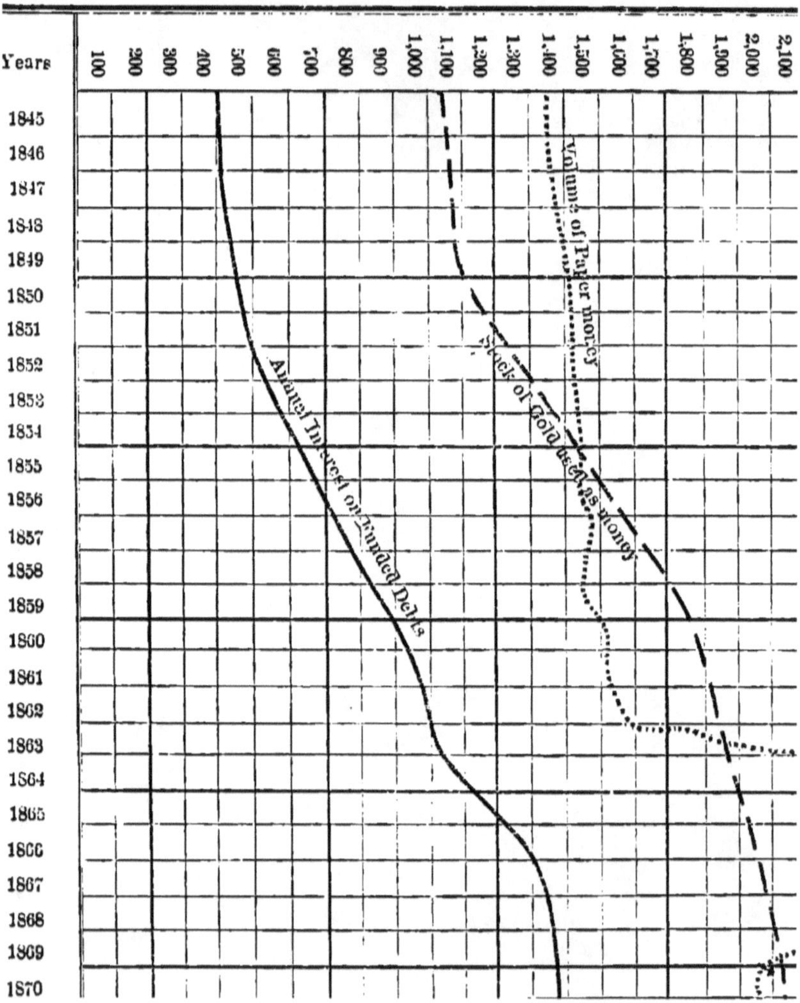

No. 2.

ER USED AS MONEY, THE ANNUAL INTEREST ON FUNDED DEBTS, AND
AND NORTH AMERICA EACH YEAR SINCE 1845.

n see page 127.

2,300 2,400 2,500 2,600 2,700 2,800 2,900 3,000 3,100 3,200 3,300 3,400 3,500 3,600 3,700 3,800 3,900 4,000 4,100 4,200 4,300 4,400 4,500 Millio of Doll

CHANGES IN THE VALUES OF THE PRECIOUS METALS, AND THEIR EFFECTS ON PRICES OF COMMODITIES.

JUST at present the commercial and financial world is perplexed with the causes of what is called the "low price of silver." Many are disposed to refer this almost wholly to the increase in the production of the metal; others more largely to the demonetization of silver in Germany; and still others claim that the decline in the value of silver, while it has been greatly increased by the above mentioned causes, was primarily an erroneous expression for a rise in the value of gold, this rise being shown not only in the decline in the gold price of silver, but of all commodities.

One of the most indisputable facts in connection with the vast increase in the production of gold from 1849 to 1854–5 was that it caused a general "rise of prices." I have made comparisons of the prices of a number of staple commodities in New York city in 1845 with those in 1854, and find that the average rise in that period was over 50 per cent (see tables of prices at the end of the book). This rise has been by some attributed to changes in the tariff, an assumption which I think is to a large extent erroneous. Aside from this there was no other feature of that period to which the rise could be attributed than the increase in the stock of gold in the world used as money. Professor Jevons compared the average of prices in 1849 with the average in 1865, and concluded there had been a rise of about 21 per cent, and his opinion was that the real permanent rise due to the increase of gold was about 21 per cent. I do not see how it is possible to avoid the conclusion, after investigation, that this estimate of the rise of prices was too low, as will be seen by the following table of average prices of thirteen leading articles in New York city either about the end of December, or in the first weeks of January following, in each one of three years of each period. Thus, the *average* price of a ton of iron in the winters of 1845–6–7 was $36; in the three winters of 1854–5–6 it was $33; in the three winters of 1873–4–5 it was $28. Coal and iron were the only exceptions to the general rise of prices. But even including these, the general rise of prices in the period 1854–6 over 1845–7 was 58 per cent.

AVERAGE PRICES OF LEADING ARTICLES AT THREE PERIODS (IN NEW YORK CITY).

Articles.	Quantities.	Periods.		
		1845–7.	1854–6.	1873–5. (Gold Prices.)
Wheat	30 bushels	$32	$65	$36
Corn	50 bushels	34	40	36
Coal	6 tons	30	24	31
Iron	1 ton	36	33	28
Salt	100 bushels	27	41	28
Pork	30 barrels	33	43	50
Beef	40 barrels	29	36	40
Rice	1000 pounds	33	36	63
Sugar (N. O.)	700 pounds	33	37	50
Cheese	500 pounds	30	45	60
Cotton	500 pounds	35	45	70
Wool	100 pounds	27	31	44
Leather	200 pounds	28	66	48
Averages		$31	$49	$45

Advance in 1854–6 over the average of 1845–7, 58 per cent.

In the period 1873–5 prices in gold were still 46 per cent above the average of 1845–7.

It is true New York was not the world; but its markets were governed by those of the rest of the world, and after making all due allowance for the effects of causes local to the United States (the tariff, the influx of emigrants, etc.), it is difficult to avoid the conclusion that the general rise of prices due to the increase of gold in 1854–6 was over 40 per cent. The values of the precious metals can be measured only by their exchangeable value for other commodities, and this general rise in the values of commodities was the index of the depreciation in the value of gold which Chevalier and others were predicting, but which in fact had already come while they were arguing about it. At the latter date, with which Professor Jevons made his comparison of prices, the average product of gold had decreased $25,000,000 or $30,000,000 per annum, and the excessive depreciation of its value was being recovered by reason of various causes. First of these was the vast increase of traffic, and the consequent necessities for the metal as a circulating medium. Second, the greatly increased use of gold in the arts. But in 1860 began a series of events which exercised an immense influence to advance prices of commodities, independent of the recovery in the value of gold. The first of these was the war of Italian liberation in 1860; next the civil war in the United States, lasting from 1861 to 1865; next the Austro-Prussian war in 1866. These three wars caused an aggregate destruction of life and property in six years scarcely equaled by any preceding period of twenty years; in fact, at the beginning of the Italian war the peace of Europe had not been disturbed by any great war since that in the Crimea, ending in 1856. These events were the main cause of a further advance in prices of commodities, which for a time concealed the rising value of gold. The waste of the wars and the diversion of industry had diminished the stocks of commodities, and their prices rose in proportion for some time after the destruction had ceased. The decline in prices of commodities was again deferred by the Franco-Prussian war, ending in 1871, the greatest effects of which, however, were apparently overcome by 1872-3. It was then that the effects of the diminishing stock of coin, the increase of obligations to pay money, together with the increasing stock of commodities, began to show themselves in various minor panics in Europe, preceding the culmination, in 1873, in the United States. From 1867 to 1872 there had been an average decline in the currency prices of all leading commodities in New York of from 30 to 35 per cent from the prices of 1867-8. This, it is true, was mainly the effect of the appreciation of the paper currency (which advanced from an average value of 70 cents on the dollar in 1867 to an average of 89 cents in 1872—27 per cent); but I think not wholly. The average of prices in 1875-6 was about the same as in 1851-2; but this latter period was before the whole rise caused by the increase of gold had been experienced. Prices had been much higher from 1854 to 1860.

It will perhaps be said that if the theory of a depreciation in the price of gold in the period from 1845 to 1854 was correct, it should have been shown in a rise in the gold value of silver. But this was prevented by the fact that at that period silver was the principal metallic currency of Europe. Great Britain had demonetized silver in 1816, but the great bulk of the metallic currency of the continent was silver. The legal value of this as compared with gold being permanent, the value of silver as money was tied to that of gold, and fell with it. Or, viewing it from the opposite side, we may say that the depreciation of gold was greatly diminished by its fixed legal value relatively to silver. Had gold been the exclusive standard of values in 1854, the rise in prices of commodities would have been twice as great. The result of the severance of the two metals, by the demonetization in Germany, and practically in France, at a period when the stock of gold is diminishing, has been a decline in prices of all commodities—including silver, which has been largely reduced in some countries to the condition of a commodity.

The demonetization of silver is not, of course, the sole cause of the decline of prices in the last four years. The vast load of war debt accumulated in Europe and the United States from 1860 to 1871 was steadily increasing the rates of interest for money. During that period the United States, Italy, Austria and France were in the market for enormous sums. The capital or wealth which they borrowed was destroyed in the wars, but the taxes were increased to pay high rates of interest on what no longer existed, and therefore was no longer the means of increasing the wealth of the world. The difference between the effects of the agencies which have produced the railroad debts and those which have produced the war debts is apparent. The former class represents something that is still in existence and operating to aid in the creation of the wealth to pay interest on the principal. The latter represents something that has been annihilated, the loss not being felt at once, but deferred and distributed over a number of years in the taxation to pay interest. It was this which, about 1872, began to make an increasing demand for the precious metals to reimburse capitalists for the cost of the wars. Philosophers may argue that gold and silver are only *measures* of values, and that one dollar of gold will measure a thousand dollars' *worth* of commodities as well as one, but it is also true that the desire for the actual *possession* of anything that seems to be getting scarce imparts to it an adventitious and phenomenal value. Such was the case in 1872–3, when capitalists began to doubt the ability of the nations to pay the greatly increased load of annual interest. It was this doubt which caused the first reaction, and the reaction once started, the cause reproduced itself and acquired momentum as it progressed. The first cause of the great reaction in 1873 was the immense load of war debts, but this has unquestionably been greatly aggravated in the last two years, and more especially in 1876, by the demonetization of silver.

The conclusion, then, is that the "decline in the value of silver" is in fact almost wholly the result of an equal divergence in the values of the two metals. The diminished stock of metallic money available in Europe, resulting from the demonetization of silver, has enhanced the value of gold and diminished the value of silver. Both metals have, for centuries, been maintained at an average value as money far above their intrinsic value as commodities. Money must be not only a standard of values, but a circulating medium.

Either increased use or diminished supply may cause a rise in the value of the thing used. Hence, if the work of $4,000,000,000 of gold and silver be delegated to $2,000,000,000 of gold, the gold will rise in value and the silver will depreciate. I conclude, therefore, that the change in the relative values of the two metals is due to the demonetization of silver; and that if gold, instead of silver, had been demonetized by Great Britain and Germany, the value of gold would have fallen and that of silver would have appreciated.

In March, 1876, a select committee was appointed by the British Parliament "to consider and report upon the causes of the depreciation of the price of silver." The committee immediately began its inquiries and continued them about one month, during which they held six sessions, and called in for examination the following persons: Messrs. Henry Waterfield, Sir Hector Hay, Stewart Pixley, Robert Giffen, Frederick G. Wilkins, Patrick Campbell, Robert Wigram Crawford, Gustavus Peitsch, Samuel Seldon, William Robinson, Colonel Henry Hyde, J. T. Mackenzie, Ernest Seyd and Walter Baghot, all persons of high repute in matters of statistics relating to money and finance. The report of the committee, printed in July, made a large folio volume of two hundred pages, equal to probably fifteen hundred pages of an ordinary 12mo book, and containing an enormous mass of figures and estimates in the papers put in by the witnesses.

The substance of the information on the question under consideration was, however, summed up in the following few paragraphs on page IV of the committee's report, viz.:

"Your committee are of the opinion that the evi-

" dence taken conclusively shews that the fall in the " price of silver is due to the following causes:

" (1) To the discovery of new silver mines of great " richness in the State of Nevada.

" (2) To the introduction of a gold currency into " Germany in place of the previous silver currency. " This operation commenced at the end of 1871.

" (3) To the decreased demand for silver for export " to India.

" (4) That the Scandinavian governments have also " substituted gold for silver in their currency.

" (5) That the Latin union, comprising France, Bel- " gium, Switzerland, Italy and Greece, have since 1874 " limited the amount of silver to be coined yearly in " the mints of each member of the union, suspending " the privilege formerly accorded to all holders of silver " bullion of claiming to have that bullion turned into " coin without restriction.

" (6) That Holland has also passed a temporary act " prohibiting, except on account of the government, the " coining of silver, and authorizing the coining of gold."

" It will be observed that two sets of causes have been " simultaneously in operation. The increased produc- " tion of the newly-discovered mines and the surplus " thrown on the market by Germany, have affected the " supply. At the same time the decreased amounts " required for India and the decreased purchases of sil- " ver by the members of the Latin union, have affected " the demand. A serious fall in the price of silver was " therefore inevitable."

" It is, however, an important and remarkable fact, to " which it may be convenient to call attention at once, " that though the increased production of silver in the

"United States is a fact beyond question, no increase "of imports of silver from the United States to Great "Britain has taken place since the year 1873, when the "average price of silver was still 59¼*d.* per ounce. "Indeed the amount of the imports of silver into Great "Britain from the United States for the year 1875, viz.: "£3,092,000, is the smallest since the year 1869. In "the same way, though the new currency laws of Germany affected a vast silver coinage, the sales of silver "actually made up to the 26th of April in the present "year do not appear to have exceeded £6,000,000 distributed over several years. Your committee, in "pointing to these circumstances, are far from saying "that the impression produced on the minds of the "dealers in silver was not justified by the causes in "operation."

It will be seen that of the "six causes" enumerated by the committee as operating to depreciate the value of silver, four are really the same thing, viz.: the movement in Europe by Germany, leading the Scandinavian States, to demonetize silver. The decreased demand for silver for export to India seems to be rather one of the results of the original decline caused by the demonetization, than an independent cause. The discovery of new mines in Nevada, mentioned by the committee as the first cause, is acknowledged to be only a source of *apprehension*, but not yet of any increased supply of silver.

It is admitted, even by those who have at times advocated an exclusive gold standard,* that it is impos-

* Probably, if there were gold enough for all the world, it would be best that there should be only a single standard of value throughout the world, and that one — gold. But this is impossible. Some have doubted whether there is gold enough even for the nations which now intend to use it; and there certainly is not enough for all the world.—*London Economist.*

sible for all nations to have the exclusive gold standard. The unavoidable result, therefore, of the adoption of the exclusive gold standard by a few of the leading nations possessing the financial preponderance of the world is to compel the remaining nations to practically adopt silver alone. But at the same time the demonetization of silver by a few leading commercial nations depreciates the metallic currency and the money obligations of the nations using silver as a standard of values. This disorganizes international trade and is a direct blow at all international relations.* The divergence in the respective values of the two metals is the measure of the divergence of national interests. The tendency of all this is to diminish the intercourse of nations and remand the world to the old narrow ideas of the necessary antagonism of the people of different countries.

The original establishment by law, in Great Britain,† France and the United States, that the legal values of

* The *London Economist* described the effects on the East India trade of the decline in the value of silver, in the first two months of 1876, as follows, viz.:

The consequence of the low value of silver is that the rate of exchange (in Calcutta) is now 1s. 9d. 1far. per rupee (or less), the lowest or almost the lowest ever known. And this operates as a direct discouragement to ship goods to India. These goods are paid for in rupees, and when the merchant wants to bring home those rupees to England he finds that they do not go so far as they used to do. He has to pay much more for every £1,000 bill on England, and this extra cost destroys or diminishes his profit.

If new silver should still continue to come into market the same process must go on. The first step must be incessantly repeated. The value of the rupee must fall as against sterling money; instead of being 1s. 9d. it may fall to 1s. 6d.

The Indian revenue is received in silver, and, therefore, the less far silver goes in buying, the poorer will the Indian government be. And this is of more instant importance to the Indian government than almost any other, because its foreign payments exceed those of most governments, and those payments are made in gold. It has to pay interest in gold on a very large debt in England, to pay home salaries, maintain home *dépôts*, and buy English goods and stores all in gold; and the less valuable silver is in comparison with gold, the less effectual for these necessary purposes will the Indian revenue be.

† Abrogated in Great Britain by the law of 1816.

gold and silver should be as 1 of gold to 15½ of silver, was the result of nearly two hundred years' observation of the following facts, viz., that the intrinsic value of each metal as a commodity, aside from its uses as currency or money, was continually fluctuating in accordance with the increase or decrease of its production, but that this increase or decrease of production, and consequent increase or decrease of value, was never the same in both metals at the same time. The experience was that when the production of gold had diminished, that of silver had either remained stationary or increased, and *vice versa*. There was no theory to show that this should necessarily be the case, but such was and had been the fact for over two hundred years. In order to prevent wide fluctuations in the standard of values, it was sought to establish a bond between the values of the two metals, so that the diminishing value of the one might be checked by either the stationary or the increasing value of the other. Experience had shown that the average commercial value of silver had been as 15½ of silver to 1 of gold, and that though either one might temporarily change in value so as to change this relative value, it would certainly come back to it sooner or later *if both metals were equally used as money*. As previously remarked, the values of both metals is to a very large extent fictitious; there is no other use, than as money, that would warrant more than one-fourth the present values of either gold or silver. The depreciation of 29 in the 100 of the value of silver (or the increase of 41 per cent in the value of gold, whichever one may choose to call it) which took place from October, 1874, to July, 1876, mainly as the result of the demonetization of silver by Germany, proves it.

It was, therefore, to prevent fluctuations in the standard of values that the two metals were, so to speak, "yoked together" by the legal establishment of their values as permanent at 15½ to 1. It was believed, and experience has proven, that if both metals were equally used as money, this relative valuation was the point from which there would be the least departure. During the discussions of this subject in Congress (1875–6) there seemed to be a disposition on the part even of the advocates of the double standard to change the relative legal values of gold and silver by the coinage of a larger silver "dollar," as compared with the gold "dollar." But any departure from the standard of 15½ to 1 is the same in principle — only less in degree — as the complete demonetization of either of the metals.* To meddle once with a rule established by the experience of centuries, only makes the necessity of meddling again at some future time.

The following table is from the annual report for 1875 of the United States Commissioner of Mining Statistics:

* The law of April, 1792, provided that the ratio of gold to silver in all coins current as money in the United States "shall be as "*fifteen to one*," and for 40 years the silver dollar of the United States was of that proportional value. But by the reduction in weight of the gold coins the ratio was increased to 16 to 1. The subsequent laws regulating the values of coins had changed this to 15.988 to 1 in 1837, which continued to be the ratio until the coinage of the trade dollar under the law of February, 1873, made it 16.27 to 1.

RELATIVE AVERAGE ANNUAL VALUES OF GOLD AND SILVER.

Date.	Ratio.		Authority.
A. D.			
1526	11.30	}	Apparent relation of market-value, as deduced from the British mint-regulations, some absurd and unsuccessful experiments in coinage being disregarded.
1543	11.10		
1561	11.70	}	French mint-regulations.
1575	11.68		
1551	11.17	}	German imperial mint-regulations.
1559	11.44		
1604	12.10	}	British mint-regulations — experiments disregarded.
1612	13.30		
1619	13.35		
1623	11 74		Upper German regulations.
1640	13.51	}	French mint-regulations.
1665	15.10		
1667	14.15	}	Upper German regulations.
1669	15.11		
1670	14.50		British regulations.
1679	15.00	}	French regulations.
1680	15.40		
1687-1700	14.97	}	Ratios calculated from the bi-weekly quotations of the Hamburg prices-current, giving the value of the gold ducats of Holland in silver thalers, down to 1771, and, after that, in fine silver bars. The nominal par of exchange during this period was 1:14.80; and the quotations show the variations of the market rate in percentage above or below this. At par, 6 silver marks-banco were equivalent to one ducat, 68 20-47 ducats containing one mark (weight) of fine gold, and 27¾ silver marks-banco containing one mark (weight) of fine silver. Hence, 6×68 20-47÷27¾=14.80, the par ratio.
1701-1720	15.21		
1721-1740	15.08		
1741-1790	14.74		
1791-1800	15.42		
1801-1810	15.61		
1811-1820	15.51		
1821-1830	15.80		
1831-1840	15 67		
1841-1850	15.83		
1851	15.46	}	The London quotations. These give the price of a given weight of standard silver in shillings and pence sterling. Bearing in mind that there is in Great Britain no charge for coinage, and, hence, that the price referred to varies exactly as the market-value of the metals, we can calculate the ratio as follows: The standard gold is $\frac{11}{12}$ fine, and its value is fixed at 77s. 10½d., or 934.5 pence per ounce troy. Hence the value of an ounce of fine gold is $\frac{12}{11}$ of this sum, or 1019.45 pence. The standard silver, on the other hand, is $\frac{37}{40}$ fine; hence an ounce of fine silver is worth 1.081 times as much as an ounce of standard silver. If the fixed value of an ounce of fine gold be divided by 1.081 times the quoted price of an ounce of standard silver, the quotient is the ratio desired. Thus, if x be the quoted price per ounce in pence, $\frac{1019.45}{1.081x}=\frac{943}{x}$ (very nearly) is the ratio. Briefly, dividing 943 by the price in pence of an ounce of standard silver gives the ratio correctly to the second decimal place. London being the acknowledged center of the commercial world, this ratio determines the relative value of the metals among civilized nations.
1852	15.57		
1853	15.33		
1854	15.33		
1855	15.36		
1856	15.33		
1857	15.27		
1858	15.36		
1859	15.21		
1860	15.30		
1861	15.47		
1862	15.36		
1863	15.38		
1864	15.40		
1865	15.33		
1866	15.44		
1867	15.57		
1868	15.60		
1869	15.60		
1870	15.60		
1871	15.59		
1872	15.63		
1873	15.90	}	The table shows annual averages only. The lowest *monthly* value of gold was 15.12 in May, 1859, and the highest 16.35, in October, 1874. The annual average for 1874 here given is calculated upon the prices of eleven months, ending November 30.
1874	16.15		

The foregoing table only gives *average annual* values; but in order to show the fluctuations caused by the increase of gold from 1848 to 1853–5, and also the much greater ones caused by the demonetization of silver in Germany, I have made the following table, showing the *per cent* of premium on each of the metals as expressed in the value of the other at various periods:

Time.	Ratio of Silver to Gold in the London Market.	Premium on Silver over 15½ to 1.	Premium on Gold over 1 to 15½.
1821 to 1830, average...	15.80 to 1	....	1.93 per cent
1851, average of year...	15.46 to 1	.25 per cent	....
1857, " " ...	15.27 to 1	1.50 "	....
1859, May............	15.12 to 1	2.45 "	....
1863, year............	15.33 to 1	1.00 "	....
1874, October..........	16.35 to 1	....	4.84 per cent
1875, January..........	16.45 to 1	....	5.48 "
1875, July............	16.97 to 1	....	9.48 "
1876, January	17.08 to 1	....	10.18 "
1876, July............	22.54 to 1	....	45.28 "
1876, September	18.84 to 1	....	21.54 "

EXPLANATION OF DIAGRAM No. 3.

In diagram No. 3 I have endeavored to make apparent what has been the progress of the values of the precious metals as compared with the values of commodities, and the principal causes which have at different times affected the values of each, the varying difference between the lines being what is understood as the "rising or falling of prices."

The upper line in the diagram — the line of dashes — begins with prices at what might be called "zero" in 1845 to 1847; the rise of the line through 1851–2–3–

DIAG

SHOWING THE FLUCTUATIONS IN THE VALUES O

Explanation.—The upper line (thus ▬ ▬ ▬) in the diagr
The two lower lines represent the values of gold and silver as com
variations in the space between the upper line and the two lower li
the prices of 1845–7. For further explanation see page 142.

OMMODITIES AND OF GOLD AND SILVER SINCE 1840.

indicates the rise and fall in values of commodities during the period.
ed to each other and as compared to the values of commodities. The
represent the rise and fall of prices of commodities as compared with

1862	1863	1864	1865	1866	1867	1868	1869	1870	1871	1872	1873	1874	1875	1876

4–5 indicates the increased demand for and consumption of all sorts of commodities incident to the gold hunting fever which prevailed throughout the world. The great rise from 1860 to 1867 was largely the effect of the general progress of civilization and the general increase in the scale of expenditure in social life. But of the special events which increased the demand for and values of commodities, the four great wars mentioned were the most potent. These were the causes which operated to increase the *values* of commodities independent of the increase or decrease of the stock of precious metals. These created a demand for new articles, viz.: munitions of war, and diverted labor from its usual employments to supply them; the result being an increased demand for labor, and consequently an increased cost. The demand for labor continued temporarily after the wars to supply the waste incident to them. But this being done there was no longer so much employment, the supply of commodities became excessive, resulting in a decline of prices and of the wages of labor. (The "rise of prices" indicated at this period refers, of course, to prices in gold—the rise in currency prices was much greater.)

But now taking the two lower lines, the continuous one representing the value of gold as compared with the values of commodities, and the dotted one representing the value of silver as compared to gold and also to the values of commodities, we see a great descent in the lines of both from 1850 to 1855–6. Silver declined because its value was "tied to the value of gold" by the laws then in force in the United States, France, and practically in the greater part of Europe, making one ounce of gold legally equal to from fourteen to sixteen of silver.* Silver being the money of nearly all Europe, its value sustained the value of gold, and prevented a much greater decline.

The whole difference between these values of the precious metals and the values of commodities was called "the rise of prices."

* The following table shows the relative legal values of gold and silver in the coinage systems of various countries:

RELATIVE VALUES OF GOLD AND SILVER IN THE COINAGE SYSTEMS OF COUNTRIES OF THE GOLD STANDARD.

Country.	Relative Coins.		Pure Metal.		Relative Value.
	Gold.	Silver.	Gold.	Silver.	
			Grains.	*Grains.*	
Bogota	peso.	½ peso.	22.49	141.009	1 to 12½
Egypt	pound.	piaster.	115.5	14.298	1 to 12.3
England	pound.	shilling.	113.001	80.727	1 to 14.2
Germany	mark.	mark.	5.531	77.16	1 to 13.
Portugal	1,000 reis	500 reis.	25.087	176.824	1 to 14.
Scandinavian Union	crown.	crown.	6.225	92.392	1 to 14.8
United States	dollar.	subsid'y	23.22	347 24	1 to 14.52
" "	dollar.	trade dol	23.22	378.00	1 to 16.27

RELATIVE VALUES OF GOLD AND SILVER IN THE COINAGE SYSTEMS OF COUNTRIES OF THE SILVER STANDARD.

Country.	Relative Coins.		Pure Metal.		Relative Value.
	Gold.	Silver.	Gold.	Silver.	
			Grains.	*Grains.*	
Austria*	gulden.	florin.	11.2006	171.466	1 to 15⅝
Mexico*	peso.	peso.	22.8477	377.1718	1 to 16½
Netherlands*	gulden.	florin.	9.3332	145.8324	1 to 15⅝
Russia*	5 rubles.	ruble.	92.5713	277.7158	1 to 14¾

* These countries issue a gold coin for commercial or trade purposes.

RELATIVE VALUES OF GOLD AND SILVER IN THE COINAGE SYSTEMS OF COUNTRIES OF THE DOUBLE STANDARD.

Country.	Relative Coins.		Pure Metal.		Relative Value.
	Gold.	Silver.	Gold.	Silver.	
Latin Union includes Belgium, France, Italy and Switzerland	5 francs.	5 francs.	22.4012	347.22	1 to 15½

The "Latin Monetary Union," mentioned in the foregoing table, was a convention ratified at Paris, December 23, 1865, between the governments named,

But the value of gold began to rise with the increase of traffic and debts. The change in the money standard of Great Britain to one of gold alone in 1816 had as yet produced but little effect on the world at large. But as great debts increased, and as immense sums began to be negotiated in London, this law of 1816 began to operate to increase the demand for gold to pay interest in the only metal that England recognized as the standard of values. The evidence of this advance in the value of gold is in the fact that it soon rose above that of 1 to 15½ of silver. The lines of the two metals, as shown in the diagram, had crossed each other about 1850, and now again they crossed about 1862, indicating that the "*golden era*" *had ended, and that the* "*era of golden debt*" *had begun.* The success of Germany in the war with France gave the former the means of attempting to follow in the footsteps of England. Germany demonetized silver, and depended upon the

this convention constituting the governments into a union for the purpose of establishing a uniform system of weights, measures and valuations and forms of currency.

The governments (Art. 2) contracted not to coin any gold moneys in any other denominations of coins than 1,000 francs, 50 francs, 20 francs, 10 francs and 5 francs, at the ratio of 1.612.90 grammes of standard gold (9-10 fine) to each 5 francs.

Silver coins of the denomination of 2 francs (or less) were made a legal tender between individuals in the state that coined the silver for sums of 50 francs; but in payments from individuals to the state which issued the silver the coins were made legal tender in any sum. It was provided that the national treasuries of the several countries should accept silver coined by any of the other states in the union to the extent of 100 francs. The convention, however, fixed the limit of total coinage of silver during the continuation of the union to its expiration in 1880. The amount allowed to be coined by each country for 1876 has been stated as follows, viz.:

	Francs.
France	54,000,000
Italy	36,000,000
Belgium	11,000,000
Switzerland	7,000,000
	108,000,000

$1,000,000,000 she was to get from France as a war penalty, for the means of substituting gold for about $300,000,000 to $400,000,000 of her silver currency. France was not only obliged to borrow gold of all the surrounding nations, but to hoard all she could to avoid being obliged to accept a metallic currency of silver which had become depreciated by the operation of the laws of England and Germany. Thus the appreciation of gold went on, but even yet was to a considerable extent held down by the use of silver in the larger part of Europe; but with the beginning of 1876, when the new laws in Germany went into full operation, and Germany began to sell off about $250,000,000 of silver, the two metals parted company. Silver declined until in July, 1876, it was nominally quoted as low as 46 pence per ounce, and gold was left as the only measure of values in the leading commercial countries of Europe, Great Britain, France and Germany. Debts and the interest on them are payable in those countries only in gold. In the United States they have been made payable (by the coinage law of February, 1873,) in promises to pay gold, viz.: in United States treasury notes. Thus this increased demand for gold, present and prospective, (made prospective in the United States by the specie resumption act of January, 1875,) has increased its value. Debts are paid with commodities, but not until the commodities have been exchanged for money—*gold.* The decline of prices since 1872–3 is explained by the increased value of gold. The first effect was to cause a collapse in "speculative securities," viz.: bonds of railroads, etc., which were based on the expectation of a continuance of high prices for commodities, or in other words, a low value for gold. The losses which followed caused panic and a decrease in manufacturing industry and improvement enterprises. This diminished employment for labor and necessarily decreased the consumptive demand for all commodities. This again caused still further cessation of industry and a further decrease of demand for commodities. Theorists have been jangling for three years about the cause of the reaction which began in 1872–3, and the decline of prices which has continued almost without interruption since. These causes are, however, not obscure. The progress of the physical sciences and of labor-saving inventions has undoubtedly had an important tendency to reduce the prices of nearly all manufactured articles and, to a small extent also, the values of raw materials. But the increased burden of debt, the increase of traffic (thus requiring a larger volume of the circulating medium), and the demonetization of silver, have all contributed to increase the value of gold beyond its equitable value as a measure for values of commodities.

The era of golden debt, like the era of gold, has had its culmination, and the causes at work now are preparing the way for some new era in financial affairs which will, in all probability, be as unique as either of the two which have preceded it. No man can yet foresee what it is to be. It is, however, not difficult to distinguish a few tendencies that must continue to operate toward the new development. The first of these is the decline in the rates of interest for money in order to reduce the burden of funded and mortgage debt everywhere. This will be accomplished partly by the repudiation and complete loss of a very large portion of the existing volume of funded debts, and partly by the concentration of capital (seeking safety rather than high rates of interest) on a smaller amount of debt. Another tendency that must continue, is the necessity for supplementing the stock of gold in the world with the stock of silver, and a universal recognition of both metals as money at about the same relative values they maintained prior to the era of gold. Until these things are accomplished, "prices" will continue to decline and the commercial world will be in distress. A great war in Europe would afford temporary relief by creating an extra demand for commodities, partly as munitions of war and partly to supply new stocks in place of those destroyed. But this would neither reduce the burden of interest on funded debts nor increase the stock of gold or silver, nor in any way decrease the demand for the precious metals. On the contrary, some nations would be obliged to pay interest in gold on the cost of the war, viz.: the value of the property destroyed and the industry diverted from its proper channels. Thus while a great war would temporarily cause a rise in prices, this would only be a reason for their ultimately declining to a lower point than before the war. Financiers and statesmen have taken an exceedingly narrow-minded view of this era of debt. While they have not failed to call attention to the magnitude of debt, it has only been in a tone of reproach to the commercial and financial community for indulging in what has been termed an "inflation of credit." The truth, however, is that the greatest part of the present burden of debt was created by *war*. The four great wars since 1860 (viz.: the Italian, the Austro-Prussian, the American and the Franco-Prussian) increased the national, municipal and State debts of the countries involved about seven thousand millions of dollars, or over 30 per cent of the total of present funded debts in the world. The increase of debt as the result of wars in the last sixteen years has been more than double the increase of debt from the expansion of the railroad system, and all other national and municipal improvements and enterprises in the same time. It is the war debts — not the debts of excessive enterprise — that have created the present burden of annual interest. It is war debts also that are represented in all the inconvertible paper money now afloat in the world. Now, it is not to be presumed that the "reign of peace" has begun, or that it will begin any time in the next hundred years. In the last quarter of a century great wars have averaged less than five years apart. The wars of this period, also, have been more largely *financial contests* than ever before in the history of modern civilization. It is a trick of capital in all countries to persuade the people that their honor is at stake in the payment of all these war debts at the highest valuation the avarice of the holders may set on them. But it is plain that a few years more of such war experience as the last sixteen, would place the burden of annual interest and the redemption of the paper money beyond the ability of the people. Indeed, with gold as the exclusive standard of values, it is extremely problematic whether "specie payments" could be maintained even in all the countries that do now propose to pay interest and redeem paper money in gold. The countries that propose to do this are Great Britain, France, Germany and the United States. The aggregate of paper money in these is about $1,700,000,000, and the total amount of gold does not exceed $1,600,000,000. Assuming that an average reserve of 50 per cent would sustain the present volume of paper money — by constant daily redemptions—at par with gold, it would require that an aggregate of $850,000,000 of gold should be evenly and constantly distributed in all the countries. But with so small a stock, outside of banks and national treasuries, the movements of foreign trade would soon disturb this distribution of the metal and cause suspension again, in one country or another.*

Even if we state the problem upon a broader basis, it is equally difficult of solution, viz.:

Europe and North America are now using an aggregate of about $7,300,000,000 of gold, silver and paper money as mediums of exchange. Of this amount over $3,100,000,000 is paper promises to pay gold or silver. But on just about three fourths of this aggregate of over $3,100,000,000 of paper money, specie payments

* Early in the current year (1876) the London *Economist*, referring to the situation of the Bank of France as compared with its position in 1860, said:

And here, just as in 1860, the principal component in the reserve is the comparatively appreciated metal. The metals have, indeed, changed places: in 1860 the metal which had augmented in value was silver; now the metal which has increased in value is gold. But the position of the Bank of France is, for the purpose now in hand, identical. It now holds an enormous amount of gold, which it would be dangerous to pay away; just as in 1860 it held a much smaller, though still considerable, amount of silver, to pay which would have been equally dangerous.

Of course, as long as the Bank of France suspends specie payments it does not feel this difficulty. If we may be permitted to say so, it is on a lower level altogether. It is not perplexed by the possibility of having to pay in the appreciated metal, for it does not, except in minor sums, and when it chooses, pay in any metal. But as soon as the Bank of France performs its legal obligations, the problem which the defective currency system of France sets before it must be solved. There is, indeed, one obvious mode of solving it. There is something very singular in a difficulty which is caused by holding a commodity which has enhanced in value. The obvious remedy is to sell it in the market and to obtain the advantage of that value. If the Bank of France could sell its gold for silver at the present price, it would get a large profit; it would have done a capital bullion transaction on a magnificent scale, and the shareholders would be large gainers in consequence. In 1860 the Emperor Napoleon, to whom the accounts of the Bank of France were then constantly submitted, would not permit the natural remedy to be tried, and, therefore, the Bank of France had to forego the profit, and to change away the dearer metal with the Bank of England. But now there can be no choice; the sums to be dealt with are so large that no such palliative by exchange can be thought of. If cash payments are to be resumed in France, large sales of gold for silver must precede and accompany it.

And the effect of such sales will, of course, be to raise the price of silver as compared with gold. The circumstances of the Bank of France will make the possession of much silver constantly essential to it, and the effect of this new large demand will be a rise of price.

have been suspended for many years. Even if it were possible for Russia, Austria, Italy, France and the United States to acquire the coin with which to resume specie payments on their respective amounts of paper currency, the amount of coin that would be drawn into national treasuries for that purpose would cause a contraction of over 20 per cent in the aggregate volume of circulating medium in the hands of the people of Europe and North America. It is beyond reasonable doubt that such a change would cause a proportionate enhancement of the vast volume of war debts, which would be shown in the corresponding decline in the prices of commodities. It would require that the peace of Europe and America should remain undisturbed for at least ten or fifteen years before the industry of the people could produce wealth enough to pay off this increase in the burden of debt and so adjust the values of commodities and the value of money to the new basis. The improbability of such a peace is the measure of the improbability of the resumption of specie payments in all the countries where they are now suspended.

PUBLIC DEBT OF THE UNITED STATES.

Statement of the Character and Amount of Bonds and Other Forms of Indebtedness, July 1, yearly, from 1861 to 1876 inclusive (omitting the years 1871-2-3-4).

COMPILED FROM THE ANNUAL STATEMENTS OF THE SECRETARY OF THE TREASURY.

Title of Loans.	Date of Authorizing Acts.	Rate.	Principal Payable.	Amount outstanding July 1, yearly—(omitting 000 at the end of each amount).											
				1861.	1862	1863.	1864.	1865.	1866.	1867.	1868.	1869.	1870.	1875.	1876.
				$	$	$	$	$	$	$	$	$	$	$	$
Old debt........	Prior to 1815	..	Demand ..	114	114	114	114	114	114	113	113	113	113	121	121
Loan of 1842	July 21, 1841	6	Dec. 31, '62	2,883	2,883	302	196	195	79	64	6	6	6	.....	....
Loan of 1847	Jan. 28, 1847.	6	Dec. 31, '67	9,415	9,415	9,415	9,415	9.415	9.415	7,160	742	26	12	1	1
Loan of 1848	Mar. 31, 1848.	6	July 1, '68.	8.908	8.908	8,908	8,908	8,908	8,908	8,020	6,151	69	43	.....	....
Texas indemnity.	Sept. 9. 1850.	5	Dec. 31, '64	3,461	3,461	3,461	2,149	842	559	263	256	242	242	181	24
Texas debt	Sept. 9, 1850.	..	Demand ..	112	112	....	.....	.....	.....	.....	. ..	......	......	260	260
Loan of 1858	June 14, 1858	5	Dec. 31, '73	20.000	20,000	20,000	20,000	20,000	20,000	20,000	20,000	20,000	20,000	17	10
Loan of 1860	June 22. 1860	5	Dec. 31, '70	7,022	7,022	7,022	7,022	7,022	7,022	7,022	7,022	7,022	7,022	10	....
Loan of Feb., 1861	Feb. 8, 1861 .	6	June 1, '81	16,339	8.415	18.415	18,415	18,415	18,415	18,415	18,415	18,415	18,415	18,415	18,415
Oregon war loan.	Mar. 2, 1861 .	6	July 1, '81.	....	998	1,021	1,016	1,016	1.016	1,016	945	945	945	945	945
Loan of July. 1861	July 17, 1861	6	June 30, '81	....	50,000	50,000	50,000	50,000	50,000	50,000	50.000	50.000	50.000 }	189,321	189,321
Bonds (for 7.30s).	Aug. 5, 1861 .	6	June 30, '81	....	.....	28	30,643	139.031	139,350	139,999	139.361	139.352	139,318 }	....	....
Five-twenty bds .	Feb. 25, 1862	6	Apr. 30, '67	....	9,907	168,880	510,780	514.780	514.780	514,780	514,780	514,771	514.771	54,897	1,111
Loan of 1863	Mar. 3, 1863 .	6	June 30, '81	....	.....	.....	42,672	75,000	75,000	75,000	75.000	75.000	75 000	75,000	75,000
Ten-forty bonds .	Mar. 3, 1864 .	5	Feb. 28, '74	....	.....	.....	73,337	172,770	171,219	171,409	194 566	194.567	194,567	194,566	194,566
Five-twenty bds .	Mar. 3, 1864 .	6	Oct. 31, '69	....	.....	.....	.....	.....	3,882	3.882	3.882	3,882	3.882	946	6
Five-twenty bds .	June 30, 1864	6	Oct. 31, '69	....	.....	.....	.....	91,789	100,000	125,561	125,561	125,561	125,561	58,046	1,854
Five-twenty bds .	Mar. 3, 1865 .	6	Oct. 31. '70	....	.....	.....	.....	.....	103,542	181,427	197.794	203.327	203.327	152,534	150,558
Five-twenty bds .	Mar. 3. 1865 .	6	June 30, '70	....	.....	.....	.....	.....	.....	301,880	332,928	332,998	332.998	202,663	202,663
Five-twenty bds .	Mar. 3, 1865 .	6	June 30, '72	....	.....	.....	.....	.....	.....	.....	365,248	379.582	379.602	310,622	310,622
Five-twenty bds .	Mar. 3, 1865 .	6	June 30, '73	....	.....	.....	.....	.....	.....	... .	17,648	42,539	42,539	37,474	37.473
5 per cents of 1881	Jan. 14 '70 } Jan. 20, '71 }	5	....	....	.....	.....	.....	.....	.....	.....	.....	.....	.....	412,306	516,859
Tot. funded debt	....	..	....	68256	131237	287568	774676	1109699	1223304	1626016	2070423	2108427	2108368	1708246	1699905

Union P. R.R. bds	July 1, 1862 ..	6	Jan. 15, '95.	....	.....	.....	.....	1,258	6,042	14,762	29,089	58,638	64,457	64,623	64,623
Treas. notes (old)	Prior to 1857.	....	Demand ...	104	104	104	104	104	104	104	104	104	89	80	90
Treas. notes of '57	Dec. 23, 1857 .	....	1 year......	2,203	18	18	8	8	8	2	2	2	2	1	.....
Treas. notes of '60	Dec. 17, 1860 .	....	1 year......	9,942	6	1	0	0	0	0	0	.....	.....	.....	.....
Treas. notes of '61	Mar. 2, 1861 ..	6	2 years.....	2,274	2,716	776	164	5	3	3	3	3	3	3	3
Treas. notes of '61	Mar. 2, 1861 ..	6	60 days. ...	5,628	3	.....	.....	.....	.....	.....	.....	.....	.....	.....	.....
Treas. notes of '63	Mar. 3, 1863 ..	5	2 years.....	....	.....	.....	108,951	42,338	3,454	1,123	555	247	218	47	43
Treas. notes of '63	Mar. 3, 1863 ..	5	60 days.....	....	.....	.....	44,520	.....	.....	.....	.....	.....	.....	.....	.....
Three years notes	July 17, 1861 .	7.30	Aug. 18, '64.	....	53,004	52,981	109356	968	649	.....	.....	.....	.....	.....	.....
Three years notes	July 17, 1861 .	7.30	Sept. 30, '64	....	69,832	86,989									
Three years notes	June 30, 1864.	7 30	Aug. 14, '67.	....	.....	.....	....								
Three years notes	Mar. 3, 1865 ..	7.30	June 14, '68.	....	.....	.....	....	671,610	806,251	488,647	37,717	1,166	641	196	183
Three years notes	Mar. 3, 1865 ..	7.30	July 14, '68.	....	.....	.....	....								
Comp'd int. notes	Mar. 3, 1863 ..	6	3 years.....	....	.....	.....	15,000	15,000	.....	.....	.....	.....	.....	.....	.....
Comp'd int. notes	June 30, 1864.	6	3 years.....	....	.....	.....	.....	178,756	159,012	122,394	28,161	2.871	2,152	367	328
Three p. c. cert's.	Mar. 2, 1867 ..	3	Demand ...	....	.....	.....	.....	.....	.....	.....	50,000	52,120	45,545	5	5
Tempor'ry loans.	Feb. 25, '62, etc	4 5 6	10 days	....	57,746	102,384	72,330	89,717	120,176	20,225	13,797	186	181	.....	.....
Certificates	Mar. 1, 1862 ..	6	1 year......	....	49,881	156,784	160,729	115,772	26,391	36	18	12	5	5	5
Tot. unf'nd debt	....	....	....	20153	233313	400034	511165	1115540	1116056	632537	159450	115352	113345	707	659
U. S. notes	July 17, 1861 .	*nil.*	Demand ..	....	53,040	3,351	780	472	272	208	141	123	106	70	66
U. S. notes	Feb. 25, 1862 .	....	....	....	96,620	147,767									
U. S. notes	July 11, 1862 .	....	....	....	.....	150,000	431178	432,687	400,619	371,783	356,000	356,000	356,000	375,771	369,772
U. S. notes	Mar. 3, 1863 ..	....	....	....	.....	89,879									
Postal currency .	July 17, 1862 .	....	....	....	.....	20,192	15,167	9,915	7,030	5,497	4,881	4,605	39878	42,129	34,446
Frac. currency...	Mar. 3, 1863 ..	....	....	....	.. ..	.....	7,727	15,090	20,040	22,809	27,745	27,508			
Tot. U. S. notes and frac. cur...	....	....	....	....	149660	411190	454854	458166	427963	400299	388768	388238	395984	417971	404285
Gold certificates .	Mar. 3, 1864 ..	....	....	....	.....	.....	.....	.....	10,713	19,207	17,678	30,489	34.547	.....	.....
Aggr. of pub. debt	....	....	....	88409	514211	1098793	1740690	2681663	2784073	2692823	2636320	2642508	2652246	2126211	2104180

N. B.—None of the "Trust Funds" are included in the above statement, such as the Navy Pension Fund, the Indian Annuity Funds, the Smithsonian Fund, etc., which are provided for by annual appropriations.

The following statement of the outstanding principal of the public debt on the 1st of January each year, from 1791 to 1876 inclusive, is taken from the annual report of the Secretary of the Treasury (B. H. Bristow) for the fiscal year ending June 30, 1875, the amount for June 30, 1876, being added from the official monthly debt statement:

Year.	Amount.	Year.	Amount.
1791	$75,463,476 52	1828	$67,475,043 87
1792	77,227,924 66	1829	58,421,413 67
1793	80,352,634 04	1830	48,565,406 50
1794	78,427,404 77	1831	39,123,191 68
1795	80,747,587 39	1832	24,322,235 18
1796	83,762,172 07	1833	7,001,698 88
1797	82,064,479 33	1834	4,760,082 08
1798	79,228,529 12	1835	37,513 05
1799	78,408,669 77	1836	336,957 83
1800	82,976,294 35	1837	3,308,124 07
1801	83,038,050 80	1838	10,434,221 14
1802	80,712,632 25	1839	3,573,343 82
1803	77,054,686 30	1840	5,250,875 54
1804	86,427,120 88	1841	13,594,480 73
1805	82,312,150 50	1842	20,601,226 28
1806	75,723,270 66	1843	32,742,922 00
1807	69,218,398 64	1844	23,461,652 50
1808	65,196,317 97	1845	15,925,303 01
1809	57,023,192 09	1846	15,550,202 97
1810	53,173,217 52	1847	38,826,534 77
1811	48,005,587 76	1848	47,044,862 23
1812	45,209,737 90	1849	63,061,858 69
1813	55,962,827 57	1850	63,452,773 55
1814	81,487,846 24	1851	68,304,796 02
1815	99,833,660 15	1852	66,199,341 71
1816	127,334,933 74	1853	59,803,117 70
1817	123,491,965 16	1854	42,242,222 42
1818	103,466,633 83	1855	35,586,956 56
1819	95,529,648 28	1856	31,972,537 90
1820	91,015,566 15	1857	28,699,831 85
1821	89,987,427 66	1858	44,911,881 03
1822	93,546,676 98	1859	58,496,837 88
1823	90,875,877 28	1860	64,842,287 88
1824	90,269,777 77	1861	90,580,873 72
1825	83,788,432 71	1862	524,176,412 13
1826	81,054,059 99	1863	1,119,772,138 63
1827	73,987,357 20	1864	1,815,784,370 57

Year.	Amount.	Year.	Amount.
1865..........	2,680,647,869 74	1871..........	2,353,211,332 32
1866..........	2,773,236,173 69	1872..........	2,253,251,328 78
1867..........	2,678,126,103 87	1873..........	*2,234,482,993 20
1868..........	2,611,687,851 19	1874..........	*2,251,690,468 43
1869..........	2,588,452,213 94	1875..........	*2,232,284,531 95
1870..........	2,480,672,427 81	1876, June 30..	*2,180,325,037 00

The total debt, including all outstanding obligations of the government, reached its maximum in 1866, when it aggregated $2,773,236,173. But the total interest-bearing portion of the debt aggregated at the same time only $2,339,954,150.

The reduction in the total annual interest since the aggregate of interest-bearing and non-interest-bearing debt reached its maximum has been as follows, viz.:

	Principal.	Interest.
1867, June 30......................	$2,678,126,603	$143,781,592
1868, "	2,611,687,851	140,404,045
1869, "	2,588,452,213	130,694,242
1870, "	2,481,672,427	129,235,498
1871, "	2,353,411,032	125,576,565
1872, "	2,253,251,328	117,357,839
1873, "	2,234,482,993	104,750,628
1874, "	2,251,690,468	98,799,144
1875, "	2,232,284,531	98,002,161
1876, "	2,178,700,111	95,104,269

* In the amount here stated as the outstanding principal of the public debt are included the certificates of deposit outstanding on the 30th of June, issued under act of June 8, 1872, amounting to $31,730,000 in 1873, $58,760,000 in 1874, and $58,415.000 in 1875, for which a like amount in United States notes was on special deposit in the treasury for their redemption, and added to the cash balance in the treasury. These certificates, as a matter of accounts, are treated as a part of the public debt, but being offset by notes held on deposit for their redemption, should properly be deducted from the principal of the public debt in making comparison with former years.

FOREIGN INDEBTEDNESS OF THE UNITED STATES.

IN 1874 Dr. Edward Young, Chief of the National Bureau of Statistics, made an estimate of the amount of American national, state and corporate bonds held in Europe at the close of 1873, and arrived at the conclusion that the amount then was, in round figures, *twelve hundred million* dollars. By a memorandum sent to the writer of this in August of this year (1876), Dr. Young estimated the amount of the foreign indebtedness of the United States at $1,350,000,000.

Dr. Young's method of arriving at the estimate of $1,200,000,000 of foreign indebtedness at the close of 1873 is somewhat elaborate, and open to some criticism, though it is perhaps as logical a method as any that can be devised for approximating to the actual amount, the most pertinent objection to his conclusions being that he has perhaps estimated the average prices at which American securities have sold in Europe higher than was actually obtained for them.* It is a tolerably well-estab-

* BALANCE OF TRADE.—It is necessary, in the outset, to consider the elements that enter into this computation. In the first place, we must ascertain the adverse balance of trade upon the actual specie values of imports and exports. As in the fiscal year 1862 the value of exports exceeded that of the imports, the period embraced in this investigation begins on the 1st July, 1862.

(Here follows a table of the total imports and exports of merchandise and specie from July 1, 1862, to December 31, 1873, which has been incorporated in a table of the same items on page 159, for the longer period from June 30, 1843, to June 30, 1876. The period selected by Dr. Young shows an excess of merchandise imports over merchandise exports, exclusive of specie, amounting to $1,040,-535,721. This adverse balance was reduced by the export of $681,946,067 of

lished fact that while a great many American state, municipal and corporate bonds negotiated in London since 1865 have sold for about par, a great many more have sold for much less, and it is well known that of the vast amount of railroad bonds negotiated there since 1870 more than half of the aggregate amount did not net the corporations in the United States over 80 cents on the dollar after deducting all expenses. The amounts "called up" each month on subscriptions to foreign loans in London, as published in the *Investors' Manual*, show that even since the crisis of 1873 the amount of American state, municipal, railroad and other corporate bonds in London has averaged at least $75,000,000 per

specie in excess of the imports of specie to $358,589,654. Beginning with this net adverse balance of $358,589,654 for the eleven and a half years, he proceeds to take into the account the following elements that increase it, viz.:)

SMUGGLING AND UNDERVALUATION.—From a careful examination of the subject during the past four years, the undersigned considers an addition of 3 per cent to the total value of the imports for undervaluation and smuggling as an ample allowance. It must be borne in mind that neither bulky nor free goods are smuggled, and that merchandise paying specific duties will not be undervalued. What kind of goods will probably be smuggled? Precious stones, jewelry, watches, silks, fine laces, etc. An examination of the official returns of the port of New York, published by this Bureau, will show that the total value of free and dutiable merchandise which entered into consumption during the fiscal year ended June 30, 1873, was, in round numbers, $438,000,000, 3 per cent on which is $13,140,000. The following were the imports of goods most easily smuggled:

Precious stones	$2,678,368
Jewelry and all manufactures of gold and silver	1,030,510
Watches and watch movements and materials	3,039,512
Silk dress goods	16,353,380
Total	$23,101,770

which, with fine laces and embroideries, probably reached $26,000,000. The $13,000,000 above estimated is equal to 50 per cent of the value of such of these articles as paid duty. Is it believed that the undervaluations and smuggling of such articles as the above named amount to $13,000,000 annually? Perhaps, of precious stones, jewelry, watches, laces and embroideries it may reach $5,000,000, but cannot amount to $8,000,000 on silk goods. It seems evident, therefore, that an addition of 3 per cent to the value of imported merchandise is sufficient to annum; and if we set the aggregate of such bonds (exclusive of national bonds) negotiated in Europe since 1870 at $800,000,000 par value, it will probably be below the actual amount, and if the average net proceeds of these received by the American corporations be estimated at say 85 cents on the dollar, it would show $120,000,000 of debt created without any return. But assuming that Dr. Young's estimate of $1,200,000,000 at the close of 1873 was nearly correct, it would place the aggregate at the present time somewhere about $1,400,000,000. But if his estimate of 80 cents on the dollar for all bonds sold prior to 1874 be 10 per cent too high, as is thought by some, it would still make the

cover the evasions of the revenue, such addition amounting in the period under review to $146,861,754.

FREIGHTS.—The values of the imports of merchandise, as presented in the first table, being those at the ports of shipment, it will be proper to add thereto the amount of freights to the several ports of the United States. As a part is brought in American vessels, and as the freight so earned is an addition to the wealth of the country, it is only necessary to consider, as another element in the computation, the amount of freight received by foreign ship-owners. As inward freights on goods vary from 100 per cent on the value of salt and some other bulky articles to 2 or 3 per cent on dress goods, and less than one-half per cent on specie, it is difficult to estimate the average *ad valorem* rate. On merchandise the average is not much less than 8 per cent; but, as nearly all the specie and the greater part of the dress goods, jewelry, watches, etc., are brought by foreign steamships, which disburse a considerable amount for fuel and ship-stores, it is believed that 6 per cent on the total value of imports is an estimate of approximate accuracy. As the imports in foreign vessels amounted to $3,531,374,280, the element of foreign freight will, therefore, cause an increment of $211,882,456.

The exports of domestic products, as given in the trade reports, are the currency values at the several ports of shipment in the United States. To make these conform to a uniform standard, the values have been reduced to gold in the tables above presented. The total amount exported in American vessels during the period under consideration was of the value of $1,450,000,000 in gold, the freight on which, estimated at 6 per cent, amounted to $87,000,000, which sum must be deducted from the aggregate of freights carried by foreign vessels.

The last item to be added to the estimate is the interest which has become due upon the debt while it has been accruing. To obtain this with approximate accuracy is the most difficult part of this investigation. The most careful aggregate at present (August, 1876) about $1,500,000,-000. Of this amount about one half is presumed to be government bonds.

FOREIGN TRADE OF THE UNITED STATES FOR 24 YEARS.

Total imports into the United States each year from 1843 to 1876 inclusive, as stated by the National Bureau of Statistics for each year ending June 30 :

Year.	Merchandise.	Specie.	Total Imports.
1843	$42,433,464	$22,320,335	$64,753,799
1844	102,604,606	5,830,429	108,435,035
1845	113,184,322	4,070,242	117,254,564
1846	117,914,065	3,777,732	121,691,797
1847	122,424,349	24,121,289	146,545,638
1848	148,638,644	6,360,284	154,998,928
1849	141,206,199	6,651,240	147,857,439
1850	173,509,526	4,628,792	178,138,318
1851	210,771,429	5,453,503	216,224,932

analysis which has been made, as a basis for an intelligent estimate, leads to the conclusion that the amount of interest is not less than $277,000,000 nor more than $290,000,000. Lest the undersigned should be charged with a desire to reduce the aggregate of our foreign debt below the actual amount, the larger sum will be used in the computation.

We have now the following items:

Adverse balance of trade for eleven and a half years	$358,589,654
Allowance for merchandise smuggled and undervalued	146,861,754
Freights on imports to foreign shipowners	211,882,456
Interest	290,000,000
	$1,007,333,864
Less freights on exports to United States shipowners	87,000.000
Aggregate	$920,333,864

From the above statement it appears that the debt we owe to Europe, incurred since July 1, 1863, amounts to $920,000,000. But owing to the fact that during the former part of that period our credit abroad was not assured, our securities sold considerably below par. Owing to the wide range in price — from 40 cents on the dollar at one time, to par at a more recent period — there

Year.	Merchandise.	Specie.	Total Imports.
1852	$207,440,398	$5,505,044	$212,945,442
1853	263,777,265	4,201,382	267,978,647
1854	297,623,039	6,939,342	304,562,381
1855	257,808,708	3,659,812	261,468,520
1856	310,432,310	4,207,632	314,639,942
1857	348,428,342	12,461,799	360,890,141
1858	263,338,654	19,274,496	282,613,150
1859	331,333,341	7,434,789	338,768,130
1860	353,616,119	8,550,135	362,166,254
1861	289,310,542	46,339,611	335,650,153
1862	189,356,677	16,415,052	205,771,729
1863	243,335,815	9,584,105	252,919,920
1864	316,447,283	13,115,612	329,562,895
1865	238,745,580	9,810,072	248,555,652
1866	434,812,066	10,700,092	445,512,158
1867	395,763,100	22,070,475	417,833,575
1868	357,436,440	14,188,368	371,624,808
1869	417,506,379	19,807,876	437,314,255
1870	435,958,408	26,419,179	462,377,587
1871	520,223,684	21,270,024	541,493,708
1872	626,595,077	13,743,689	640,338,766
1873	642,136,210	21,480,937	663,617,147
1874	567,406,342	28,454,906	595,861,248
1875	535,005,336	18,900,717	553,906,153
1876	460,713,761	15,935,453	476,649,214

is great difficulty in ascertaining the average rate of discount. But a careful estimate establishes the fact that the average discount for the whole period (eleven and a half years) under consideration was *less than 20 per cent.* In computing the aggregate of this debt, the par value of these securities must be ascertained, and as they sold at an average rate of at least 80 cents on the dollar, it follows that our debt to foreign nations, incurred in the past dozen years, amounts to about $1,150,000,000. Although there were no national securities held abroad at the commencement of our late war, yet some of the bonds of the Commonwealth of Pennsylvania, and probably of Massachusetts and other States, as well as railroad shares and securities, were owned in Europe. In the absence of accurate data on the subject, it is believed that fifty millions is an ample estimate for these *ante bellum* securities. With this addition, our aggregate foreign debt amounts to nearly TWELVE HUNDRED MILLION DOLLARS!

[It will be borne in mind that the foregoing is an *unofficial estimate* of the amount of the United States securities — national, state, municipal and corporation — held in foreign countries. The figures in the tables have, however, been taken from the records of the bureau, and are, therefore, trustworthy.]

EDWARD YOUNG.

—*Monthly Report of the Bureau of Statistics for February, 1874.*

TOTAL EXPORTS (SPECIE VALUES).

Year.	Merchandise.	Specie and Bullion.	Total Exports.
1843....................	....	....	$ 84,346,474
1844....................	....	....	111,200,046
1845....................	....	....	114,646,606
1846....................	....	....	113,488,516
1847....................	....	....	158,648,622
1848....................	....	....	154,032,131
1849....................	....	....	145,755,820
1850....................	....	....	151,898,720
1851....................	....	....	218,388,011
1852....................	....	....	209,658,366
1853....................	....	....	230,976,157
1854....................	....	....	273,898,000
1855....................	....	....	275,156,846
1856....................	....	....	326,964,908
1857....................	....	....	362,960,682
1858....................	....	....	324,644.421
1859....................	....	....	356,789,462
1860....................	....	....	400,122,292
1861....................	....	....	249,344,913
1862....................	....	....	227,558,141
1863....................	$203,964,447	$ 64,156,611	268,121,058
1864....................	158,837,988	105,396,541	264,234,529
1865....................	166,029,303	67,643,226	233,672,529
1866....................	348,859,522	86,044,071	434,903,593
1867....................	292,361,225	60,868,372	353,229,597
1868....................	281,952,899	93,784,105	375,737,004
1869....................	286,117,697	57,138,380	343,256,077
1870....................	392,771,768	58,155,666	450,927,434
1871....................	442,820,178	98,441,988	541,262,166
1872....................	444,177,586	79,877,534	524,055,120
1873....................	522,479,922	84,608,574	607,088,496
1874....................	646,856,926	59,699,686	706,556,612
1875....................	579,367,543	73,857,129	653,224,672
1876....................	540,338,693	56,506,302	596,844,995

The following figures show the debtor balances against and the creditor balances in favor of the United States each year for twenty-four years:

Debtor Balance.		Creditor Balance.
....	1843	$19,590,675
....	1844	2,765,011
$2,607,958	1845	....
8,203,281	1846	....
....	1847	12,102,984
966,797	1848	....
2,101,619	1849	....
26,239,598	1850	....
....	1851	2,163,079
3,287,076	1852	....
37,002,490	1853	....
30,664,381	1854	....
....	1855	13,688,326
....	1856	12,324,966
....	1857	2,070,541
....	1858	42,031,271
....	1859	18,021,332
....	1860	37,955,938
86,305,240	1861	....
....	1862	21,786,412
....	1863	15,201,138
65,328,366	1864	....
14,883,123	1865	....
10,608,565	1866	....
64,603,978	1867	....
....	1868	4,112,196
94,058,178	1869	....
11,450,153	1870	....
231,542	1871	....
116,283,646	1872	....
56,528,651	1873	....
....	1874	108,695,364
....	1875	99,318,519
....	1876	120,195,781

TABLE I.—ANNUAL REVENUE AND EXPENDITURES OF THE UNITED STATES.

Receipts of the Government from July 1, 1865, to July 1, 1876, inclusive—Net Revenue by Fiscal Years.

Year.	Customs.	Internal revenue.	Direct tax.	Sales of public lands.	Premium on loans and sales of gold.	Miscellaneous items.	Net revenue.
1866	$179,046,651 58	$309,226,813 42	$1,974,754 12	$665,031 03	$38,083,055 68	$29,036,314 23	$558,032,620 06
1867	176,417,810 88	266,027,537 43	4,200,233 70	1,163,575 76	27,787,330 35	15,037,522 15	490,634,010 27
1868	164,464,599 56	191,087,589 41	1,788,145 85	1,348,715 41	29,203,629 50	17,745,403 59	405,638,083 32
1869	180,048,426 63	158,356,460 86	765,685 61	4,020,344 34	13,755,491 12	18,997,338 65	370,943,747 21
1870	194,538,374 44	184,899,756 49	229,102 88	3,350,481 76	15,295,643 76	12,942,118 30	411,255,477 63
1871	206,270,408 05	143,098,153 63	580,355 37	2,388,646 68	8,892,839 95	22,093,541 21	383,323,944 89
1872	216,370,286 77	130,642,177 72	....	2,575,714 19	9,412,637 65	15,106,051 23	374,106,867 56
1873	188,089,522 70	113,729,314 14	315,254 51	2,882,312 38	11,560,530 89	17,161,270 05	333,738,204 67
1874	163,103,833 69	102,409,784 90	....	1,852,428 93	5,037,665 22	17,075,042 73	289,478,755 47
1875	157,167,722 35	110,007,493 58	....	1,413,640 17	3,979,279 69	15,431,915 31	288,000,051 10
1876	148,071,984 61	116,700,732 03	93,798 80	1,129,466 95	4,029,280 58	17,456,776 19	287,482,039 16
	1,973,589,621 26	1,826,185,813 61	9,947,330 84	22,790,357 60	167,037,384 39	193,083,293 64	4,192,633,801 34

Expenditures of the Government for the same period.

Year.	Total expended.	For interest on debts.	Civil service.	Pensions and Indians.	War.	Navy.
1866	$520,750,940	$133,067,741	$41,056,961	$18,852,416	$284,449,701	$43,324,118
1867	346,729,124	131,034,011	51,110,027	25,579,083	95,224,415	43,781,591
1868	377,340,284	140,424,045	60,011,018	27,883,069	123,246,648	25,775,502
1869	321,490,597	130,964,242	56,471,061	35,519,544	78,501,990	20,000,757
1870	309,653,560	129,235,498	69,234,017	31,748,140	57,655,675	21,780,229
1871	292,177,188	125,576,565	69,498,710	34,443,894	35,799,991	19,431,027
1872	270,559,695	117,357,839	60,984,757	35,595,130	35,372,157	21,249,809
1873	290,345,245	109,856,607	73,328,109	37,311,120	46,323,158	23,526,256
1874	302,633,873	107,119,815	69,641,593	35,730,876	42,313,927	30,932,587
1875	274,623,392	103,093,544	69,100,884	38,840,875	41,120,645	21,497,626
1876	*293,166,177	....	....	....	....	....
Total	3,599,469,985	....	....	....	....	....

* Amount appropriated.

MONETARY LAWS

OF THE

UNITED STATES.

Revision of all Laws in 1873; Coinage Laws; Laws Authorizing United States Notes and Bonds; Laws for National Banks and Bank Currency.

AND

REFERENCE TABLES:

Tables of Prices for 54 years; Tables of Values of Coins and Monetary Units of all Nations; Table of the Average Annual Price of Gold from 1862 to 1876; Table of the Value of United States Notes with Gold at any Price.

REVISION OF ALL THE PERMANENT LAWS OF THE UNITED STATES IN 1873.

BY an act of Congress, June 27, 1866, the President was authorized to appoint three commissioners, "three persons learned in the law," "to revise, simplify, arrange and consolidate all statutes of the United States, general and permanent in their nature." This act was "revived" by the act of May 4, 1870, under authority of which the President appointed the three commissioners.

This commission prosecuted its important work by striking out all that was obsolete and all that had been repealed down to December 1, 1873, and then brought the parts of the various laws relating to the same subjects together under their respective new titles. This work was presented to the forty-second Congress, and adopted by act of June 20, 1874, which repealed all *general* laws in existence prior to December 1, 1873, as follows, viz.:

(SEC. 5596) All acts of Congress passed prior to said 1st day of December, 1873, any portion of which is embraced in any section of said revision, are hereby repealed, and the section applicable thereto shall be in force in lieu thereof; all parts of such acts not contained in such revision having been repealed or suspended by subsequent acts, or not being general or permanent in their nature; provided, that the incorporation into said revision of any general and permanent provision, taken from an act making appropriations, or from an act containing other provisions of a private, local, or temporary character, shall not repeal or in any way affect any appropriation, or any provision of a private, local, or temporary character, contained in any of said acts, but the same shall remain in force; and all acts of Congress passed prior to said last named day, no part of which are embraced in said revision, shall not be affected or changed by its enactment.

The repeal above referred to, it will be seen, related back to December 1, 1873. But in the interim to the date of adoption many important amendments had been made to the laws that were revised. Thus the "National Currency Act," or "National Bank Act," was amended by act of June 20, 1874, abolishing the reserve to be held against circulation. This amendment was itself partly repealed by the specie resumption act of January 14, 1875. None of this legislation appears in the Revised Statutes, and these changes only appear in the Statutes at Large in the form of amendments to a law that does not exist in its original form and arrangement of sections.

Unlike the laws in regard to the coinage and in regard to the issue and redemption of United States notes and bonds, there are no questions of general importance in connection with the history of the legislation in regard to the national banks and to national bank currency.

THE PLAN OF COMPILATION

pursued in the following pages has, therefore, been to divide the monetary laws under three heads, viz.: *Coinage*, *United States Notes and Bonds*, and *National Banks and Bank Currency*,— each of these three divisions being compiled with a different view. Under the head of Coinage are given only such clauses of the laws as relate to the weight, fineness and legal tender value of United States and foreign coins. Under the head of United States Notes and Bonds are given only such clauses as relate to the character of the obligation on the part of the government as a borrower, and the kind of payment provided for in the redemption of such obligations; all minor points not having any inportant bearing on these are omitted. But under the head of National Banks and Bank Currency are given all the laws now in force regarding the organization and management of National Banks and the issue and redemption of National Bank Currency. The object, therefore, in the compilation of laws under the last mentioned head has been to embody in their proper places in the Revised Statutes all the amendments passed in the interim between December 1, 1873, and June 20, 1874, and to strike out all that was repealed in the same time, thus making the compilation of laws under the head of National Banks and Bank Currency the same as if the revision of laws had been continued to June 20, 1874, instead of terminating at December 1, 1873.

COINAGE.

THE following includes all the clauses of all the laws of the United States (and the previous Confederation of States) from 1781 to 1876, as they relate to the *Weight*, *Fineness* and *Legal-Tender Value* of United States and Foreign Coins. This summary is intended as historic of the policy of the government in regard to gold and silver coins and the relative values of the two metals:

Articles of Confederation between the States, adopted March 1, 1781.

§ 1. The United States in Congress assembled shall also have the sole and exclusive right and power of regulating the alloy and value of coin struck by their own authority or by that of the respective States, fixing the standard of weights and measures throughout the United States.

[By act of the Congress of the Confederation passed August 8, 1786, and by the ordinance of October 16, 1786, a silver dollar, containing 375.64 grains of pure silver, was established as the "unit of account," though the Confederation had not established any mint and no such coins as were specified by the act were coined anywhere. The dollar thus established was intended to be the equivalent of 4s. 6d. sterling, but fell short of it by about two per cent.]

The Constitution, adopted September 17, 1787.

The Congress shall have power—

§ 2. To borrow money on the credit of the United States.

§ 3. To coin money, regulate the value thereof, and of foreign coin, and fix the standard of weights and measures.

No State shall coin money; emit bills of credit; make anything but gold and silver coin a tender in payment of debts; pass any *ex post facto* law, or law impairing the obligation of contracts.

ACTS OF CONGRESS.

Act April 2, 1792.

That the money of account of the United States shall be expressed in dollars or units, dimes or tenths, cents or hundredths, and mills or thousandths, a dime being the tenth part of a dollar, a cent the hundredth part of a dollar, a mill the thousandth part of a dollar, and that all accounts in the public offices and all proceedings in the courts of the United States shall be kept and had in conformity to this regulation.

§ 4. That a mint for the purpose of a national coinage be and the same is established; to be situate and carried on at the seat of government of the United States for the time being.

§ 5. There shall be, from time to time, struck and coined at the said mint, coins of gold, silver and copper, of the following denominations, values and descriptions, viz.: *Eagles*—each to be of the value of ten dollars or units, and to contain $247\frac{4}{8}$ grains of pure or 270 grains of standard gold. *Half eagles*—each to be of the value of five dollars or units, and to contain $123\frac{6}{8}$ grains of pure or 135 grains of standard gold. *Quarter eagles*—each to be of the value of two dollars and a half dollar, and to contain $61\frac{7}{8}$ grains of pure or $67\frac{4}{8}$ grains of standard gold. *Dollars or units*—each to be of the value of a Spanish milled dollar, as the same is now current, and to contain $371\frac{4}{16}$ grains of pure or 416 grains of standard silver. *Half dollars*—each to be of half the value of the dollar or unit, and to contain $185\frac{10}{16}$ grains of pure or 208 grains of standard silver. *Quarter dollars*—each to be of one fourth the value of the dollar or unit, and to contain $92\frac{13}{16}$ grains of pure or 104 grains of standard silver. *Dismes*—each to be of one tenth the value of a dollar or unit, and to contain $37\frac{2}{16}$ grains of pure or $41\frac{3}{5}$ grains of standard silver. *Half dismes*—each to be of the value of one twentieth of a dollar, and to contain $18\frac{9}{16}$ grains of pure or $20\frac{4}{5}$ grains of standard silver. *Cents*—each to be of the value of one hundredth part of a dollar, and to contain 11 pennyweights of copper. *Half cents*—each to be of the value of half a cent, and to contain $5\frac{1}{2}$ pennyweights of copper.

§ 6. The proportional value of gold to silver in all coins which shall, by law, be current as money within the United States shall be as fifteen to one, according to quantity in weight of pure gold or pure silver: that is to say, every fifteen pounds weight of pure silver shall be of equal value in all payments with one pound weight of pure gold, and so in proportion as to greater or less quantities of the respective metals.

Act February 9, 1793.

§ 7. At the expiration of three years next ensuing from the time when the coinage of gold and silver, agreeably to the act entitled "An act establishing a mint and regulating the coins of the United States," shall commence at the mint of the United States (which shall be announced by proclamation of the President of the United States), all foreign gold coins and all foreign silver coins, except Spanish milled dollars and parts of such dollars, shall cease to be legal tender as aforesaid. (See § 13.)

§ 8. All foreign gold and silver coins, except Spanish milled dollars and parts of such dollars, which shall be received in payment for moneys due to the United States after the said time when the coining of gold and silver coins shall begin at the mint of the United States, shall, previously to their being issued in circulation, be coined anew, in conformity to the act entitled "An act establishing a mint and regulating the coins of the United States." (See § 19.)

Act March 2, 1799.

§ 9. All foreign coins and currencies shall be estimated at the following rates, viz.: each *pound sterling* of Great Britain at four dollars and forty-four cents ($4.44); each *livre tournois* of France at eighteen and a half cents (18½); each *florin* or *guilder* of the Union Netherlands at forty cents (40); each *mark-banco* of Hamburg at thirty-three and one-third cents (33⅓); each *rix dollar* of Denmark at one hundred (100) cents; each *real* of plate and each *rial of vellon* of Spain, the former at ten cents and the latter at five cents each; each *milree* of Portugal at one dollar and twenty-four cents; each *pound sterling* of Ireland at four dollars and ten cents; each *tale* of China at one dollar and forty-eight cents; each *pagoda* of India at one dollar and ninety-four cents; each *rupee* of Bengal at fifty-five and one-half cents; and all other denominations of money, as nearly as may be to the said rates or the intrinsic value thereof, compared with money of the United States.

§ 10. All duties and fees to be collected shall be payable in money of the United States, or in foreign gold and silver coins at the following rates, that is to say: the gold coins of Great Britain and Portugal of the standard prior to the year 1792 at the rate of one hundred cents for every twenty-seven grains of the actual weight thereof; the gold coins of France, Spain and the dominions of Spain, of the standard prior to the year 1792, at the rate of one hundred cents for every twenty-seven grains and two-fifths of a grain of the actual weight thereof; Spanish milled dollars at the rate of one hundred cents for each dollar, the actual weight whereof shall not be less than seventeen (17) pennyweights and seven (7) grains—and in proportion for the parts of a dollar; crowns of France at the rate of one hundred and ten cents for each crown, the actual weight whereof shall not be less than eighteen (18) pennyweights and seventeen (17) grains, and in proportion for the parts of a crown. *Provided*, that no foreign coins shall be receivable which are not by law a legal tender for the payment of all debts—except in consequence of a proclamation of the President of the United States authorizing such foreign coins to be received in payment of duties and fees as aforesaid.

Act March 3, 1801.

§ 11. The foreign coins and currencies hereinafter mentioned shall be estimated in the computation of duties at the following rates: each sicca rupee of Bengal and each rupee of Bombay at fifty cents, and each star pagoda of Madras at one hundred and eighty-four cents.

Act April 10, 1806.

§ 12. Foreign gold and silver coins shall pass current as money within the United States, and be a legal tender for the payment of all debts and demands at the several and respective rates following, and not otherwise, viz.: The gold coins of Great Britain and Portugal of their present standard at the rate of one hundred cents for every twenty-seven grains of the standard weight thereof; the gold coins of France, Spain and the dominions of Spain, of their present standard, at the rate of one hundred cents for every twenty-seven grains and two-fifths of a grain of the actual weight thereof. Spanish milled dollars at the rate of one hundred cents for each, the actual weight whereof shall not be less than seventeen (17) pennyweights and seven (7) grains, and in proportion for the parts of a dollar. Crowns of France at the rate of one hundred and ten cents for each crown, the actual weight whereof shall not be less than eighteen (18) pennyweights and seventeen (17) grains, and in proportion for the parts of a crown. And it shall be the duty of the Secretary of the Treasury to cause assays of the foreign gold and silver coins of the description made current by this act, and which shall issue subsequently to the passage of this act, and shall circulate in the United States—at the mint aforesaid, at least once in every year, and to make report of the result thereof to Congress, for the purpose of enabling Congress to make such coins current—if they shall deem the same to be proper—at their real standard value.

§ 13. That the first section of the act entitled "An act regulating foreign coins and for other purposes," passed the 9th day of February, 1793, be and the same is hereby repealed, and the operation of the second section of the same act is hereby suspended for and during the space of three years from the passage of this act. (See § 7–8.)

Act March 3, 1823.

§ 14. The following gold coins shall be received in all payments on account of public lands at the several and respective rates following and not otherwise, viz.: the gold coins of Great Britain and Portugal of their present standard, at the rate of one hundred cents for every twenty-seven grains, or eighty-eight cents and eight-ninths ($88\frac{8}{9}$) per pennyweight; the gold coins of France, of their present standard, at the rate of one hundred cents for every twenty-seven and one-half grains or eighty-seven and a quarter ($87\frac{1}{4}$) cents per pennyweight, and the gold coins of Spain, of their present standard, at the rate of one hundred cents for every twenty-eight and a half grains, or eighty-four cents per pennyweight.

§ 15. It shall be the duty of the secretary of the treasury to cause assays of the foregoing coins to be made at the mint of the United States at least once in every year, and make report of the result thereof to Congress.

Act June 25, 1834.

§ 16. The following silver coins shall be of the legal value, and shall pass current as money within the United States, by tale for the payment of all debts and demands at the rate of one hundred cents the dollar, that is to say, the *dollars* of Mexico, Peru, Chili and Central America, of not less weight than four hundred and fifteen grains each, and those re-stamped in Brazil of the like weight, of not less fineness than ten ounces fifteen pennyweights of pure silver in the troy pound of twelve ounces of standard silver; and the five-franc pieces of France, when of not less fineness than ten (10) ounces and sixteen (16) pennyweights in twelve ounces troy weight of standard silver, and weighing not less than three hundred and eighty-four grains each — at the rate of ninety-three (93) cents each.

§ 17. The following gold coins shall pass current as money in the United States, and be receivable in all payments by weight for the payment of all debts and demands at the rates following, that is to say: the gold coins of Great Britain, Portugal and Brazil, of not less than twenty-two (22) carats fine, at the rate of ninety-four cents and eight-tenths of a cent ($94\frac{8}{10}$) per pennyweight; the gold coins of France, nine-tenths fine, at the rate of ninety-three cents and one-tenth of a cent ($93\frac{1}{10}$) per pennyweight, and the gold coins of Spain, Mexico and Columbia, of the fineness of twenty (20) carats, three grains and seven-sixteenths ($3\frac{7}{16}$) of a grain, at the rate of eighty-nine cents and nine-tenths of a cent ($89\frac{9}{10}$) per pennyweight.

Act January 18, 1837.

§ 18. The standard for both gold and silver coins of the United States shall hereafter be such that of one thousand parts by weight nine hundred shall be of pure metal and one hundred of alloy, and the alloy of silver coins shall be of copper, and the alloy of the gold coins shall be of copper and silver, provided that the silver do not exceed one-half the alloy.

§ 19. Of the silver coins, the *Dollar* shall be of the weight of 412½ grains; the *Half Dollar* of the weight of 206¼ grains; the *Quarter Dollar* of the weight of 103⅛ grains; the *Dime*, or tenth part of a dollar, of the weight of 41¼ grains, and the *Half Dime*, or twentieth part of a dollar, of the weight of 20⅝ grains.

§ 20. And that Dollars, Half Dollars, Quarter Dollars, Dimes and Half Dimes shall be legal tenders of payment according to their nominal value for any sums whatever.

§ 21. Of the gold coins, the weight of the *Eagle* shall be 258 grains; that of the *Half Eagle* 129 grains, and of the *Quarter Eagle* 64½ grains.

§ 22. And that for all sums whatever the Eagle shall be a legal tender of payment for ten dollars, the Half Eagle for five dollars, and the Quarter Eagle for two and a half dollars.

Act July 27, 1842.

§ 23. In all payments by or to the treasury, whether made here or in foreign countries where it becomes necessary to compute the value of the pound sterling, it shall be deemed equal to four dollars and eighty-four cents ($4.84).

Act March 3, 1843.

§ 24. The following gold coins shall pass current as money in the United States and be receivable by weight for the payment of all debts and demands at the rates following, that is to say: the gold coins of Great Britain, of not less than nine hundred and fifteen and a half thousandths (915½-1,000) in fineness, at ninety-four cents and six-tenths ($94\frac{6}{10}$) of a cent per pennyweight, and the gold coins of France, of not less than eight hundred and ninety-nine thousandths ($\frac{899}{1000}$) in fineness, at ninety-two cents and nine-tenths of a cent ($92\frac{9}{10}$) per pennyweight.

The following foreign silver coins shall pass current as money within the United States and be receivable by tale for the payment of all debts and demands at the rates following, that is to say: the Spanish pillar dollars, and the dollars of Mexico, Peru and Bolivia, of not less than eight hundred and ninety-seven thousandths ($\frac{897}{1000}$) in fineness and four hundred and fifteen (415) grains in weight, at one hundred cents each, and the five-franc pieces of France, of not less than nine hundred thousandths ($\frac{900}{1000}$) in fineness and three hundred and eighty-four (384) grains in weight, at ninety-three (93) cents each.

Act March 3, 1849.

§ 25. There shall be from time to time struck and coined at the mint of the United States and the branches thereof—conformably in all respects to law, and conformably in all respects to the standard for gold coins now established by law—coins of gold of the following denominations and value, viz.: *Double Eagles*, each to be of the value of twenty dollars or units, and *Gold Dollars*, each to be of the value of one dollar, or unit.

§ 26. For all sums whatever the Double Eagle shall be a legal tender for twenty dollars, and the Gold Dollar shall be a legal tender for one dollar.

§ 27. In adjusting the weights of gold coins henceforward the following deviations from the standard weight shall not be exceeded in any of the single pieces, namely: in the double eagles, the eagle and the half eagle, one half of a grain; and in the quarter eagle and gold dollar, one quarter of a grain; and that in weighing a large number of pieces together, when delivered from the chief coiner to the treasurer, and from the treasurer to the depositors, the deviation from the standard weight shall not exceed three pennyweights in one thousand double eagles; two pennyweights in one thousand eagles; one and one-half pennyweights in one thousand half eagles; one pennyweight in one thousand quarter eagles, and one-half of a pennyweight in one thousand gold dollars.

Act March 3, 1851.

§ 28. It shall be lawful to coin at the mint of the United States and its branches a piece of the denomination and legal value of three cents, or three-hundredths of a dollar, to be composed of three-fourths silver and one-fourth copper, and to weigh twelve (12) grains and three-eighths (⅜) of a grain; that it shall be a legal tender in payment of debts for all sums of thirty cents and under.

Act February 21, 1853.

§ 29. That the weight of the *Half Dollar*, or piece of fifty cents, shall be one hundred and ninety-two (192) grains; and the *Quarter Dollar*, *Dime* and *Half Dime* shall be respectively one-half, one-fifth and one-tenth of the weight of the Half Dollar.

§ 30. The silver coins issued in conformity with the above section shall be legal tenders in payment of debts for all sums not exceeding five dollars.

§ 31. From time to time there shall be struck and coined at the mint of the United States and the branches thereof, conformably in all respects to the standard of gold coins now established by law, a coin of gold of the value of *Three Dollars or Units.*

§ 32. And that hereafter the Three Cent piece now authorized by law shall be made of the weight of three-fiftieths of the weight of the half dollar, as provided in said act, and of the same standard of fineness. And said act, entitled "An act amendatory of existing laws relative to the *Half Dollar, Quarter Dollar, Dime and Half Dime*," shall take effect and be in full force from and after the first day of April, 1853, anything to the contrary notwithstanding.

Act February 21, 1857.

§ 33. The standard weight of the *Cent* coined at the mint shall be seventy-two (72) grains, or three-twentieths of an ounce troy, with no greater deviation than four grains in each piece; and said *Cent* shall be composed of eighty-eight (88) per centum of copper and twelve (12) per centum of nickel. And the coinage of the *Half Cent* shall cease.

Act February 21, 1857.

§ 34. The pieces commonly known as the quarter, eighth and sixteenth of the Spanish *pillar dollar* and of the Mexican dollar shall be receivable at the Treasury of the United States and its several offices, and at the several post offices and land offices, at the rates of valuation following, viz.: the fourth of a dollar, or piece of two reals, at twenty cents; the eighth of a dollar, or piece of one real, at ten cents; and the sixteenth of a dollar, or half real, at five cents.

§ 35. *All former acts* authorizing the currency of foreign gold or silver coins, and declaring the same a legal tender in payment of debts, *are hereby repealed;* but it shall be the duty of the director of the mint to cause assays to be made from time to time of such foreign coins as may be known to commerce, to determine their average weight, fineness and value, and to embrace in his annual report a statement of the results thereof.

Act April 22, 1864.

§ 36. The standard weight of the cent coined at the mint of the United States shall be forty-eight grains, or one tenth of one ounce troy, and said cent shall be composed of ninety-five per centum of copper and five per centum of tin and zinc in such proportions as shall be determined by the director of the mint; and there shall be from time to time struck and coined at the mint a two-cent piece of the same composition, the standard weight of which shall be ninety-six grains, or one fifth of an ounce troy, with no greater deviation than four grains to each piece.

§ 37. The said coins shall be a legal tender in any payment, the one cent coin to the amount of ten cents, and the two cent coin to the amount of twenty cents; and it shall be lawful to pay out said coins in exchange for the lawful currency of the United States (except cents or half cents issued under former acts of Congress) in suitable sums, by the treasurer of the mint, and by such other depositaries as the secretary of the treasury may designate.

Act March 3, 1865.

§ 38. There shall be coined at the mint of the United States a *three cent piece* composed of copper and nickel in such proportion — not exceeding twenty-five (25) per centum of nickel — as shall be determined by the director of the mint, the standard weight of which shall be thirty grains, with no greater deviation than four grains to each piece.

§ 39. The said coin shall be a legal tender in any payment to the amount of sixty cents; and it shall be lawful to pay out said coins in exchange for the lawful currency of the United States (except cents or half cents or two cent pieces issued under former acts of Congress) in suitable sums, by the treasurer of the mint, and by such other depositaries as the secretary of the treasury may designate. *Provided*, that from and after the passage of this act no issues of fractional notes of the United States shall be of less denomination than five cents.

§ 40. The one and two cent coins of the United States shall not be a legal tender for any payment exceeding four cents in amount, (previous laws to the contrary repealed).

Act May 16, 1866.

§ 41. There shall be coined at the mint of the United States a five cent piece, composed of copper and nickel in such proportion — not exceeding twenty-five per centum of nickel — as shall be determined by the director of the mint, the standard weight of which shall be seventy-seven and sixteen hundredths grains, with no greater deviation than two grains to each piece.

§ 42. Said coins shall be a legal tender in any payment to the amount of one dollar; and it shall be lawful to pay out said coins for lawful currency of the United States, in suitable sums, by the treasurer of the mint, and by such other depositaries as the secretary of the treasury may designate.

§ 43. That from and after the passage of this act no issues of fractional notes of the United States shall be of less denomination than ten cents.

§ 44. It shall be lawful for the treasurer and the several assistant treasurers of the United States to *redeem in national currency*, under such rules and regulations as may be prescribed by the secretary of the treasury, the coins herein authorized to be issued when presented in sums of not less than one hundred dollars.

Act March 3, 1871.

§ 45. That the secretary of the treasury is required to redeem in lawful money all copper, bronze, copper-nickel and base-metal coinage of every kind hitherto authorized by law, when presented in sums of not less than twenty dollars.

Act February 12, 1873.

§ 46. That the gold coins of the United States shall be a One Dollar Piece, which, at the standard weight of twenty-five and eight-tenths ($25\frac{8}{10}$) grains, shall be the *Unit of Value;* a Quarter Eagle, or two and a half dollar piece; a Three Dollar Piece; a Half Eagle, or five dollar piece; an Eagle, or ten dollar piece; and a Double Eagle, or twenty dollar piece. And the standard weight of the Gold Dollar shall be twenty-five and eight-tenths grains; of the Quarter Eagle sixty-four and one-half grains; of the Three Dollar Piece seventy-seven and four-tenths grains; of the Half Eagle one hundred and twenty-nine grains; of the Eagle two hundred and fifty-eight grains; of the Double Eagle five hundred and sixteen grains, which coins shall be a legal tender in all payments at their nominal value when not below the standard weight and limit of tolerance provided in this act, and that when reduced in weight below said standard and tolerance shall be a legal tender in proportion to their actual weight.

Any gold coins of the United States, if reduced by natural abrasion not more than a half of one per cent below the standard weight after twenty years' circulation, and at a ratable proportion for any less period, shall be received at their nominal value at the United States treasury.

§ 47. The silver coins of the United States shall be a Trade Dollar, a Half Dollar, a Quarter Dollar, a Dime. And the weight of the Trade Dollar shall be four hundred and twenty (420) grains troy; the weight of the Half Dollar shall be twelve *grams* and one half of a *gram;* the Quarter Dollar and the Dime shall be respectively one half and one fifth the weight of said half dollar; and *said coins* shall be a legal tender at their nominal value for any amount not exceeding five dollars in one payment.

§ 48. The standard for both gold and silver coins of the United States shall be such that of one thousand parts by weight nine hundred shall be of pure metal and one hundred of alloy. The alloy of the silver coins shall be of copper. The alloy of the gold coins shall be of copper or of copper and silver, but the silver shall in no case exceed one tenth of the whole alloy.

§ 49. The minor coins of the United States shall be a Five Cent Piece, a Three Cent Piece and a One Cent Piece. The alloy for the five and three cent pieces shall be of copper and nickel, to be composed of three-fourths copper and one-fourth nickel. The alloy of the one cent piece shall be ninety-five per centum of copper and five per centum of tin and zinc, in such proportions as shall be determined by the director of the mint. The weight of the five cent piece shall be seventy-seven and sixteen-hundredths grains troy; of the three cent piece thirty grains, and of the one cent piece forty-eight grains.

§ 50. No coins, either of gold, silver or minor coinage, shall hereafter be issued from the mint other than those of the denominations, standards and weights set forth in this title.

§ 51. Silver coins, other than the trade dollars, shall be paid out at the several mints and at the assay office in New York city in exchange for gold coins at par, in sums not less than one hundred dollars.

§ 52. Nothing herein contained shall, however, prevent the payment of silver coins at their nominal value for silver parted from gold, as provided in this title, or for change less than one dollar in settlement of gold deposits.

§ 53. In adjusting the weights of the gold coins the following deviations shall not be exceeded in any single piece: In the double eagle and the eagle, one half of a grain; in the half eagle, the three dollar piece, the quarter eagle and the one dollar piece, one fourth of a grain, and in weighing a number of pieces together, when delivered by the coiner to the superintendent and by the superintendent to the depositor, the deviation from the standard weight shall not exceed one hundredth of an ounce in five thousand dollars in double eagles, eagles, half eagles or quarter eagles, or in one thousand dollars in three dollar pieces or one dollar pieces.

§ 54. In adjusting the weight of the silver coins the following deviations shall not be exceeded in any single piece: In *the dollar*, the half dollar, the quarter dollar and in the dime, one and one-half grains, and in weighing a large number of pieces the deviations shall not exceed two hundredths of an ounce in one thousand *dollars*, half dollars, or quarter dollars, and one hundredth of an ounce in one thousand dimes.

§ 55. In adjusting the weight of the minor coins provided by this title, there shall be no greater deviation allowed than three grains for the five cent piece, and two grains for the three and one cent pieces.

§ 56. That all other acts and parts of acts pertaining to the mints, assay offices and coinage of the United States, inconsistent with the provisions of this act, are hereby repealed: *Provided*, That this act shall not be construed to affect any act done, right accrued, or penalty incurred under former acts, but every such right is hereby saved.

Act March 3, 1873.

§ 57. The value of the sovereign, or pound sterling, shall be deemed equal to four dollars eighty-six cents and six and one-half mills; and all contracts made after the first day of January, 1874, based on an assumed par of exchange with Great Britain, of fifty-four pence to the dollar, or four dollars forty-four cents and four-ninths cents to the sovereign, or pound sterling, shall be null and void.

Act March 3, 1875.

§ 58. That there shall be from time to time coined at the mints of the United States, conformably in all respects to the coinage act of 1873, a coin of silver of the denomination of twenty cents, and of the weight of five grams. That the twenty cent piece shall be a legal tender at its nominal value for any amount not exceeding five dollars in any one payment. That in adjusting the weight of the twenty cent piece, the deviation from the standard weight shall not exceed one and one-half grains.

Act July 13, 1876.

§ 59. That the trade dollar shall not hereafter be a legal tender. (See Subsidiary Silver Coin Bill, page 201.)

UNITED STATES NOTES AND BONDS.

IN the preparation of the following digest of the laws of the United States relating to the issue and redemption of United States notes and bonds, it was not deemed necessary to cite any legislation prior to 1861. The amount of national obligations assumed to be yet "outstanding" that were authorized by acts prior to 1861, is unimportant, and it is moreover believed that a large proportion of such notes and bonds has been destroyed and lost. As far as the public have any real interest in the laws relating to the national debt, it is confined exclusively to the war debt created since 1860 and to the Pacific Railroad debt created since 1862.

None of the laws, except a few of the most important, such as the "Sinking Fund Act," the "Public Credit Act," the "Specie Resumption Act" and a few others, are given in full, as the details of printing, issuing, signing, and a multitude of other minor provisions, are not deemed pertinent to the greater questions of the contract between the government as a borrower and the note and bond holders as creditors, nor to the legal-tender character of notes intended to circulate as money. But the object in this division of the compilation of laws has been to give all the clauses in the acts of Congress which have any important bearing on the character and redemption of the obligations of the United States issued since 1860.

Act June 22, 1860.

[This act authorized the issue of $21,000,000 of 6 per cent bonds to be used in the redemption of outstanding treasury notes.]

Act December 17, 1860.

That the President of the United States be authorized to cause treasury notes to be issued for such sums as the exigencies of the public service may require, but not to exceed at any time the amount of ten millions ($10,000,000). That such notes shall be redeemed after the expiration of one year. They shall bear interest, 6 per cent per annum.

Act February 8, 1861.

That the President of the United States be authorized to borrow, on the credit of the United States, a sum not exceeding twenty-five millions ($25,000,000). That stock shall be issued for the amount so borrowed, bearing interest not exceeding 6 per centum per annum, and to be reimbursed within a period not beyond twenty years and not less than ten years.

Act March 2, 1861.

That the President of the United States be, and hereby is, authorized, at any time within twelve months from the passage of this act, to borrow, on the credit of the United States, a sum not exceeding ten millions of dollars: *Provided*, That no stipulation or contract shall be made to prevent the United States from reimbursing any sum borrowed under the authority of this act at any time after the expiration of ten years from the 1st day of July next, by the United States giving three months' notice, to be published in some newspaper published at the seat of government, of their readiness to do so; and no contract shall be made to prevent the redemption of the same at any time after the expiration of twenty years from the said 1st day of July next, without notice. That stock shall be issued for the amount so borrowed, bearing interest not exceeding 6 per cent per annum.

Act July 17, 1861.

That the Secretary of the Treasury be authorized to borrow, on the credit of the United States, within twelve months, a sum not exceeding $250,000,000, for which he is authorized to issue *coupon bonds* or registered bonds or treasury notes in such proportion as he may deem advisable. The bonds to bear interest not exceeding seven per cent per annum, payable semi-annually, irredeemable for twenty years, and after that at the pleasure of the United States, and the treasury notes to be of denominations not less than $50, payable three years after date, with interest at the rate of seven and three-tenths per cent per annum. And the Secretary may also issue, in exchange for coin, treasury notes of a less denomination than $50, not bearing interest but payable on demand at the assistant treasuries of the United States — or treasury notes bearing interest at the rate of 3.65 per cent per annum, payable in one year from date and exchangeable at any time for treasury notes (7-30s) for $50 and upward.

That the Secretary is authorized, whenever he shall deem it expedient, to issue, in exchange for coin or in payment of public dues, treasury notes of any of the denominations hereinbefore specified, bearing interest not exceeding six per cent per annum, and payable at any time not exceeding twelve months from date: that the amount of notes so issued shall at no time exceed $20,000,000.

Act August 5, 1861.

That the Secretary of the Treasury is authorized to issue bonds of the United States, bearing interest at six per cent per annum, and payable at the pleasure of the United States after twenty years from date. If any holder of treasury notes bearing interest at the rate of seven and three-tenths per cent per annum desire to exchange the same for said bonds, the Secretary may, at any time before the maturity of said treasury notes, issue to said holder, in payment thereof, an amount of said bonds equal to the amount due on said treasury notes; nor shall the whole amount of such bonds exceed the whole amount of treasury notes bearing seven and three-tenths per cent interest issued under said act (of July 17, 1861).

Act February 12, 1862.

That the Secretary of the Treasury, in addition to the $50,000,000 of notes payable on demand of denominations not less than five dollars, authorized by the acts of July 17 and August 5, 1861, is authorized to issue like notes to the amount of $10,000,000 — said notes shall be deemed part of the loan of $250,000,000 authorized by said acts.

Act February 25, 1862.

That the Secretary of the Treasury is hereby authorized to issue, on the credit of the United States, one hundred and fifty millions of dollars of United States notes, not bearing interest, payable to bearer, at the Treasury of the United States, and of such denominations as he may deem expedient, not less than five dollars each: *Provided, however*, That fifty millions of said notes shall be in lieu of the demand treasury notes authorized to be issued by the act of July seventeen, eighteen hundred and sixty-one; which said demand notes shall be taken up as rapidly as practicable, and the notes herein provided for substituted for them: *And provided further*, That the amount of the two kinds of notes together shall at no time exceed the sum of one hundred and fifty millions of dollars, and such notes herein authorized shall be receivable in payment of all taxes, internal duties, excises, debts and demands of every kind due to the United States, except duties on imports, and of all claims and demands against the United States of every kind whatsoever, except for interest upon bonds and notes, which shall be paid in coin, and shall also be lawful money and a legal tender in payment of all debts, public and private, within the United States, except duties on imports and interest as aforesaid. And any holders of said United States notes depositing any sum not less than fifty dollars, or some multiple of fifty dollars, with the Treasurer of the United States, or either of the assistant treasurers, shall receive in exchange therefor duplicate certificates of deposit, one of which may be transmitted to the Secretary of the Treasury, who shall thereupon issue to the holder an equal amount of bonds of the United States, coupon or registered, as may by said holder be desired, bearing interest at the rate of six per centum per annum, payable semi-annually, and redeemable at the pleasure of the United States after five years, and payable twenty years from the date thereof. And such United States notes shall be received the same as coin, at their par value, in payment for any loans that may be hereafter sold or negotiated by the Secretary of the Treasury, and may be re-issued from time to time as the exigencies of the public interest shall require.

That to enable the Secretary to fund the floating debt of the United States he be authorized to issue, on the credit of the United States, bonds to an amount not exceeding $500,000,000, redeemable at the pleasure of the United States after five years, and payable twenty years after date, bearing interest at the rate of six per cent per annum.

Sinking Fund Act, February 25, 1862.

That all duties on imported goods shall be paid in coin, or in notes payable on demand, heretofore authorized to be issued and by law receivable in payment of public dues, and the *coin* so paid shall be set apart as a special fund and shall be applied as follows:

First, To the payment in coin of the interest on the bonds and notes of the United States.

Second, To the purchase or payment of one per centum of the entire debt of the United States to be made within each fiscal year after the first day of July, 1862, which is to be set apart as a sinking fund, and the interest of which shall in like manner be applied to the purchase or payment of the public debt as the Secretary of the Treasury shall from time to time direct.

Third, The residue thereof to be paid into the Treasury.

Act March 17, 1862.

That the Secretary may purchase coin with any of the bonds or notes of the United States authorized by law, at such rates and upon such terms as he may deem most advantageous to the public interest.

(By Sec. 2 of this act, the demand notes authorized by the acts of July 17, 1861, and February 12, 1862, are declared lawful money and a legal tender, same as the treasury notes issued under act of February 25, 1862.)

Pacific Railroad Bonds, Act July 1, 1862.

Sec. 5. That for the purposes herein mentioned the Secretary of the Treasury shall, upon the certificate in writing of said commissioners of the completion and equipment of forty consecutive miles of said railroad and telegraph, in accordance with the provisions of this act, issue to said company bonds of the United States of one thousand dollars each, payable in thirty years after date, bearing six per centum per annum interest (said interest payable semi-annually), which interest may be paid in United States treasury notes or any other money or currency which the United States have or shall declare lawful money and a legal tender, to the amount of sixteen of said bonds per mile for such section of forty miles; and to secure the repayment to the United States, as hereinafter provided, of the amount of said bonds so issued and delivered to said company, together with all interest therein which shall have been paid by the United States, the issue of said bonds and delivery to the company shall ipso facto constitute a first mortgage on the whole line of the railroad and telegraph, together with the rolling stock, fixtures and property of every kind and description, and in consideration of which said bonds may be issued; and on the refusal or failure of said company to redeem said bonds, or any part of them, when required so to do by the Secretary of the Treasury, in accordance with the provisions of this act, the said road, with all the rights, functions, immunities and appurtenances thereunto belonging, and also all lands granted to the said company by the United States, which, at the time of said default, shall remain in the ownership of said company, may be taken possession of by the Secretary of the Treasury, for the use and benefit of the United States: *Provided*, this section shall not apply to that part of any road now constructed.

SEC. 6. That the grants aforesaid are made upon condition that said company shall pay said bonds at maturity, and shall keep said railroad and telegraph line in repair and use, and shall at all times transmit dispatches over said telegraph line, and transport mails, troops and munitions of war, supplies and public stores upon said railroad for the government, whenever required to do so by any department thereof, and that the government shall at all times have the preference in the use of the same for all the purposes aforesaid (at fair and reasonable rates of compensation, not to exceed the amounts paid by private parties for the same kind of service); and all compensation for services rendered for the government shall be applied to the payment of said bonds and interest until the whole amount is fully paid. Said company may also pay the United States, wholly or in part, in the same or other bonds, treasury notes, or other evidences of debt against the United States, to be allowed at par; and after said road is completed, until said bonds and interest are paid, at least five per centum of the net earnings of said road shall also be annually applied to the payment thereof.

Act July 11, 1862.

That the Secretary of the Treasury is hereby authorized to issue, in addition to the amounts heretofore authorized, on the credit of the United States, one hundred and fifty millions of dollars of United States notes, not bearing interest, payable to bearer at the Treasury of the United States, and of such denominations as he may deem expedient: *Provided*, That no note shall be issued for the fractional part of a dollar, and not more than thirty-five millions shall be of lower denominations than five dollars; and such notes shall be receivable in payment of all loans made to the United States, and of all taxes, internal duties, excises, debts and demands of every kind due to the United States, except duties on imports and interest, and of all claims and demands against the United States, except for interest upon bonds, notes, and certificates of debt or deposit; and shall also be lawful money and a legal tender in payment of all debts, public and private, within the United States, except duties on imports and interest, as aforesaid. And any holder of said United States notes depositing any sum not less than fifty dollars, or some multiple of fifty dollars, with the Treasurer of the United States, or either of the assistant treasurers, shall receive in exchange therefor duplicate certificates of deposit, one of which may be transmitted to the Secretary of the Treasury, who shall thereupon issue to the holder an equal amount of bonds of the United States, coupon or registered, as may by said holder be desired, bearing interest at the rate of six per centum per annum, payable semi-annually, and redeemable at the pleasure of the United States after five years, and payable twenty years from the date thereof: *Provided, however*, That any notes issued under this act may be paid in coin, instead of being received in exchange for certificates of deposit as above specified, at the direction of the Secretary of the Treasury. And the Secretary of the Treasury may exchange for such notes, on such terms as he shall think most beneficial to the public interest, any bonds of the United States bearing six per centum interest, and redeemable after five and payable in twenty years, which have been or may be lawfully issued under the provisions of any existing act; may reissue the notes so received in exchange; may receive and cancel any notes heretofore lawfully issued under any act of Congress, and in lieu thereof issue an equal amount in notes such as are authorized by this act; and may purchase, at rates not exceeding that of the current market, and cost of purchase not exceeding one-eighth of one per centum, any bonds or certificates of debt of the United States as he may deem advisable.

Joint Resolution January 17, 1863.

That the Secretary of the Treasury is hereby authorized, if required by the exigencies of the public service, to issue on the credit of the United States the sum of one hundred millions of dollars of United States notes in such form as he may deem expedient, not bearing interest, payable to bearer on demand, and of such denominations, not less than one dollar, as he may prescribe, which notes so issued shall be lawful money and a legal tender, like the similar notes heretofore authorized, in payment of all debts, public and private, within the United States, except duties on imports and interest on the public debt.

Act March 3, 1863.

That the Secretary of the Treasury be, and is hereby, authorized to borrow, from time to time, on the credit of the United States, a sum not exceeding three hundred millions of dollars for the current fiscal year, and six hundred millions for the next fiscal year, and to issue therefor coupon or registered bonds, payable at the pleasure of the government after such periods as may be fixed by the Secretary, not less than ten nor more than forty years from date, in coin, and of such denominations, not less than fifty dollars, as he may deem expedient, bearing interest at a rate not exceeding six per centum per annum, payable on bonds not exceeding one hundred dollars, annually, and on all other bonds semi-annually, in coin; and he may, in his discretion, dispose of such bonds at any time, upon such terms as he may deem most advisable, for lawful money of the United States, or for any of the certificates of indebtedness or deposit that may at any time be unpaid, or for any of the treasury notes heretofore issued or which may be issued under the provisions of this act. And all the bonds and treasury notes or United States notes issued under the provisions of this act shall be exempt from taxation by or under state or municipal authority: *Provided*, That there shall be outstanding of bonds, treasury notes, and United States notes, at any time, issued under the provisions of this act, no greater amount altogether than the sum of nine hundred millions of dollars.

That the Secretary of the Treasury be, and he is hereby, authorized to issue, on the credit of the United States, four hundred millions of dollars in treasury notes, payable at the pleasure of the United States, or at such time or times not exceeding three years from date as may be found most beneficial to the public interests, and bearing interest at a rate not exceeding six per centum per annum, payable at periods expressed on the face of said treasury notes; and the interest on the said treasury notes and on certificates of indebtedness and deposit hereafter issued, shall be paid in lawful money. The treasury notes thus issued shall be of such denominations as the Secretary may direct, not less than ten dollars, and may be disposed of on the best terms that can be obtained, or may be paid to any creditor of the United States willing to receive the same at par. And said treasury notes may be made a legal tender to the same extent as United States notes, for their face value, excluding interest; or they may be made exchangeable under regulations prescribed by the Secretary of the Treasury, by the holder thereof, at the treasury in the city of Washington, or at the office of any assistant treasurer or depositary designated for that purpose, for United States notes equal in amount to the treasury notes offered for exchange, together with the interest accrued and due thereon, at the date of interest payment next preceding such exchange. And in lieu of any amount of said treasury notes thus exchanged, or redeemed or paid at maturity, the Secretary may issue an equal amount of other treasury notes; and the treasury notes so exchanged, redeemed or paid, shall be canceled and destroyed as the Secretary may direct. In order to secure certain and prompt exchanges of United States notes for treasury notes when required as above provided, the Secretary shall have power to issue United States notes to the amount of one hundred and fifty millions of dollars, which may be used if necessary for such exchanges; but no part of the United States notes authorized by this section shall be issued for or applied to any other purposes than said exchanges; and whenever any amount shall have been so issued and applied, the same shall be replaced as soon as practicable from the sales of treasury notes for United States notes.

That the Secretary of the Treasury be, and he is hereby, authorized, if required by the exigencies of the public service, for the payment of the army and navy, and other creditors of the government, to issue on the credit of the United States the sum of one hundred and fifty millions of dollars of United States notes, including the amount of such notes heretofore authorized by the joint resolution approved January seventeen, eighteen hundred and sixty-three, in such form as he may deem expedient, not bearing interest, payable to bearer, and of such denominations, not less than one dollar, as he may prescribe, which notes so issued shall be lawful money and a legal tender in payment of all debts, public and private, within the United States, except for duties on imports and interest on the public debt; and any of the said notes, when returned to the treasury, may be reissued from time to time as the exigencies of the public service may require. And in lieu of any of said notes, or any other United States notes, returned to the treasury, and canceled or destroyed, there may be issued equal amounts of United States notes, such as are authorized by this act. And so much of the act to authorize the issue of United States notes, and for other purposes, approved February twenty-five, eighteen hundred and sixty-two, and of the act to authorize an additional issue of United States notes, and for other purposes, approved July eleven, eighteen hundred and sixty-two, as restricts the negotiation of bonds to market value, is hereby repealed. And the holders of United States notes, issued under and by virtue of said acts, shall present the same for the purpose of exchanging the same for bonds, as therein provided, on or before the first day of July, eighteen hundred and sixty-three, and thereafter the right so to exchange the same shall cease and determine.

That in lieu of postage and revenue stamps for fractional currency, and of fractional notes, commonly called postage currency, issued or to be issued, the Secretary of the Treasury may issue fractional notes of like amounts in such form as he may deem expedient, and may provide for the engraving, preparation and issue thereof in the treasury department building. And all such notes issued shall be exchangeable by the assistant treasurers and designated depositaries for United States notes, in sums not less than three dollars, and shall be receivable for postage and revenue stamps, and also in payment of any dues to the United States less than five dollars, except duties on imports, and shall be redeemed on presentation at the treasury of the United States in such sums and under such regulations as the Secretary of the Treasury shall prescribe: *Provided*, that the whole amount of fractional currency issued, including postage and revenue stamps issued as currency, shall not exceed fifty millions of dollars.

That the Secretary of the Treasury is hereby authorized to receive deposits of gold coin and bullion with the treasurer or any assistant treasurer of the United States, in sums not less than twenty dollars, and to issue certificates therefor in denominations of not less than twenty dollars each, corresponding with the denominations of the United States notes. The coin and bullion deposited for or representing the certificates of deposit shall be retained in the treasury for the payment of the same on demand. And certificates representing coin in the treasury may be issued in payment of interest on the public debt, which certificates, together with those issued for coin and bullion deposited, shall not at any time exceed twenty per centum beyond the amount of coin and bullion in the treasury; and the certificates for coin or bullion in the treasury shall be received at par in payment for duties on imports.

Act March 3, 1864.

That in lieu of so much of the loan authorized by the act of March 3, 1863, the Secretary of the Treasury be and is hereby authorized to borrow, on the credit of the United States, not exceeding two hundred millions of dollars during the current fiscal year, bearing date March first, eighteen hundred and sixty-four, or any subsequent period, redeemable at the pleasure of the government after any period not less than five years, and payable at any period not more than forty years from date, in coin, bearing interest not exceeding six per centum a year—and he may dispose of such bonds at any time, on such terms as he may deem most advisable, for lawful money of the United States, or, at his discretion, for treasury notes, certificates of indebtedness or certificates of deposit issued under any act of Congress.

Joint Resolution March 17, 1864.

That the Secretary of the Treasury be authorized to anticipate the payment of interest on the public debt, by a period not exceeding one year, from time to time, either with or without a rebate of interest upon the coupons, as to him may seem expedient, and he is hereby authorized to dispose of any *gold* * in the Treasury of the United States not necessary for the payment of interest on the public debt.

Act June 30, 1864.

That the Secretary of the Treasury be authorized to borrow four hundred millions of dollars, and to issue bonds of the United States, redeemable at the pleasure of the government after any period not less than five nor more than forty years from date, and bear an annual interest not exceeding six per centum, payable semi-annually in coin.

The Secretary of the Treasury may issue on the credit of the United States, and in lieu of an equal amount of bonds authorized by the preceding section, and as a part of said loan, not exceeding two hundred millions of dollars, in treasury notes of any denomination not less than ten dollars, payable at any time not exceeding three years from date, or, if thought more expedient, redeemable at any time after three years from date, and bearing interest not exceeding

* This is the first instance of the use of the word "gold" instead of "coin" or "gold and silver" in any of the laws of the United States with regard to money obligations of the government issued since 1860.

the rate of seven and three-tenths per centum, payable in lawful money at maturity. And such of them as shall be made payable, principal and interest, at maturity, shall be a legal tender to the same extent as United States notes, for their face value, excluding interest, and may be paid to any creditor of the United States at their face value, excluding interest, or to *any creditor willing to receive them* at par, including interest.

That the total amount of bonds and treasury notes authorized by the first and second sections of this act shall not exceed four hundred millions of dollars, in addition to the amounts heretofore issued; nor shall the total amount of United States notes, issued or to be issued, ever exceed four hundred millions of dollars, and such additional sum, not exceeding fifty millions of dollars, as may be temporarily required for the redemption of temporary loan; nor shall any treasury note bearing interest, issued under this act, be a legal tender in payment or redemption of any notes issued by any bank, banking association, or banker, calculated or intended to circulate as money.

The Secretary of the Treasury may issue notes of the fractions of a dollar as now used for currency, in such form, with such inscriptions, and with such safeguards against counterfeiting, as he may judge best; but the whole amount of all descriptions of notes or stamps less than one dollar issued as currency, shall not exceed fifty millions of dollars.

Amendment to Pacific Railroad Act, July 2, 1864.

That section five of said act be so modified and amended that the Union Pacific Railroad Company, the Central Pacific Railroad Company, and any other company authorized to participate in the construction of said road, may, on the completion of each section of said road, as provided in this act and the act to which this act is an amendment, issue their first mortgage bonds on their respective railroad and telegraph lines to an amount not exceeding the amount of the bonds of the United States, and of even tenor and date, time of maturity, rate and character of interest, with the bonds authorized to be issued to said railroad companies respectively. *And the lien of the United States bonds* shall be subordinate to that of the bonds of any or either of said companies hereby authorized to be issued on their respective roads, property and equipments, except as to the provisions of the sixth section of the act to which this act is an amendment, relating to the transmission of dispatches and the transportation of mails, troops, munitions of war, supplies and public stores for the government of the United States.

Act January 28, 1865.

That in lieu of any bonds authorized to be issued by the first section of the act entitled "An act to provide ways and means for the support of the government," approved June 30, 1864, that may remain unsold at the date of this act, the Secretary of the Treasury may issue, under the authority of said act, treasury notes of the description and character authorized by the second section of said act: *Provided*, That the whole amount of bonds authorized as aforesaid and treasury notes issued and to be issued in lieu thereof shall not exceed the sum of four hundred millions of dollars; and such treasury notes may be disposed of for lawful money, or for any other treasury notes or certificates of indebtedness or certificates of deposit issued under any previous act of Congress; and such notes shall be exempt from taxation by or under State or municipal authority.

Act March 3, 1865.

That the Secretary of the Treasury be, and he is hereby, authorized to borrow, from time to time, on the credit of the United States, in addition to the amounts heretofore authorized, any sums not exceeding, in the aggregate, six hundred millions of dollars, and to issue therefor bonds or treasury notes of the United States in such form as he may prescribe; and so much thereof as may be issued in bonds shall be of denominations not less than fifty dollars, and may be made payable at any period not more than forty years from date of issue, or may be made redeemable, at the pleasure of the government, at or after any period not less than five years nor more than forty years from date, or may be made redeemable and payable as aforesaid, as may be expressed upon their face; and so much thereof as may be issued in treasury notes may be made convertible into any bonds authorized by this act.

Provided, That the rate of interest on any such bonds or treasury notes, when payable in coin, shall not exceed six per centum per annum; and when not payable in coin shall not exceed seven and three-tenths per centum per annum.

Provided, That nothing herein contained shall be construed as authorizing the issue of legal-tender notes in any form.

Act April 12, 1866.

That the act approved March 3, 1865, shall be extended and construed to authorize the Secretary of the Treasury, at his discretion, to receive any treasury notes or other obligations issued under any act of Congress, whether bearing interest or not, in exchange for any description of bonds authorized by the act to which this is an amendment; and also to dispose of any description of bonds authorized by said act, either in the United States or elsewhere, to such an amount, in such manner and at such rates as he may think advisable, for lawful money of the United States or for any treasury notes, certificates of indebtedness or certificates of deposit, or other representatives of value which have been or which may be issued under any act of Congress, the proceeds thereof to be used only for retiring treasury notes or other obligations issued under any act of Congress; but nothing herein contained shall be construed to authorize any increase of the public debt: *Provided*, That of United States notes not more than ten millions of dollars may be retired and canceled within six months from the passage of this act, and thereafter not more than four millions of dollars in any one month.

Act March 2, 1867.

That for the purpose of redeeming and retiring any compound-interest notes outstanding, the Secretary of the Treasury is hereby authorized and directed to issue temporary loan certificates in the manner prescribed by section four of the act entitled "An act to authorize the issue of United States notes and for the redemption or funding thereof, and for funding the floating debt of the United States," approved February twenty-fifth, eighteen hundred and sixty-two; bearing interest at a rate not exceeding three per centum per annum, principal and interest payable in lawful money on demand; and said certificates of temporary loan may constitute and be held, by any national bank holding or owning the same, as a part of the reserve provided for in sections thirty-one and thirty-two of the act entitled "An act to provide a national currency, secured by a pledge of United States bonds, and to provide for the circulation and redemption thereof:" *Provided*, that the amount of such certificates outstanding at any time shall not exceed fifty millions of dollars.

Act July 25, 1868.

That for the sole purpose of redeeming and retiring the remainder of the compound interest notes outstanding, the Secretary of the

Treasury is authorized to issue an additional amount of temporary loan certificates not exceeding twenty-five millions of dollars, said certificates to bear three per cent interest, payable in lawful money

An Act to strengthen the public credit, approved March 18, 1869.

Be it enacted by the Senate and House of Representatives of the United States of America, in Congress assembled: That in order to remove any doubt as to the purpose of the government to discharge all just obligations to the public creditors, and to settle conflicting questions and interpretations by the laws by virtue of which such obligations have been contracted, it is hereby provided and declared that the faith of the United States is solemnly pledged to the payment in coin or its equivalent of all the obligations of the United States not bearing interest, known as the United States notes, and of all the interest-bearing obligations of the United States, except in cases where the law authorizing the issue of such obligations has expressly provided that the same may be paid in lawful money, or other currency than gold and silver. But none of said interest-bearing obligations not already due shall be redeemed or paid before maturity, unless at such time United States notes shall be convertible into coin at the option of the holder, or unless at such time bonds of the United States bearing a lower rate of interest than the bonds to be redeemed can be sold at par in coin. And the United States also solemnly pledges its faith to make provisions at the earliest practicable period for the redemption of the United States notes in coin.

Funding Act July 14, 1870.

That the Secretary of the Treasury is hereby authorized to issue in a sum or sums not exceeding in the aggregate two hundred millions of dollars, coupon or registered bonds of the United States, in such form as he may prescribe, and of denominations of fifty dollars, or some multiple of that sum, redeemable in coin of the present standard value, at the pleasure of the United States, after ten years from the date of their issue, and bearing interest. payable semi-annually in such coin, at the rate of five per cent per annum; also a sum or sums not exceeding in the aggregate three hundred millions of dollars of like bonds, the same in all respects, but payable at the pleasure of the United States, after fifteen years from their issue, and bearing interest at the rate of four and a half per cent per annum; also a sum or sums not exceeding in the aggregate one thousand millions of dollars of like bonds, the same in all respects, but payable at the pleasure of the United States after thirty years from the date of their issue, and bearing interest at the rate of four per cent per annum; all of which said several classes of bonds and the interest thereon shall be exempt from the payment of all taxes or duties of the United States, as well as from taxation in any form by or under State, municipal or local authority; and the said bonds shall have set forth and expressed upon their face the above-specified conditions, and shall, with their cc pons, be made payable at the Treasury of the United States. But nothing in this act, or in any other law now in force, shall be construed to authorize any increase whatever of the bonded debt of the United States.

That the Secretary of the Treasury is hereby authorized to sell and dispose of any of the bonds issued under this act, at not less than their par value for coin, and to apply the proceeds thereof to the redemption of any of the bonds of the United States outstanding, and known as five-twenty bonds, at their par value; or he may exchange the same for such five-twenty bonds, par for par; but the bonds hereby authorized shall be used for no other purpose whatsoever. And a sum not exceeding one-half of one per cent of the bonds herein authorized is hereby appropriated to pay the expense of preparing, issuing, advertising and disposing of the same.

That the payment of any of the bonds hereby authorized after the expiration of the said several terms of ten, fifteen and thirty years, shall be made in amounts to be determined from time to time by the Secretary of the Treasury at his discretion, the bonds so to be paid to be distinguished and described by the dates and numbers, beginning for each successive payment with the bonds of each class last dated and numbered, of the time of which intended payment or redemption the Secretary of the Treasury shall give public notice, and the interest on the particular bonds so selected at any time to be paid shall cease at the expiration of three months from the date of such notice.

That the Secretary of the Treasury is hereby authorized, with any coin in the Treasury of the United States which he may lawfully apply to such purpose, or which may be derived from the sale of any of the bonds, the issue of which is provided for in this act, to pay at par and cancel any six per cent bonds of the United States of the kind known as five-twenty bonds, which have become or shall hereafter become redeemable by the terms of their issue. But the particular bonds so to be paid and canceled shall in all cases be indicated and specified by class, date and number, in the order of their numbers and issue, beginning with the first numbered and issued, in public notice to be given by the Secretary of the Treasury, and in three months after the date of such public notice the interest on the bonds so selected and advertised to be paid shall cease.

That the Secretary of the Treasury is hereby authorized, at any time within two years from the passage of this act, to receive gold coin of the United States on deposit for not less than thirty days, in sums of not less than one hundred dollars, with the Treasurer, or any assistant treasurer of the United States authorized by the Secretary of the Treasury to receive the same, who shall issue therefor certificates of deposit, made in such form as the Secretary of the Treasury shall prescribe, and said certificates of deposit shall bear interest at a rate not exceeding two and a half per cent per annum; and any amount of gold coin so deposited may be withdrawn from deposit at any time after thirty days from the date of deposit, and after ten days' notice and on the return of said certificates: *Provided*, That the interest on all such deposits shall cease and determine at the pleasure of the Secretary of the Treasury. And not less than twenty-five per cent of the coin deposited for or represented by said certificates of deposit shall be retained in the treasury for the payment of said certificates; and the excess beyond twenty-five per cent may be applied, at the discretion of the Secretary of the Treasury, to the payment or redemption of such outstanding bonds of the United States heretofore issued and known as the five-twenty bonds, as he may designate under the provisions of the fourth section of this act; and any certificates of deposit issued as aforesaid may be received at par, with the interest accrued thereon, in payment for any bonds authorized to be issued by this act.

Act January 20, 1871.

That the amount of bonds authorized by the act approved July 14, 1870, entitled "An act to authorize the refunding of the national debt," to be issued bearing five per centum interest per annum, be, and the same is, increased to five hundred millions of dollars, and the interest of any portion of the bonds issued under said act, or this act, may, at the discretion of the Secretary of the Treasury, be made payable quarter-yearly: *Provided, however*, that this act shall not be construed to authorize any increase of the total amount of bonds provided for by the act to which this act is an amendment.

Act June 8, 1872.

That the Secretary of the Treasury is hereby authorized to receive United States notes on deposit without interest from banking associations, and to issue certificates therefor. The certificates issued may be held and counted by national banks as part of their reserve.

That nothing contained in this act shall be construed to authorize any expansion or contraction of the currency; and the United States notes for which such certificates are issued, or other United States notes of like amount, shall be held as special deposits in the treasury and used only for the redemption of such certificates.

Act December 17, 1873.

That for the purpose of redeeming the bonds called the loan of 1858, it is hereby declared to be the pleasure of the United States to pay all the coupon bonds of said loan on the first day of January, 1874. That the Secretary of the Treasury may issue an equal amount at par of principal and interest of five per cent bonds of the funded loan under the act for refunding the national debt, approved January 20, 1871, for any of the bonds of the loan of 1858, which the holders thereof may, on or before the 1st of February, 1874, elect to exchange.

Specie Resumption Act of January 14, 1875.

§ 1. That the Secretary of the Treasury is hereby authorized and required, as rapidly as practicable, to cause to be coined at the mints of the United States, silver coins of the denominations of ten, twenty-five and fifty cents, of standard value, and to issue them in redemption of an equal number and amount of fractional currency of similar denominations, or, at his discretion, he may issue such silver coins through the mints, the subtreasuries, public depositories and post-offices of the United States; and upon such issue he is hereby authorized and required to redeem an equal amount of such fractional currency until the whole amount of such fractional currency outstanding shall be redeemed.

§ 2. That so much of section 3524 of the Revised Statutes of the United States as provides for a charge of one sixth of one per centum for converting standard gold bullion into coin is hereby repealed, and hereafter no charge shall be made for that service.

§ 3. That section 5777 of the Revised Statutes of the United States, limiting the aggregate amount of the circulating notes of the national banking associations, be, and is hereby, repealed, and each existing banking association may increase its circulating notes in accordance with the existing law, without respect to said aggregate limit; and new banking associations may be organized in accordance with the existing law, without respect to the aggregate limit; and the provisions of the law for the withdrawal and redistribution of national-bank currency among the several States and Territories are hereby repealed; and whenever and so often as circulating notes shall be issued to any such banking association, so increasing its capital or circulating notes, or so newly organized as aforesaid, it shall be the duty of the Secretary of the Treasury to redeem the legal-tender United States notes in excess only of $300,-000,000 to the amount of eighty per centum of the sum of national-bank notes so issued to any such banking association as aforesaid, and to continue such redemption as such circulating notes are issued until there shall be outstanding the sum of $300,000,000 of such legal-tender United States notes, and no more. And on and after the 1st day of January, A.D. 1879, the Secretary of the Treasury shall redeem in coin the United States legal-tender notes then outstanding on their presentation for redemption at the office of the assistant treasurer of the United States, in the city of New York, in sums of not less than $50. And to enable the Secretary of the Treasury to prepare and provide for the redemption in this act authorized or required, he is authorized to use any surplus revenues from time to time in the treasury not otherwise appropriated, and to issue, sell and dispose of, at not less than par in coin, either of the description of bonds of the United States described in the act of Congress approved July 14, 1870, entitled "An act to authorize the refunding of the national debt," with like privileges and exemptions, to the extent necessary to carry this act into effect, and to use the proceeds thereof for the purposes aforesaid. And all provisions of law inconsistent with the provisions of this act are hereby repealed.

Subsidiary Silver Coin Law, Joint Resolution of Congress July 13, 1876.

§ 1. That the Secretary of the Treasury, under such limits and regulations as will best secure a just and fair distribution of the same through the country, may issue the silver coin at any time in the treasury, to an amount not exceeding $10,000,000, in exchange for an equal amount of legal-tender notes, and notes so received in exchange shall be kept as a special fund, separate and apart from all other money in the treasury, and be issued only upon the retirement and destruction of a like sum of fractional currency received at the treasury in payment of dues to the United States, and said fractional currency, when so substituted, shall be destroyed and held as part of the sinking fund, as provided in the act approved April 17, 1876.

§ 2. That the trade dollar shall not hereafter be a legal tender, and the Secretary of the Treasury is hereby authorized to limit from time to time the coinage thereof to such an amount as he may deem sufficient to meet the export demand for the same.

§ 3. That in addition to the amount of subsidiary silver coin authorized by law to be issued in redemption of the fractional currency, it shall be lawful to manufacture at the several mints, and issue through the treasury and its several offices, such coin to an amount that, including the amount of subsidiary silver coin and of fractional currency outstanding, shall in the aggregate not exceed at any time $50,000,000.

§ 4. That the silver bullion required for the purposes of this act shall be purchased from time to time at the market rate by the Secretary of the Treasury with any money in the treasury not otherwise appropriated, but no purchase of bullion shall be made under this resolution when the market rate for the same shall be such as will not admit of the coinage and issue as herein provided without loss to the treasury, and any gain or seigniorage arising from this coinage shall be accounted for and paid into the treasury as provided under existing laws relative to subsidiary coinage, provided that the amount of money at any time invested in such silver bullion, exclusive of such resulting coin, shall not exceed $200,000.

NATIONAL BANKS AND BANK CURRENCY.

LAWS IN FORCE AUGUST, 1876.

THE following compilation embraces all the laws in force August, 1876, governing the organization and management of national banks and the issue and redemption of national-bank currency, under the following heads, viz.:

Chapter I. Organization and Powers of National Banks.
II. Obtaining and Issuing Circulating Notes.
III. Regulation of the Banking Business.
IV. Dissolution and Receivership.
V. Tax on Circulation and on Bank Checks.
VI. Crimes and Misdemeanors.
VII. Interest Laws.

The numbers of the sections are the same as in the Revised Statutes.

CHAPTER I.

ORGANIZATION AND POWERS OF NATIONAL BANKS.

Formation of national banking associations.

(SEC. 5133.) Associations for carrying on the business of banking under this title may be formed by any number of natural persons, not less in any case than five. They shall enter into articles of association, which shall specify in general terms the object for which the association is formed, and may contain any other provisions, not inconsistent with law, which the association may see fit to adopt for the regulation of its business and the conduct of its affairs. These articles shall be signed by

Articles of association.

the persons uniting to form the association, and a copy of them shall be forwarded to the Comptroller of the Currency, to be filed and preserved in his office.

Organization certificate.

(SEC. 5134.) The persons uniting to form such an association shall, under their hands, make an organization certificate, which shall specifically state:

Name of association.

First. The name assumed by such association; which name shall be subject to the approval of the Comptroller of the Currency.

Place of business.

Second. The place where its operations of discount and deposit are to be carried on, designating the State, Territory, or district, and the particular county and city, town, or village.

Capital stock.

Third. The amount of capital stock and the number of shares into which the same is to be divided.

Shareholders.

Fourth. The names and places of residence of the shareholders, and the number of shares held by each of them.

Object of certificate.

Fifth. The fact that the certificate is made to enable such persons to avail themselves of the advantages of this title.

Acknowledgment of organization certificate.

(SEC. 5135.) The organization certificate shall be acknowledged before a judge of some court of record, or notary public; and shall be, together with the acknowledgment thereof, authenticated by the seal of such court, or notary, transmitted to the Comptroller of the Currency, who shall record and carefully preserve the same in his office.

Corporate powers of associations. 2 Abb., U.S., 416.

(SEC. 5136.) Upon duly making and filing articles of association and an organization certificate, the association shall become, as from the date of the execution of its organization certificate, a body corporate, and as such, and in the name designated in the organization certificate, it shall have power:

Seal.

First. To adopt and use a corporate seal.

Succession.

Second. To have succession for the period of twenty years from its organization, unless it is sooner dissolved according to the provisions of its articles of association, or by the act of its shareholders owning two-thirds of its stock, or unless its franchise becomes forfeited by some violation of law.

Third. To make contracts. Contracts.

Fourth. To sue and be sued, complain and defend, in any court of law and [or] equity, as fully as natural persons. Suits.

Fifth. To elect or appoint directors, and by its board of directors to appoint a president, vice-president, cashier, and other officers, define their duties, require bonds of them and fix the penalty thereof, dismiss such officers or any of them at pleasure, and appoint others to fill their places. Appointment of officers.

Sixth. To prescribe, by its board of directors, by-laws not inconsistent with law, regulating the manner in which its stock shall be transferred, its directors elected or appointed, its officers appointed, its property transferred, its general business conducted, and the privileges granted to it by law exercised and enjoyed. By-laws.

Seventh. To exercise by its board of directors, or duly authorized officers or agents, subject to law, all such incidental powers as shall be necessary to carry on the business of banking; by discounting and negotiating promissory notes, drafts, bills of exchange, and other evidences of debt; by receiving deposits; by buying and selling exchange, coin and bullion; by loaning money on personal security; and by obtaining, issuing and circulating notes according to the provisions of this Title. Incidental powers.

But no association shall transact any business except such as is incidental and necessarily preliminary to its organization, until it has been authorized by the Comptroller of the Currency to commence the business of banking. When may commence business.

(SEC. 5137.) A national banking association may purchase, hold, and convey real estate for the following purposes, and for no others: Power to hold real property.

First. Such as shall be necessary for its immediate accommodation in the transaction of its business.

Second. Such as shall be mortgaged to it in good faith by way of security for debts previously contracted.

Third. Such as shall be conveyed to it in satisfaction of debts previously contracted in the course of its dealings.

Fourth. Such as it shall purchase at sales under judgments, decrees or mortgages held by the association, or shall purchase to secure debts due to it.

Limitation as to mortgages, etc.

But no such association shall hold the possession of any real estate under mortgage, or the title and possession of any real estate purchased to secure any debts due to it, for a longer period than five years.

Minimum capital required.

(SEC. 5138.) No association shall be organized under this Title with a less capital than one hundred thousand dollars; except that banks with a capital of not less than fifty thousand dollars may, with the approval of the Secretary of the Treasury, be organized in any place the population of which does not exceed six thousand inhabitants. No association shall be organized in a city the population of which exceeds fifty thousand persons with a less capital than two hundred thousand dollars.

Value and transfer of shares of stock.

(SEC. 5139.) The capital stock of each association shall be divided into shares of one hundred dollars each, and be deemed personal property, and transferable on the books of the association in such manner as may be prescribed in the by-laws or articles of association. Every person becoming a shareholder by such transfer shall, in proportion to his shares, succeed to all the rights and liabilities of the prior holder of such shares; and no change shall be made in the articles of association by which the rights, remedies or security of the existing creditors of the association shall be impaired.

Rights and liabilities of persons holding shares by transfer. Van Allen vs. The Assessors, 3 Wall. 573.

When capital stock must be paid in and certified.

(SEC. 5140.) At least fifty per centum of the capital stock of every association shall be paid in before it shall be authorized to commence business; and the remainder of the capital stock of such association shall be paid in installments of at least ten per centum each, on the whole amount of the capital, as frequently as one installment at the end of each succeeding month from the time it shall be authorized by the Comptroller of the Currency to commence business; and the payment of each installment shall be certified to the Comptroller, under oath, by the president or cashier of the association.

Proceedings if shareholder fails to pay installments.

(SEC. 5141.) Whenever any shareholder, or his assignee, fails to pay any installment on the stock when the same is required by the preceding section to be paid, the directors of such association may sell the stock of such delinquent shareholder at public auction, having given three weeks' previous notice thereof in a newspaper published and of general circulation in the city or county where the association is located, or if no newspaper is published in said city or county, then in a newspaper published nearest thereto, to any person who will pay the highest price therefor, to be not less than the amount then due thereon, with the expenses of advertisement and sale; and the excess, if any, shall be paid to the delinquent shareholder. If no bidder can be found who will pay for such stock the amount due thereon to the association, and the cost of advertisement and sale, the amount previously paid shall be forfeited to the association, and such stock shall be sold as the directors may order, within six months from the time of such forfeiture, and if not sold it shall be canceled and deducted from the capital stock of the association. If any such cancellation and reduction shall reduce the capital of the association below the minimum of capital required by law, the capital stock shall, within thirty days from the date of such cancellation, be increased to the required amount; in default of which a receiver may be appointed, according to the provisions of section fifty-two hundred and thirty-four, to close up the business of the association.

Capital to be restored if reduced below minimum or receiver appointed.

(Sec. 5168.) Whenever a certificate is transmitted to the Comptroller of the Currency, as provided in this Title, and the association transmitting the same notifies the Comptroller that at least fifty per centum of its capital stock has been duly paid in, and that such association has complied with all the provisions of this Title required to be complied with before an association shall be authorized to commence the business of banking, the Comptroller shall examine into the condition of such association, ascertain especially the amount of money paid in on account of its capital, the name and place of residence of each of its directors, and the amount of the capital stock of which each is the owner in good faith, and generally whether such association has complied with all the provisions of this Title required to entitle it to engage in the business of banking; and shall cause to be made and

Comptroller to determine if association is entitled to commence business.

Certificate of officers and directors.

attested by the oaths of a majority of the directors, and by the president or cashier of the association, a statement of all the facts necessary to enable the Comptroller to determine whether the association is lawfully entitled to commence the business of banking.

Certificate of authority to commence business, when to be issued.

(SEC. 5169.) If, upon a careful examination of the facts so reported, and of any other facts which may come to the knowledge of the Comptroller, whether by means of a special commission appointed by him for the purpose of inquiring into the condition of such association, or otherwise, it appears that such association is lawfully entitled to commence the business of banking, the Comptroller shall give to such association a certificate, under his hand and official seal, that such association has complied with all the provisions required to be complied with before commencing the business of banking, and that such association is authorized to commence such business.

When certificate of authority may be withheld.

But the Comptroller may withhold from an association his certificate authorizing the commencement of business whenever he has reason to suppose that the shareholders have formed the same for any other than the legitimate objects contemplated by this Title.

Publication of certificate.

(SEC. 5170.) The association shall cause the certificate issued under the preceding section to be published in some newspaper printed in the city or county where the association is located for at least sixty days next after the issuing thereof; or, if no newspaper is published in such city or county, then in the newspaper published nearest thereto.

Increase of capital stock.

(SEC. 5142.) Any association formed under this Title may, by its articles of association, provide for an increase of its capital from time to time, as may be deemed expedient, subject to the limitations of this Title. But the maximum of such increase to be provided in the articles of association shall be determined by the Comptroller of the Currency; and no increase of capital shall be valid until the whole amount of such increase is paid in, and notice thereof has been transmitted to the Comptroller of the Currency, and his certificate obtained specifying the amount of such increase of capital stock, with his approval thereof, and that it has been duly paid in as part of the capital of such association.

(SEC. 5143.) Any association formed under this Title may, by the vote of shareholders owning two-thirds of its capital stock, reduce its capital to any sum not below the amount required by this Title to authorize the formation of associations; but no such reduction shall be allowable which will reduce the capital of the association below the amount required for its outstanding circulation, nor shall any such reduction be made until the amount of the proposed reduction has been reported to the Comptroller of the Currency and his approval thereof obtained.

Reduction of capital stock.

(SEC. 5144.) In all elections of directors, and in deciding all questions at meetings of shareholders, each shareholder shall be entitled to one vote on each share of stock held by him. Shareholders may vote by proxies duly authorized in writing; but no officer, clerk, teller or bookkeeper of such association shall act as proxy; and no shareholder whose liability is past due and unpaid shall be allowed to vote.

Rights of shareholders to vote at elections.

Proxies.

(SEC. 5145.) The affairs of each association shall be managed by not less than five directors, who shall be elected by the shareholders at a meeting to be held at any time before the association is authorized by the Comptroller of the Currency to commence the business of banking; and afterward at meetings to be held on such day in January of each year as is specified therefor in the articles of association. The directors shall hold office for one year, and until their successors are elected and have qualified.

Number and election of directors.

Term of office.

(SEC. 5146.) Every director must, during his whole term of service, be a citizen of the United States, and at least three-fourths of the directors must have resided in the State, Territory or District in which the association is located for at least one year immediately preceding their election, and must be residents therein during their continuance in office. Every director must own, in his own right, at least ten shares of the capital stock of the association of which he is a director. Any director who ceases to be the owner of ten shares of the stock, or who

Qualifications of directors.

becomes in any other manner disqualified, shall thereby vacate his place.

Oath required from directors.

(SEC. 5147.) Each director, when appointed or elected, shall take an oath that he will, so far as the duty devolves on him, diligently and honestly administer the affairs of such association, and will not knowingly violate, or willingly permit to be violated, any of the provisions of this Title, and that he is the owner in good faith, and in his own right, of the number of shares of stock required by this Title, subscribed by him, or standing in his name on the books of the association, and that the same is not hypothecated, or in any way pledged, as security for any loan or debt. Such oath, subscribed by the director making it, and certified by the officer before whom it is taken, shall be immediately transmitted to the Comptroller of the Currency, and shall be filed and preserved in his Office.

Vacancies, how filled.

(SEC. 5148.) Any vacancy in the board shall be filled by appointment by the remaining directors, and any director so appointed shall hold his place until the next election.

Proceedings where no election is held on the proper day.

(SEC. 5149.) If from any cause an election of directors is not made at the time appointed, the association shall not for that cause be dissolved, but an election may be held on any subsequent day, thirty days' notice thereof in all cases having been given in a newspaper published in the city, town or county in which the association is located; and if no newspaper is published in such city, town or county, such notice shall be published in a newspaper published nearest thereto. If the articles of association do not fix the day on which the election shall be held, or if no election is held on the day fixed, the day for the election shall be designated by the board of directors in their by-laws, or otherwise; or if the directors fail to fix the day, shareholders representing two-thirds of the shares may do so.

The president must be a director.

(SEC. 5150.) One of the directors, to be chosen by the board, shall be the president of the board.

Individual liability of shareholders.

(SEC. 5151.) The shareholders of every national banking association shall be held individually responsible, equally and ratably, and not one for another, for all contracts, debts and engagements of such association, to the extent of the amount of their stock therein, at the par value thereof, in addition to the amount invested in such shares; except that shareholders of any banking association now existing under State laws, having not less than five millions of dollars of capital actually paid in, and a surplus of twenty per centum on hand, both to be determined by the Comptroller of the Currency, shall be liable only to the amount invested in their shares; and such surplus of twenty per centum shall be kept undiminished, and be in addition to the surplus provided for in this Title; and if at any time there is a deficiency in such surplus of twenty per centum, such association shall not pay any dividends to its shareholders until the deficiency is made good; and in case of such deficiency the Comptroller of the Currency may compel the association to close its business and wind up its affairs under the provisions of chapter four of this Title.

Exception as to individual liability.

Receiver may be appointed for deficiency in surplus.

(SEC. 5152.) Persons holding stock as executors, administrators, guardians, or trustees, shall not be personally subject to any liabilities as stockholders; but the estates and funds in their hands shall be liable in like manner and to the same extent as the testator, intestate, ward, or person interested in such trust-funds would be, if living and competent to act and hold the stock in his own name.

Executors, trustees, etc., not personally liable.

(SEC. 5153.) All national banking associations, designated for that purpose by the Secretary of the Treasury, shall be depositaries of public money, except receipts from customs, under such regulations as may be prescribed by the Secretary; and they may also be employed as financial agents of the government; and they shall perform all such reasonable duties as depositaries of public moneys and financial agents of the government, as may be required of them. The Secretary of the Treasury shall require the associations thus designated to give satisfactory security, by the deposit of United States bonds and otherwise, for the safe-keeping and prompt payment of the public money deposited with them, and for the faithful performance of their duties as financial agents of the government. And every associa-

Duties and liabilities of associations when designated as depositaries of public moneys.

tion so designated as receiver or depositary of the public money shall take and receive at par all of the national currency bills, by whatever association issued, which have been paid into the government for internal revenue, or for loans or stocks.

Organization of State banks as national banking associations.

(SEC. 5154.) Any bank incorporated by special law, or any banking institution organized under a general law of any State, may become a national association under this Title by the name prescribed in its organization certificate; and in such case the articles of association and the organization certificate may be executed by a majority of the directors of the bank or banking institution; and the certificate shall declare that the owners of two-thirds of the capital stock have authorized the directors to make such certificate, and to change and convert the bank or banking institution into a national association. A majority of the directors, after executing the articles of association and organization certificate, shall have power to execute all other papers, and to do whatever may be required to make its organization perfect and complete as a national association. The shares of any such bank may continue to be for the same amount each as they were before the conversion, and the directors may continue to be the directors of the association until others are elected or appointed in accordance with the provisions of this chapter; and any State bank which is a stockholder in any other bank, by authority of State laws, may continue to hold its stock, although either bank, or both, may be organized under and have accepted the provisions of this Title. When the Comptroller of the Currency has given to such association a certificate, under his hand and official seal, that the provisions of this Title have been complied with, and that it is authorized to commence the business of banking, the association shall have the same powers and privileges, and shall be subject to the same duties, responsibilities, and rules, in all respects, as are prescribed for other associations originally organized as national banking associations, and shall be held and regarded as such an association. But no such association shall have a less capital than the amount prescribed for associations organized under this Title.

Mode of procedure.

To have the same rights liabilities, etc., as other national associations.

Minimum capital.

(SEC. 5155.) It shall be lawful for any bank or banking association, organized under State laws, and having branches, the capital being joint and assigned to and used by the mother-bank and branches in definite proportions, to become a national banking association in conformity with existing laws, and to retain and keep in operation its branches, or such one or more of them as it may elect to retain; the amount of the circulation redeemable at the mother-bank, and each branch, to be regulated by the amount of capital assigned to and used by each.

State banks having branches.

(SEC. 5156.) Nothing in this Title shall affect any appointments made, acts done, or proceedings had or commenced prior to the third day of June, eighteen hundred and sixty-four, in or toward the organization of any national banking association under the act of February twenty-five, eighteen hundred and sixty-three; but all associations which, on the third day of June, eighteen hundred and sixty-four, were organized or commenced to be organized under that act, shall enjoy all the rights and privileges granted, and be subject to all the duties, liabilities, and restrictions imposed by this Title, notwithstanding all the steps prescribed by this Title for the organization of associations were not pursued, if such associations were duly organized under that act.

Reservation of rights of associations organized under act of 1863.

(SEC. 5185.) Associations may be organized in the manner prescribed by this Title for the purpose of issuing notes payable in gold; and upon the deposit of any United States bonds bearing interest payable in gold with the Treasurer of the United States, in the manner prescribed for other associations, it shall be lawful for the Comptroller of the Currency to issue to the association making the deposit circulating notes of different denominations, but none of them of less than five dollars, and not exceeding in amount eighty per centum of the par value of the bonds deposited, which shall express the promise of the association to pay them, upon presentation at the office at which they are issued, in gold coin of the United States, and shall be so redeemable.

Organization of associations for issuing gold-notes.

Denominations of circulating notes, and ratio of to bonds deposited.

(SEC. 5186.) Every association organized under the preceding section shall at all times keep on hand not less than twenty-five per centum of its outstanding cir-

Reserve required on circulation of gold-banks.

culation, in gold or silver coin of the United States; and shall receive at par in the payment of debts the gold-notes of every other such association which at the time of such payment is redeeming its circulating notes in gold coin of the United States, and shall be subject to all the provisions of this Title: *Provided*, That, in applying the same to associations organized for issuing gold-notes, the terms "lawful money" and "lawful money of the United States" shall be construed to mean gold or silver coin of the United States.

Gold-notes to be received at par by all gold-banks.

"Lawful money," how construed for gold-banks.

CHAPTER II.

OBTAINING AND ISSUING CIRCULATING NOTES.

What associations are governed by Chapters II, III and IV of this Title.*

(SEC. 5157.) The provisions of chapters two, three and four* of this Title, which are expressed without restrictive words, as applying to "national banking associations," or to "associations," apply to all associations organized to carry on the business of banking under any act of Congress.

United States bonds defined.

(SEC. 5158.) The term "United States bonds," as used throughout this chapter, shall be construed to mean registered bonds of the United States.

United States bonds to be deposited before commencing business.

(SEC. 5159.) Every association, after having complied with the provisions of this Title, preliminary to the commencement of the banking business, and before it shall be authorized to commence banking business under this Title, shall transfer and deliver to the Treasurer of the United States any United States registered bonds, bearing interest, to an amount not less than thirty thousand dollars and not less than one third of the capital stock paid in. Such bonds shall be received by the Treasurer upon deposit, and shall be by him safely kept in his office, until they shall be otherwise disposed of, in pursuance of the provisions of this Title.

Bonds to be increased upon

(SEC. 5160.) The deposits of bonds made by each association shall be increased as its capital may be paid

* Chapters II, III and IV of this compilation and of the Revised Statutes.

up or increased, so that every association shall at all times have on deposit with the Treasurer registered United States bonds to the amount of at least one third of its capital stock actually paid in. And any association that may desire to reduce its capital or to close up its business and dissolve its organization, may take up its bonds upon returning to the Comptroller its circulating notes in the proportion hereinafter required, or may take up any excess of bonds beyond one third of its capital stock, and upon which no circulating notes have been delivered.

Increase of capital.

May be diminished upon reduction of capital.

That any association organized under this act, or any of the acts of which this is an amendment, desiring to withdraw its circulating notes, in whole or in part, may, upon the deposit of lawful money with the Treasurer of the United States in sums of not less than nine thousand dollars, take up the bonds which said association has on deposit with the Treasurer for the security of such circulating notes, which bonds shall be assigned to the bank in the manner specified in sections 5162 and 5163 of the Revised Statutes; and the outstanding notes of said association, to an amount equal to the legal-tender notes deposited, shall be redeemed at the Treasury of the United States, and destroyed as now provided by law: *Provided*; that the amount of the bonds on deposit for circulation shall not be reduced below fifty thousand dollars.

June 20, 1874.

Provisions for retiring circulation and withdrawing bonds.

Limit of withdrawal of bonds.

(SEC. 5161.) To facilitate a compliance with the two preceding sections, the Secretary of the Treasury is authorized to receive from any association, and cancel, any United States coupon bonds, and to issue in lieu thereof registered bonds of like amount, bearing a like rate of interest, and having the same time to run.

Exchange of coupon for registered bonds.

(SEC. 5162.) All transfers of United States bonds, made by any association under the provisions of this Title, shall be made to the Treasurer of the United States in trust for the association, with a memorandum written or printed on each bond, and signed by the cashier, or some other officer of the association making the deposit. A receipt shall be given to the association by the Comptroller of the Currency, or by a clerk appointed by him

Transfer of bonds to Treasurer.

for that purpose, stating that the bond is held in trust for the association on whose behalf the transfer is made, and as security for the redemption and payment of any circulating notes that have been or may be delivered to such association. No assignment or transfer of any such bond by the Treasurer shall be deemed valid unless countersigned by the Comptroller of the Currency.

Registry of transfers.

(SEC. 5163.) The Comptroller of the Currency shall keep in his office a book in which he shall cause to be entered, immediately upon countersigning it, every transfer or assignment by the Treasurer, of any bonds belonging to a national banking association, presented for his signature. He shall state in such entry the name of the association from whose accounts the transfer is made, the name of the party to whom it is made, and the par value of the bonds transferred.

Notice of transfer to be given to association.

(SEC. 5164.) The Comptroller of the Currency shall, immediately upon countersigning and entering any transfer or assignment by the Treasurer, of any bonds belonging to a national banking association, advise by mail the association from whose accounts the transfer is made, of the kind and numerical designation of the bonds, and the amount thereof so transferred.

Comptroller to have access to bonds, and to books of Treasurer.

Treasurer to have access to books of Comptroller.

(SEC. 5165.) The Comptroller of the Currency shall have at all times, during office hours, access to the books of the Treasurer of the United States for the purpose of ascertaining the correctness of any transfer or assignment of the bonds deposited by an association, presented to the Comptroller to countersign; and the Treasurer shall have the like access to the book mentioned in section fifty-one hundred and sixty-three, during office hours, to ascertain the correctness of the entries in the same; and the Comptroller shall also at all times have access to the bonds on deposit with the Treasurer, to ascertain their amount and condition.

Annual examination of bonds by associations.

(SEC. 5166.) Every association having bonds deposited in the office of the Treasurer of the United States shall, once or oftener in each fiscal year, examine and compare the bonds pledged by the association with the books of the Comptroller of the Currency and with the accounts of the association, and, if they are found correct, to execute to the Treasurer a certificate setting forth the different kinds and the amounts thereof, and that the same are in the possession and custody of the Treasurer at the date of the certificate. Such examination shall be made at such time or times, during the ordinary business hours, as the Treasurer and the Comptroller, respectively, may select, and may be made by an officer or agent of such association, duly appointed in writing for that purpose; and his certificate before mentioned shall be of like force and validity as if executed by the president or cashier. A duplicate of such certificate, signed by the Treasurer, shall be retained by the association.

Bonds to be held to secure circulation.

(SEC. 5167.) The bonds transferred to and deposited with the Treasurer of the United States, by any association, for the security of its circulating notes, shall be held exclusively for that purpose, until such notes are redeemed, except as provided in this Title. The Comptroller of the Currency shall give to any such association powers of attorney to receive and appropriate to its own use the interest on the bonds which it has so transferred to the Treasurer; but such powers shall become inoperative whenever such association fails to redeem its circulating notes. Whenever the market or cash value of any bonds thus deposited with the Treasurer is reduced below the amount of the circulation issued for the same, the Comptroller may demand and receive the amount of such depreciation in other United States bonds at cash value, or in money, from the association, to be deposited with the Treasurer as long as such depreciation continues. And the Comptroller, upon the terms prescribed by the Secretary of the Treasury, may permit an exchange to be made of any of the bonds deposited with the Treasurer by any association, for other bonds of the United States authorized to be received as security for circulating notes, if he is of opinion that such an exchange can be made without prejudice to the United States; and he may direct the return of any bonds to the association which transferred the same, in sums of not less than one thousand dollars, upon the surrender to him and the cancellation of a proportionate amount of such circulating notes: *Provided*, That the remaining bonds which shall

Interest on bonds, how collected.

If bonds depreciate, deposit to be increased.

Exchange or return of bonds.

have been transferred by the association offering to surrender circulating notes are equal to the amount required for the circulating notes not surrendered by such association, and that the amount of bonds in the hands of the Treasurer is not diminished below the amount required to be kept on deposit with him, and that there has been no failure by the association to redeem its circulating notes, nor any other violation by it of the provisions of this Title, and that the market or cash value of the remaining bonds is not below the amount required for the circulation issued for the same.

Delivery of circulating notes to associations.

(SEC. 5171.) Upon a deposit of bonds as prescribed by sections fifty-one hundred and fifty-nine and fifty-one hundred and sixty, the association making the same shall be entitled to receive from the Comptroller of the Currency circulating notes of different denominations, in blank, registered and countersigned as hereinafter provided, equal in amount to ninety per centum of the current market value of the United States bonds so transferred and delivered, but not exceeding ninety per centum of the amount of the bonds at the par value thereof, if bearing interest at a rate not less than five per centum per annum: *Provided*, That the amount of circulating notes to be furnished to each association shall be in proportion to its paid-up capital, as follows, and no more:

Ratio to capital of circulating notes issued.

First. To each association whose capital does not exceed five hundred thousand dollars, ninety per centum of such capital.

Second. To each association whose capital exceeds five hundred thousand dollars, but does not exceed one million of dollars, eighty per centum of such capital.

Third. To each association whose capital exceeds one million of dollars, but does not exceed three million[s] of dollars, seventy-five per centum of such capital.

Fourth. To each association whose capital exceeds three millions of dollars, sixty per centum of such capital.

Form, denominations and printing of circulating notes.

(SEC. 5172.) In order to furnish suitable notes for circulation, the Comptroller of the Currency shall, under the direction of the Secretary of the Treasury, cause plates and dies to be engraved, in the best manner to guard against counterfeiting and fraudulent alterations, and shall have printed therefrom, and numbered, such quantity of circulating notes, in blank, of the denominations of one dollar, two dollars, three dollars, five dollars, ten dollars, twenty dollars, fifty dollars, one hundred dollars, five hundred dollars, and one thousand dollars, as may be required to supply the associations entitled to receive the same. Such notes shall express upon their face that they are secured by United States bonds, deposited with the Treasurer of the United States, by the written or engraved signatures of the Treasurer and Register, and by the imprint of the seal of the Treasury; and shall also express upon their face the promise of the association receiving the same to pay on demand, attested by the signatures of the president or vice-president and cashier; and shall bear such devices and such other statements, and shall be in such form, as the Secretary of the Treasury shall, by regulation, direct.

June 20, 1874. The charter numbers of banks to be printed upon their notes.

That the Comptroller of the Currency shall, under such rules and regulations as the Secretary of the Treasury may prescribe, cause the charter numbers of the association to be printed upon all national-bank notes which may be hereafter issued by him.

Control of plates and dies, and expenses of bureau.

(SEC. 5173.) The plates and special dies to be procured by the Comptroller of the Currency for the printing of such circulating notes shall remain under his control and direction, and the expenses necessarily incurred in executing the laws respecting the procuring of such notes, and all other expenses of the Bureau of the Currency, shall be paid out of the proceeds of the taxes or duties assessed and collected on the circulation of national banking associations under this Title.

Annual examination of plates, dies, etc.

(SEC. 5174.) The Comptroller of the Currency shall cause to be examined, each year, the plates, dies, butpieces [bed-pieces], and other material from which the national-bank circulation is printed, in whole or in part, and file in his office annually a correct list of the same.

Certain printing material to be destroyed.

Such material as shall have been used in the printing of the notes of associations which are in liquidation, or have closed business, shall be destroyed under such regulations as shall be prescribed by the Comptroller of the Currency and approved by the Secretary of the Treasury. The expenses of any such examination or destruction shall be paid out of any appropriation made by Congress for the special examination of national banks and bank-note plates.

Issue of notes under five dollars, limited.

(SEC. 5175.) Not more than one-sixth part of the notes furnished to any association shall be of a less denomination than five dollars. After specie payments are resumed no association shall be furnished with notes of a less denomination than five dollars.

Circulation of certain banks limited to $500,000.

(SEC. 5176.) No banking association organized subsequent to the twelfth day of July, eighteen hundred and seventy, shall have a circulation in excess of five hundred thousand dollars.

June 20, 1874. Repeal of limitation of aggregate amount of circulating notes.

* That section five thousand one hundred and seventy-seven of the Revised Statutes, limiting the aggregate amount of circulating notes of national banking associations, be and is hereby repealed; and each existing banking association may increase its circulating notes in accordance with existing law without respect to said aggregate limit; and new banking associations may be organized in accordance with existing law without respect to said aggregate limit. And whenever, and so often, as circulating notes shall be issued to any such banking association, so increasing its capital or circulating notes, or so newly organized as aforesaid, it shall be the duty of the Secretary of the Treasury to redeem the legal-tender United States notes in excess only of three hundred million of dollars, to the amount of eighty per centum of the sum of national-bank notes so issued to any such banking association as aforesaid, and to continue such redemption as such circulating notes are issued until there shall be outstanding the sum of three hundred million dollars of such legal-tender United States notes, and no more.

Redemption of legal-tender notes in proportion to the issue of national-bank notes.

Legal-tenders not to be reduced below $300,000,000.

Maximum amount of U. S. notes outstanding.

That the amount of United States notes outstanding and to be used as a part of the circulating medium shall not exceed the sum of three hundred and eighty-two million dollars, which said sum shall appear in each

* Sections 5177, 5178, 5179, 5180 and 5181, repealed by act of June 20, 1874.

monthly statement of the public debt, and no part thereof shall be held or used as a reserve.

Circulating notes, when may be issued.

(SEC. 5182.) After any association receiving circulating notes under this Title has caused its promise to pay such notes on demand to be signed by the president or vice-president and cashier thereof, in such manner as to make them obligatory promissory notes, payable on demand, at its place of business, such association may issue and circulate the same as money. And the same shall be received at par in all parts of the United States in payment of taxes, excises, public lands, and all other dues to the United States, except duties on imports; and also for all salaries and other debts and demands owing by the United States to individuals, corporations and associations within the United States, except interest on the public debt, and in redemption of the national currency.

For what demands shall be received.

Issue of other notes prohibited.

Act of Feb. 18, 1875, correcting Rev. Stat.

Merchants' Bank *vs.* State Bank, 10 Wall. 604.

(SEC. 5183.) No national banking association shall issue post-notes or any other notes to circulate as money than such as are authorized by the provisions of this Title.

(SEC. 5184.) It shall be the duty of the Comptroller of the Currency to receive worn-out or mutilated circulating notes issued by any banking association, and also, on due proof of the destruction of any such circulating notes, to deliver in place thereof to the association other blank circulating notes to an equal amount. Such worn-out or mutilated notes, after a memorandum has been entered in the proper books, in accordance with such regulations as may be established by the Comptroller, as well as all circulating notes which shall have been paid or surrendered to be canceled, shall be destroyed by maceration instead of burning to ashes in presence of four persons, one to be appointed by the Secretary of the Treasury, one by the Comptroller of the Currency, one by the Treasurer of the United States, and one by the association, under such regulations as the Secretary of the Treasury may prescribe. A certificate of such maceration, signed by the parties so appointed, shall be made in the books of the Comptroller, and a duplicate thereof forwarded to the association whose notes are thus canceled.

Destroying and replacing worn-out and mutilated notes.

Act of June 23, 1874.

CHAPTER III.

REGULATION OF THE BANKING BUSINESS.

Place of business. Merchants' Bank vs. State Bank, 10 Wall. 604.

(SEC. 5190.) The usual business of each national banking association shall be transacted at an office or banking-house located in the place specified in its organization certificate.

Requirements as to lawful money reserve.

(SEC. 5191.) Every national banking association in either of the following cities: Albany, Baltimore, Boston, Cincinnati, Chicago. Cleveland, Detroit, Louisville, Milwaukee, New Orleans, New York, Philadelphia, Pittsburgh, Saint Louis, San Francisco and Washington, shall at all times have on hand, in lawful money of the United States, an amount equal to at least twenty-five per centum of the aggregate amount of its deposits; and every other association shall at all times have on hand, in lawful money of the United States, an amount equal to at least fifteen per centum of the aggregate amount of its deposits. Whenever the lawful money of any association in any of the cities named shall be below the amount of twenty-five per centum of its deposits, and whenever the lawful money of any other association shall be below fifteen per centum of its deposits, such association shall not increase its liabilities by making any new loans or discounts otherwise than by discounting or purchasing bills of exchange payable at sight, nor make any dividend of its profits until the required proportion, between the aggregate amount of its deposits and its lawful money of the United States, has been restored. And the Comptroller of the Currency may notify any association, whose lawful-money reserve shall be below the amount above required to be kept on hand, to make good such reserve; and if such association shall fail for thirty days thereafter so to make good its reserve of lawful money, the Comptroller may, with the concurrence of the Secretary of the Treasury, appoint a receiver to wind up the business of the association, as provided in section fifty-two hundred and thirty-four.

Act June 20, 1874.

No loans or dividends to be made while reserve is below limit.

Receiver may be appointed for failure to make good the reserve.

That every association organized, or to be organized, under the provisions of the said act, and of the several acts amendatory thereof, shall at all times keep and have on deposit in the Treasury of the United States, in lawful money of the United States, a sum equal to five per centum of its circulation, to be held and used for the redemption of such circulation; which sum shall be counted as a part of its lawful reserve, as provided in section two of this act (Sec. 5191 Revised Statutes); and when the circulating notes of any such associations, assorted or unassorted, shall be presented for redemption, in sums of one thousand dollars or any multiple thereof, to the Treasurer of the United States, the same shall be redeemed in United States notes. All notes so redeemed shall be charged by the Treasurer of the United States to the respective associations issuing the same, and he shall notify them severally, on the first day of each month, or oftener, at his discretion, of the amount of such redemptions; and whenever such redemptions for any association shall amount to the sum of five hundred dollars, such association so notified shall forthwith deposit with the Treasurer of the United States a sum in United States notes equal to the amount of its circulating notes so redeemed. And all notes of national banks, worn, defaced, mutilated, or otherwise unfit for circulation, shall, when received by any assistant treasurer or at any designated depository of the United States, be forwarded to the Treasurer of the United States for redemption as provided herein. And when such redemptions have been so reimbursed, the circulating notes so redeemed shall be forwarded to the respective associations by which they were issued; but if any of such notes are worn, mutilated, defaced, or rendered otherwise unfit for use, they shall be forwarded to the Comptroller of the Currency and destroyed, and replaced as now provided by law: *Provided*, That each of said associations shall reimburse to the Treasury the charges for transportation, and the costs for assorting such notes; and the associations hereafter organized shall also severally reimburse to the Treasury the cost of engraving such plates as shall be ordered by each association respectively; and the amount

June 20, 1874. Redemption fund to be deposited with Treasurer.

May be counted as lawful reserve.

Provisions relative to redemption of notes by Treasurer.

Mutilated notes to be returned by assistant treasurers.

Associations to reimburse the Treasury for cost of redemption, new plates, etc.

assessed upon each association shall be in proportion to the circulation redeemed, and be charged to the fund on deposit with the Treasurer.

Redemption cities and proportion of reserve which may be kept therein. See act of June 20, 1874.

(SEC. 5192.) Three-fifths of the reserve of fifteen per centum required by the preceding section to be kept, may consist of balances due to an association, available for the redemption of its circulating notes, from associations approved by the Comptroller of the Currency, organized under the act of June three, eighteen hundred and sixty-four, or under this Title, and doing business in the cities of Albany, Baltimore, Boston, Charleston, Chicago, Cincinnati, Cleveland, Detroit, Louisville, Milwaukee, New Orleans, New York, Philadelphia, Pittsburgh, Richmond, Saint Louis, San Francisco and Washington.

Clearing-house certificates deemed lawful money.

Clearing-house certificates, representing specie or lawful money specially deposited for the purpose, of any clearing-house association, shall also be deemed to be lawful money in the possession of any association belonging to such clearing-house, holding and owning such certificate, within the preceding section.

U. S. certificates of deposit may be issued, and may count as reserve.

(SEC. 5193.) The Secretary of the Treasury may receive United States notes on deposit, without interest, from any national banking associations, in sums of not less than ten thousand dollars, and issue certificates therefor in such form as he may prescribe, in denominations of not less than five thousand dollars, and payable on demand in United States notes at the place where the deposits were made. The notes so deposited shall not be counted as part of the lawful-money reserve of the association; but the certificates issued therefor may be counted as part of its lawful-money reserve, and may be accepted in the settlement of clearing-house balances at the places where the deposits therefor were made.

Limitation upon the issue of certificates of deposit.

(SEC. 5194.) The power conferred on the Secretary of the Treasury, by the preceding section, shall not be exercised so as to create any expansion or contraction of the currency. And United States notes for which certificates are issued under that section, or other United States notes of like amount, shall be held as special deposits in the Treasury, and used only for the redemption of such certificates.

(SEC. 5195.) Each association organized in any of the cities named in section fifty-one hundred and ninety-one may keep one-half of its lawful-money reserve in cash deposits in the city of New York. But the foregoing provision shall not apply to associations organized and located in the city of San Francisco for the purpose of issuing notes payable in gold. Each association not organized within the cities named, shall select, subject to the approval of the Comptroller, an association in either of the cities named, at which it will redeem its circulating notes at par. The Comptroller shall give public notice of the names of the associations selected, at which redemptions are to be made by the respective associations, and of any change that may be made of the association at which the notes of any association are redeemed. Whenever any association fails either to make the selection or to redeem its notes as aforesaid, the Comptroller of the Currency may, upon receiving satisfactory evidence thereof, appoint a receiver in the manner provided for in section fifty-two hundred and thirty-four, to wind up its affairs. But this section shall not relieve any association from its liability to redeem its circulating notes at its own counter, at par, in lawful money on demand.

Agents for redemption of circulating notes to be designated. See act of June 20, 1874.

Receiver may be appointed for failure to redeem notes.

(SEC. 5196.) Every national banking association formed or existing under this Title, shall take and receive at par, for any debt or liability to it, any and all notes or bills issued by any lawfully organized national banking association. But this provision shall not apply to any association organized for the purpose of issuing notes payable in gold.

National banks to receive notes of all other national banks.

(SEC. 5197.) Any association may take, receive, reserve, and charge on any loan or discount made, or upon any note, bill of exchange, or other evidences of debt, interest at the rate allowed by the laws of the State, Territory, or district where the bank is located, and no more, except that where by the laws of any State a different rate is limited for banks of issue organized under State laws,* the rate so limited shall be allowed for associations organized or existing in any such State under

Limitations upon rate of interest which may be taken. Tiffany *vs.* National Bank of Missouri, 18 Wall. 409.

* See table of Interest Laws of the States, page 254.

this Title. When no rate is fixed by the laws of the State, or Territory, or district, the bank may take, receive, reserve, or charge a rate not exceeding seven per centum, and such interest may be taken in advance, reckoning the days for which the note, bill, or other evidence of debt has to run. And the purchase, discount, or sale of a bona-fide bill of exchange, payable at another place than the place of such purchase, discount, or sale, at not more than the current rate of exchange for sight drafts in addition to the interest, shall not be considered as taking or receiving a greater rate of interest.

The purchase or discount of bills of exchange not usury.

Penalty for taking usurious interest.

(SEC. 5198.) The taking, receiving, reserving, or charging a rate of interest greater than is allowed by the preceding section, when knowingly done, shall be deemed a forfeiture of the entire interest which the note, bill, or other evidence of debt carries with it, or which has been agreed to be paid thereon. In case the greater rate of interest has been paid, the person by whom it has been paid, or his legal representatives, may recover back, in an action in the nature of an action of debt, twice the amount of the interest thus paid from the association taking or receiving the same; provided such action is commenced within two years from the time the usurious transaction occurred.

In what courts suits may be brought.

See act of Feb. 18, 1875, correcting Rev. Stat.

Suits, actions and proceedings against any association under this Title may be had in any circuit, district, or territorial court of the United States held within the district in which such association may be established, or in any State, county, or municipal court in the county or city in which said association is located, having jurisdiction in similar cases.

Dividends and surplus fund.

(SEC. 5199.) The directors of any association may, semi-annually, declare a dividend of so much of the net profits of the association as they shall judge expedient; but each association shall, before the declaration of a dividend, carry one-tenth part of its net profits of the preceding half-year to its surplus fund until the same shall amount to twenty per centum of its capital stock.

Limit of liabilities

(SEC. 5200.) The total liabilities to any association, of any person, or of any company, corporation, or firm, for money borrowed, including, in the liabilities of a company or firm, the liabilities of the several members thereof, shall at no time exceed one-tenth part of the amount of the capital stock of such association actually paid in. But the discount of bills of exchange drawn in good faith against actually existing values, and the discount of commercial or business paper actually owned by the person negotiating the same, shall not be considered as money borrowed.

to an association of any person, firm, or corporation.

The discount of bills of exchange, etc., not a loan.

(SEC. 5201.) No association shall make any loan or discount on the security of the shares of its own capital stock, nor be the purchaser or holder of any such shares, unless such security or purchase shall be necessary to prevent loss upon a debt previously contracted in good faith; and stock so purchased or acquired shall, within six months from the time of its purchase, be sold or disposed of at public or private sale; or, in default thereof, a receiver may be appointed to close up the business of the association, according to section fifty-two hundred and thirty-four.

Associations not to loan upon or purchase their own stock. Bank *vs.* Lanier, 11 Wall. 369; Ballard *vs.* Bank, 18 Wall. 589.

Receiver may be appointed for failure to sell stock.

(SEC. 5202.) No association shall at any time be indebted, or in any way liable, to an amount exceeding the amount of its capital stock at such time actually paid in and remaining undiminished by losses or otherwise, except on account of demands of the nature following:

Limit of indebtedness of association.

First. Notes of circulation.

Exceptions.

Second. Moneys deposited with or collected by the association.

Third. Bills of exchange or drafts drawn against money actually on deposit to the credit of the association, or due thereto.

Fourth. Liabilities to the stockholders of the association for dividends and reserve profits.

(SEC. 5203.) No association shall, either directly or indirectly, pledge or hypothecate any of its notes of circulation, for the purpose of procuring money to be paid in on its capital stock, or to be used in its banking operations, or otherwise; nor shall any association use its circulating notes, or any part thereof, in any manner or form, to create or increase its capital stock.

Circulating notes not to be hypothecated, nor used to increase capital.

Withdrawal of capital prohibited.

(SEC. 5204.) No association, or any member thereof, shall, during the time it shall continue its banking operations, withdraw, or permit to be withdrawn, either in the form of dividends or otherwise, any portion of its capital. If losses have at any time been sustained by any such association, equal to or exceeding its undivided profits then on hand, no dividend shall be made; and no dividend shall ever be made by any association, while it continues its banking operations, to an amount greater than its net profits then on hand, deducting therefrom its losses and bad debts. All debts due to any associations, on which interest is past due and unpaid for a period of six months, unless the same are well secured, and in process of collection, shall be considered bad debts within the meaning of this section. But nothing in this section shall prevent the reduction of the capital stock of the association under section fifty-one hundred and forty-three.

Dividend not to exceed net profits.

Bad debts defined.

Enforcing payment of deficiency in capital stock.

(SEC. 5205). Every association which shall have failed to pay up its capital stock, as required by law, and every association whose capital stock shall have become impaired by losses or otherwise, shall, within three months after receiving notice thereof from the Comptroller of the Currency, pay the deficiency in the capital stock, by assessment upon the shareholders pro rata for the amount of capital stock held by each; and the Treasurer of the United States shall withhold the interest upon all bonds held by him in trust for any such association, upon notification from the Comptroller of the Currency, until otherwise notified by him. If any such association shall fail to pay up its capital stock, and shall refuse to go into liquidation, as provided by law, for three months after receiving notice from the Comptroller, a receiver may be appointed to close up the business of the association, according to the provisions of section fifty-two hundred and thirty-four.

Receiver may be appointed for failure to pay up capital.

June 30, 1876.

And provided, that if any shareholder or shareholders of such bank shall neglect or refuse, after three months' notice to pay the assessment, as provided in this section, it shall be the duty of the board of directors to cause a sufficient amount of the capital stock of such shareholder or shareholders to be sold at public auction (after thirty days' notice shall be given by posting such notice of sale in the office of the bank, and by publishing such notice in a newspaper of the city or town in which the bank is located, or in a newspaper published nearest thereto) to make good the deficiency; and the balance, if any, shall be returned to such delinquent shareholder or shareholders.

That all United States officers charged with the receipt or disbursement of public moneys, and all officers of national banks, shall stamp or write in plain letters the word "counterfeit," "altered" or "worthless," upon all fraudulent notes issued in the form of, and intended to circulate as money, which shall be presented at their places of business; and if such officers shall wrongfully stamp any genuine note of the United States, or of the national banks, they shall, upon presentation, redeem such notes at the face value thereof.

Bank officers to stamp counterfeit and altered notes.

SEC. 6. That all savings banks or savings and trust companies organized under authority of any act of Congress shall be, and are hereby, required to make, to the Comptroller of the Currency, and publish, all the reports which national banking associations are required to make and publish under the provisions of sections fifty-two hundred and eleven, fifty-two hundred and twelve and fifty-two hundred and thirteen of the Revised Statutes, and shall be subject to the same penalties for failure to make or publish such reports as are therein provided; which penalties may be collected by suit before any court of the United States in the district in which said savings banks or savings and trust companies may be located. And all savings or other banks now organized, or which shall hereafter be organized, in the District of Columbia, under any act of Congress, which shall have capital stock paid up in whole or in part, shall be subject to all the provisions of the Revised Statutes, and of all acts of Congress applicable to national banking associations, so far as the same may be applicable to such savings or other banks: *Provided*, that such savings banks now established shall not be required

Act June 30, 1876. Savings Banks and Trust Co's to make reports to the Comptroller of the Currency.

to have a paid in capital exceeding one hundred thousand dollars.

Associations not to pay out uncurrent notes.

(SEC. 5206.) No association shall at any time pay out on loans or discounts, or in purchasing drafts or bills of exchange, or in payment of deposits, or in any other mode pay or put in circulation, the notes of any bank or banking association which are not, at any such time, receivable, at par, on deposit, and in payment of debts by the association so paying out or circulating such notes; nor shall any association knowingly pay out or put in circulation any notes issued by any bank or banking association which at the time of such paying out or putting in circulation is not redeeming its circulating notes in lawful money of the United States.

Penalty for falsely certifying checks.

(SEC. 5208.) It shall be unlawful for any officer, clerk, or agent of any national banking association to certify any check drawn upon the association unless the person or company drawing the check has on deposit with the association, at the time such check is certified, an amount of money equal to the amount specified in such check. Any check so certified by duly authorized officers shall be a good and valid obligation against the association; but the act of any officer, clerk or agent of any association, in violation of this section, shall subject such bank to the liabilities and proceedings on the part of the Comptroller as provided for in section fifty-two hundred and thirty-four.

Receiver may be appointed for false certification.

List of shareholders to be kept, subject to inspection.

(SEC. 5210.) The president and cashier of every national banking association shall cause to be kept at all times a full and correct list of the names and residences of all the shareholders in the association, and the number of shares held by each, in the office where its business is transacted. Such list shall be subject to the inspection of all the shareholders and creditors of the association, and the officers authorized to assess taxes under State authority, during business-hours of each day in which business may be legally transacted. A copy of such list, on the first Monday of July of each year, verified by the oath of such president or cashier, shall be transmitted to the Comptroller of the Currency.

List to be sent to Comptroller annually.

Provisions relative to reports of associations to Comptroller.

(SEC. 5211.) Every association shall make to the Comptroller of the Currency not less than five reports during each year according to the form which may be prescribed by him, verified by the oath or affirmation of the president or cashier of such association, and attested by the signature of at least three of the directors. Each such report shall exhibit, in detail and under appropriate heads, the resources and liabilities of the associations at the close of business on any past day by him specified; and shall be transmitted to the Comptroller within five days after the receipt of a request or requisition therefor from him, and in the same form in which it is made to the Comptroller shall be published in a newspaper published in the place where such association is established, or if there is no newspaper in the place, then in the one published nearest thereto in the same county, at the expense of the association; and such proof of publication shall be furnished as may be required by the Comptroller. The Comptroller shall also have power to call for special reports from any particular association whenever in his judgment the same are necessary in order to a full and complete knowledge of its condition.

Reports of dividends and earnings.

(SEC. 5212.) In addition to the reports required by the preceding section, each association shall report to the Comptroller of the Currency, within ten days after declaring any dividend, the amount of such dividend, and the amount of net earnings in excess of such dividend. Such reports shall be attested by the oath of the president or cashier of the association.

Penalty for failure to make reports to Comptroller.

(SEC. 5213.) Every association which fails to make and transmit any report required under either of the two preceding sections shall be subject to a penalty of one hundred dollars for each day after the periods, respectively, therein mentioned, that it delays to make and transmit its report. Whenever any association delays or refuses to pay the penalty herein imposed, after it has been assessed by the Comptroller of the Currency, the amount thereof may be retained by the Treasurer of the United States, upon the order of the Comptroller of the Currency, out of the interest, as it may become due to the association, on the bonds deposited with him to secure circulation. All sums of money collected for penalties under this section shall be paid into the Treasury of the United States.

Duty on circulation, deposits, and capital stock.

(SEC. 5214.) In lieu of all existing taxes, every association shall pay to the Treasurer of the United States, in the months of January and July, a duty of one-half of one per centum each half year upon the average amount of its notes in circulation, and a duty of one-quarter of one per centum each half year upon the average amount of its deposits, and a duty of one-quarter of one per centum each half year on the average amount of its capital stock, beyond the amount invested in United States bonds.

Semi-annual return of circulation, deposits, and capital stock.

(SEC. 5215.) In order to enable the Treasurer to assess the duties imposed by the preceding section, each association shall, within ten days from the first days of January and July of each year, make a return, under the oath of its president or cashier, to the Treasurer of the United States, in such form as the Treasurer may prescribe, of the average amount of its notes in circulation, and of the average amount of its deposits, and of the average amount of its capital stock, beyond the amount invested in United States bonds, for the six months next preceding the most recent first day of January or July.

Penalty for failure to make return.

Every association which fails so to make such return shall be liable to a penalty of two hundred dollars, to be collected either out of the interest as it may become due such association on the bonds deposited with the Treasurer, or, at his option, in the manner in which penalties are to be collected of other corporations under the laws of the United States.

Method of assessment if return is not made.

(SEC. 5216.) Whenever any association fails to make the half-yearly return required by the preceding section, the duties to be paid by such association shall be assessed upon the amount of notes delivered to such association by the Comptroller of the Currency, and upon the highest amount of its deposits and capital stock, to be ascertained in such manner as the Treasurer may deem best.

How tax may be collected if association fails to pay.

(SEC. 5217.) Whenever an association fails to pay the duties imposed by the three preceding sections, the sums due may be collected in the manner provided for the collection of United States taxes from other corporations; or the Treasurer may reserve the amount out of the interest, as it may become due, on the bonds deposited with him by such defaulting association.

Refunding excess of duties paid.

(SEC. 5218.) In all cases where an association has paid or may pay in excess of what may be or has been found due from it, on account of the duty required to be paid to the Treasurer of the United States, the association may state an account therefor, which, on being certified by the Treasurer of the United States, and found correct by the First Comptroller of the Treasury, shall be refunded in the ordinary manner by warrant on the Treasury.

Provisions relative to State taxation of associations. Bank of Commerce *vs.* New York City, 2 Bl. 620; Van Allen *vs.* The Assessors, 3 Wall. 573; People *vs.* The Commissioners, 4 Wall. 244; Bradley *vs.* The People, 4 Wall. 459; National Bank *vs.* The Commonwealth, 9 Wall. 353; Lionberger *vs.* Rouse, 9 Wall. 468.

(SEC. 5219.) Nothing herein shall prevent all the shares in any association from being included in the valuation of the personal property of the owner or holder of such shares, in assessing taxes imposed by authority of the State within which the association is located; but the legislature of each State may determine and direct the manner and place of taxing all the shares of national banking associations located within the State, subject only to the two restrictions, that the taxation shall not be at a greater rate than is assessed upon other moneyed capital in the hands of individual citizens of such State, and that the shares of any national banking association owned by non-residents of any State shall be taxed in the city or town where the bank is located, and not elsewhere. Nothing herein shall be construed to exempt the real property of associations from either State, county, or municipal taxes, to the same extent, according to its value, as other real property is taxed.

Appointment, powers and duties of bank examiners.

(SEC. 5240.) The Comptroller of the Currency, with the approval of the Secretary of the Treasury, shall, as often as shall be deemed necessary or proper, appoint a suitable person or persons to make an examination of the affairs of every banking association, who shall have power to make a thorough examination into all the affairs of the association, and, in doing so, to examine any of the officers and agents thereof on oath: and shall make a full and detailed report of the condition of the association to the Comptroller. All persons appointed to be examiners

Compensation of examiners. Act of Feb. 19, 1875, amending Rev. Stat.

of national banks not located in the redemption-cities specified in section five thousand one hundred and ninety-two of the Revised Statutes of the United States, or in any one of the States of Oregon, California and Nevada, or in the Territories, shall receive compensation for such examination as follows: For examining national banks having a capital less than one hundred thousand dollars, twenty dollars; those having a capital of one hundred thousand dollars and less than three hundred thousand dollars, twenty-five dollars; those having a capital of three hundred thousand dollars and less than four hundred thousand dollars, thirty-five dollars; those having a capital of four hundred thousand dollars and less than five hundred thousand dollars, forty dollars; those having a capital of five hundred thousand dollars and less than six hundred thousand dollars, fifty dollars; those having a capital of six hundred thousand dollars and over, seventy-five dollars; which amounts shall be assessed by the Comptroller of the Currency upon, and paid by, the respective associations so examined, and shall be in lieu of the compensation and mileage heretofore allowed for making said examinations; and persons appointed to make examination of national banks in the cities named in section five thousand one hundred and ninety-two of the Revised Statutes of the United States, or in any one of the States of Oregon, California and Nevada, or in the Territories, shall receive such compensation as may be fixed by the Secretary of the Treasury upon the recommendation of the Comptroller of the Currency; and the same shall be assessed and paid in the manner hereinbefore provided.

Not to examine banks of which they are officers.

But no person shall be appointed to examine the affairs of any banking association of which he is a director or other officer.

Limitation of visitorial powers.

(SEC. 5241.) No association shall be subject to any visitorial powers other than such as are authorized by this Title, or are vested in the courts of justice.

Use of the word "national" in title, prohibited to other than national banks.

(SEC. 5243.) All banks not organized and transacting business under the national-currency laws, or under this Title, and all persons or corporations doing the business of bankers, brokers, or savings institutions, except savings-banks authorized by Congress to use the word "national" as a part of their corporate name, are prohibited from using the word "national" as a portion of the name or title of such bank, corporation, firm or partnership; and any violation of this prohibition committed after the third day of September, eighteen hundred and seventy-three, shall subject the party chargeable therewith to a penalty of fifty dollars for each day during which it is committed or repeated.

CHAPTER IV.

DISSOLUTION AND RECEIVERSHIP.

(SEC. 5220.) Any association may go into liquidation and be closed by the vote of its shareholders owning two-thirds of its stock. **Voluntary liquidation.**

(SEC. 5221.) Whenever a vote is taken to go into liquidation it shall be the duty of the board of directors to cause notice of this fact to be certified, under the seal of the association, by its president or cashier, to the Comptroller of the Currency, and publication thereof to be made for a period of two months in a newspaper published in the city of New York, and also in a newspaper published in the city or town in which the association is located, or if no newspaper is there published, then in the newspaper published nearest thereto, that the association is closing up its affairs, and notifying the holders of its notes and other creditors to present the notes and other claims against the association for payment. **Notice of intention to go into liquidation.**

(SEC. 5222.) Within six months from the date of the vote to go into liquidation, the association shall deposit with the Treasurer of the United States, lawful money of the United States sufficient to redeem all its outstanding circulation. The Treasurer shall execute duplicate receipts for money thus deposited, and deliver one to the association and the other to the Comptroller of the Currency, stating the amount received by him, and the purpose for which it has been received; and the money shall be paid into the Treasury of the United States, and placed to the credit of such association upon redemption account. **Deposit of lawful money to redeem circulation.**

Consolidating banks need not deposit lawful money.

(Sec. 5223.) An association which is in good faith winding up its business for the purpose of consolidating with another association shall not be required to deposit lawful money for its outstanding circulation; but its assets and liabilities shall be reported by the association with which it is in process of consolidation.

Re-assignment of bonds to closed banks.

Notes to be redeemed at Treasury.

Proceedings when association fails to deposit lawful money.

See act of Feb. 18, 1875, correcting Rev. Stat.

(Sec. 5224.) Whenever a sufficient deposit of lawful money to redeem the outstanding circulation of an association proposing to close its business has been made, the bonds deposited by the association to secure payment of its notes shall be re-assigned to it, in the manner prescribed by section fifty-one hundred and sixty-two. And thereafter the association and its shareholders shall stand discharged from all liabilities upon the circulating notes, and those notes shall be redeemed at the Treasury of the United States. And if any such bank shall fail to make the deposit and take up its bonds for thirty days after the expiration of the time specified, the Comptroller of the Currency shall have power to sell the bonds pledged for the circulation of said bank, at public auction in New York city, and, after providing for the redemption and cancellation of said circulation, and the necessary expenses of the sale, to pay over any balance remaining to the bank or its legal representative.

Destruction of redeemed notes.

Act of June 23, 1874.

(Sec. 5225.) Whenever the Treasurer has redeemed any of the notes of an association which has commenced to close its affairs under the six [five] preceding sections, he shall cause the notes to be mutilated and charged to the redemption account of the association; and all notes so redeemed by the Treasurer shall, every three months, be certified to and destroyed in the manner prescribed in section fifty-one hundred and eighty-four.

Mode of protesting notes.

(Sec. 5226.) Whenever any national banking association fails to redeem in the lawful money of the United States any of its circulating notes, upon demand of payment duly made during the usual hours of business, at the office of such association, or at its designated place of redemption, the holder may cause the same to be protested, in one package, by a notary public, unless the president or cashier of the association whose notes are presented for payment, or the president or cashier of the association at the place at which they are redeemable offers to waive demand and notice of the protest, and, in pursuance of such offer, makes, signs, and delivers to the party making such demand an admission in writing, stating the time of the demand, the amount demanded, and the fact of the non-payment thereof. The notary public, on making such protest, or upon receiving such admission, shall forthwith forward such admission or notice of protest to the Comptroller of the Currency, retaining a copy thereof. If, however, satisfactory proof is produced to the notary public that the payment of the notes demanded is restrained by order of any court of competent jurisdiction, he shall not protest the same. When the holder of any notes causes more than one note or package to be protested on the same day, he shall not receive pay for more than one protest.

One protest fee, only, on same day.

(SEC. 5227.) On receiving notice that any national banking association has failed to redeem any of its circulating notes, as specified in the preceding section, the Comptroller of the Currency, with the concurrence of the Secretary of the Treasury, may appoint a special agent, of whose appointment immediate notice shall be given to such association, who shall immediately proceed to ascertain whether it has refused to pay its circulating notes in the lawful money of the United States, when demanded, and shall report to the Comptroller the fact so ascertained. If, from such protest, and the report so made, the Comptroller is satisfied that such association has refused to pay its circulating notes and is in default, he shall, within thirty days after he has received notice of such failure, declare the bonds deposited by such association forfeited to the United States, and they shall thereupon be so forfeited.

Examination by special agent, after notice of protest.

Forfeiture of bonds.

(SEC. 5228.) After a default on the part of an association to pay any of its circulating notes has been ascertained by the Comptroller, and notice thereof has been given by him to the association, it shall not be lawful for the association suffering the same to pay out any of its notes, discount any notes or bills, or otherwise prosecute the business of banking, except to receive and

Association not to do business after notice of protest.

Act of Feb. 18, 1875, correcting Rev. Stat.

safely keep money belonging to it, and to deliver special deposits.

Notice to noteholders.

(SEC. 5229.) Immediately upon declaring the bonds of an association forfeited for non-payment of its notes, the Comptroller shall give notice, in such manner as the Secretary of the Treasury shall, by general rules or otherwise, direct, to the holders of the circulating notes of such association, to present them for payment at the Treasury of the United States; and the same shall be paid as presented in lawful money of the United States; whereupon the Comptroller may, in his discretion, cancel an amount of bonds pledged by such association equal at current market rates, not exceeding par, to the notes paid.

Redemption of notes at Treasury, and cancellation of bonds.

Sale of bonds at auction.

(SEC. 5230.) Whenever the Comptroller has become satisfied, by the protest or the waiver and admission specified in section fifty-two hundred and twenty-six, or by the report provided for in section fifty-two hundred and twenty-seven, that any association has refused to pay its circulating notes, he may, instead of canceling its bonds, cause so much of them as may be necessary to redeem its outstanding notes to be sold at public auction in the city of New York, after giving thirty days' notice of such sale to the association. For any deficiency in the proceeds of all the bonds of an association, when thus sold, to reimburse to the United States the amount expended in paying the circulating notes of the association, the United States shall have a paramount lien upon all its assets; and such deficiency shall be made good out of such assets in preference to any and all other claims whatsoever, except the necessary costs and expenses of administering the same.

The United States to have a paramount lien upon assets of associations.

Sale of bonds at private sale.

(SEC. 5231.) The Comptroller may, if he deems it for the interest of the United States, sell at private sale any of the bonds of an association shown to have made default in paying its notes, and receive therefor either money or the circulating notes of the association. But no such bonds shall be sold by private sale for less than par, nor for less than the market value thereof at the time of sale; and no sales of any such bonds, either public or private, shall be complete until the transfer of

Transfer of bonds sold.

the bonds shall have been made with the formalities prescribed by sections fifty-one hundred and sixty-two, fifty-one hundred and sixty-three, and-fifty-one hundred and sixty-four.

(SEC. 5232.) The Secretary of the Treasury may, from time to time, make such regulations respecting the disposition to be made of circulating notes after presentation at the Treasury of the United States for payment, and respecting the perpetuation of the evidence of the payment thereof, as may seem to him proper. Disposition to be made of notes redeemed by Treasurer.

(SEC. 5233.) All notes of national banking associations presented at the Treasury of the United States for payment shall, on being paid, be canceled. Cancellation of notes.

(SEC. 5234.) On becoming satisfied, as specified in sections fifty-two hundred and twenty-six and fifty-two hundred and twenty-seven, that any association has refused to pay its circulating notes as therein mentioned, and is in default, the Comptroller of the Currency may forthwith appoint a receiver, and require of him such bond and security as he deems proper. Such receiver, under the direction of the Comptroller, shall take possession of the books, records, and assets of every description of such association, collect all debts, dues, and claims belonging to it, and, upon the order of a court of record of competent jurisdiction, may sell or compound all bad or doubtful debts, and, on a like order, may sell all the real and personal property of such association, on such terms as the court shall direct; and may, if necessary to pay the debts of such association, enforce the individual liability of the stockholders. Such receiver shall pay over all money so made to the Treasurer of the United States, subject to the order of the Comptroller, and also make report to the Comptroller of all his acts and proceedings. Appointment and duties of receivers. Kennedy *vs.* Gibson, 8 Wall. 498; Bank of Bethel *vs.* Pahquioque Bank, 14 Wall. 383; Bank *vs.* Kennedy, 16 Wall. 19; *In re.* Platt, Receiver, etc., 1 Ben. 534.

That whenever any national banking association shall be dissolved, and its rights, privileges, and franchises declared forfeited, as prescribed in section fifty-two hundred and thirty-nine of the Revised Statutes of the United States, or whenever any creditor of any national banking association shall have obtained a judgment against it in any court of record, and made application, accompanied June 30, 1876.

by a certificate from the clerk of the court stating that such judgment has been rendered and has remained unpaid for the space of thirty days; or whenever the Comptroller shall become satisfied of the insolvency of a national banking association, he may, after due examination of its affairs, in either case, appoint a receiver, who shall proceed to close up such association, and enforce the personal liability of the shareholders, as provided in section fifty-two hundred and thirty-four of said statutes.

When the Comptroller may appoint a receiver.

Liability of stockholders of liquidating banks.

That when any national banking association shall have gone into liquidation under the provisions of section five thousand two hundred and twenty of said statutes, the individual liability of the shareholders provided for by section fifty-one hundred and fifty-one of said statutes may be enforced by any creditor of such association, by bill in equity in the nature of a creditor's bill, brought by such creditor on behalf of himself and of all other creditors of the association, against the shareholders thereof, in any court of the United States having original jurisdiction in equity for the district in which such association may have been located or established.

That whenever any association shall have been or shall be placed in the hands of a receiver, as provided in section fifty-two hundred and thirty-four and other sections of said statutes, and when, as provided in section fifty-two hundred and thirty-six thereof, the Comptroller shall have paid to each and every creditor of such association, not including shareholders who are creditors of such association, whose claim or claims as such creditor shall have been proved, or allowed as therein prescribed, the full amount of such claims and all expenses of the receivership, and the redemption of the circulating notes of such association shall have been provided for by depositing lawful money of the United States with the Treasurer of the United States, the Comptroller of the Currency shall call a meeting of the shareholders of such association by giving notice thereof for thirty days in a newspaper published in the town, city, or county where the business of such association was carried on, or if no newspaper is there published, in the newspaper published

Comptroller shall call meetings of shareholders of banks in the hands of receivers.

nearest thereto, at which meeting the shareholders shall elect an agent, voting by ballot, in person or by proxy, each share of stock entitling the holder to one vote; and when such agent shall have received votes representing at least a majority of the stock in value and number of shares, and when any of the shareholders of the association shall have executed and filed a bond to the satisfaction of the Comptroller of the Currency, conditioned for the payment and discharge in full of any and every claim that may hereafter be proved and allowed against such association by and before a competent court, and for the faithful performance and discharge of all and singular the duties of such trust, the Comptroller and the receiver shall thereupon transfer and deliver to such agent all the undivided or uncollected or other assets and property of such association then remaining in the hands or subject to the order or control of said Comptroller and said receiver, or either of them; and for this purpose, said Comptroller and said receiver are hereby severally empowered to execute any deed, assignment, transfer, or other instrument in writing that may be necessary and proper; whereupon the said Comptroller and the said receiver shall, by virtue of this act, be discharged and released from any and all liabilities to such association, and to each and all of the creditors and shareholders thereof; and such agent is hereby authorized to sell, compromise, or compound the debts due to such association upon the order of a competent court of record or of the United States circuit court for the district where the business of the association was carried on. Such agent shall hold, control, and dispose of the assets and property of any association which he may receive as hereinbefore provided for the benefit of the shareholders of such association as they, or a majority of them in value or number of shares, may direct, distributing such assets and property among such shareholders in proportion to the shares held by each; and he may, in his own name or in the name of such association, sue and be sued, and do all other lawful acts and things necessary to finally settle and distribute the assets and property in his hands. In selecting an agent

Transfer of assets of bank to agent of the shareholder.

as hereinbefore provided, administrators or executors of deceased shareholders may act and sign as the decedent might have done if living, and guardians may so act and sign for their ward or wards.

Notice by Comptroller to creditors.

(SEC. 5235.) The Comptroller shall, upon appointing a receiver, cause notice to be given, by advertisement in such newspapers as he may direct, for three consecutive months, calling on all persons who may have claims against such association to present the same, and to make legal proof thereof.

Dividends by Comptroller to creditors. Bank of Bethel *vs.* Pahquioque Bank, 14 Wall. 383.

(SEC. 5236.) From time to time, after full provision has been first made for refunding to the United States any deficiency in redeeming the notes of such association, the Comptroller shall make a ratable dividend of the money so paid over to him by such receiver on all such claims as may have been proved to his satisfaction or adjudicated in a court of competent jurisdiction, and, as the proceeds of the assets of such association are paid over to him, shall make further dividends on all claims previously proved or adjudicated; and the remainder of the proceeds, if any, shall be paid over to the shareholders of such association, or their legal representatives, in proportion to the stock by them respectively held.

Injunction upon receivership.

(SEC. 5237.) Whenever an association against which proceedings have been instituted, on account of any alleged refusal to redeem its circulating notes as aforesaid, denies having failed to do so, it may, at any time within ten days after it has been notified of the appointment of an agent, as provided in section fifty-two hundred and twenty-seven, apply to the nearest circuit, or district, or territorial court of the United States to enjoin further proceedings in the premises; and such court, after citing the Comptroller of the Currency to show cause why further proceedings should not be enjoined, and after the decision of the court or finding of a jury that such association has not refused to redeem its circulating notes, when legally presented, in the lawful money of the United States, shall make an order enjoining the Comptroller, and any receiver acting under his direction, from all further proceedings on account of such alleged refusal.

(SEC. 5238.) All fees for protesting the notes issued by any national banking association shall be paid by the person procuring the protest to be made, and such association shall be liable therefor; but no part of the bonds deposited by such association shall be applied to the payment of such fees. All expenses of any preliminary or other examinations into the condition of any association shall be paid by such association. All expenses of any receivership shall be paid out of the assets of such association before distribution of the proceeds thereof. **Fees and expenses of protest and receivership.**

(SEC. 5239.) If the directors of any national banking association shall knowingly violate, or knowingly permit any of the officers, agents or servants of the association to violate any of the provisions of this Title, all the rights, privileges and franchises of the association shall be thereby forfeited. Such violation shall, however, be determined and adjudged by a proper circuit, district or territorial court of the United States, in a suit brought for that purpose by the Comptroller of the Currency, in his own name, before the association shall be declared dissolved. And in cases of such violation, every director who participated in or assented to the same shall be held liable in his personal and individual capacity for all damages which the association, its shareholders, or any other person, shall have sustained in consequence of such violation. **Penalty for violation of provisions of this Title.** **Violation, how determined.** **Liability of directors for violation.**

(SEC. 5242.) All transfers of the notes, bonds, bills of exchange, or other evidences of debt owing to any national banking association, or of deposits to its credit; all assignments of mortgages, sureties on real estate, or of judgments or decrees in its favor; all deposits of money, bullion, or other valuable thing for its use, or for the use of any of its shareholders or creditors; and all payments of money to either, made after the commission of an act of insolvency, or in contemplation thereof, made with a view to prevent the application of its assets in the manner prescribed by this chapter, or with a view to the preference of one creditor to another, except in payment of its circulating notes, shall be utterly null and void. **Transfers, assignments, etc., after an act of insolvency, void.**

Attachment not to issue before final judgment in State court.

No attachment, injunction, or execution, shall be issued against such association or its property before final judgment in any suit, action, or proceeding, in any State, county, or municipal court.

CHAPTER V.

TAX ON CIRCULATION NOT AUTHORIZED BY CONGRESS.

Capital of State bank converted into national association.

(Sec. 3410.) The capital of any State bank or banking association which has ceased or shall cease to exist, or which has been or shall be converted into a national bank, shall be assumed to be the capital as it existed immediately before such bank ceased to exist or was converted as aforesaid.

Circulation, when exempted from tax.

(Sec. 3411.) Whenever the outstanding circulation of any bank, association, corporation, company, or person is reduced to an amount not exceeding five per centum of the chartered or declared capital existing at the time the same was issued, said circulation shall be free from taxation; and whenever any bank which has ceased to issue notes for circulation, deposits in the Treasury of the United States, in lawful money, the amount of its outstanding circulation, to be redeemed at par, under such regulations as the Secretary of the Treasury shall prescribe, it shall be exempt from any tax upon such circulation.

Tax on notes of persons or State banks, used for circulation. See act of Feb. 8, 1875.

(Sec. 3412.) Every national banking association, State bank, or State banking association, shall pay a tax of ten per centum on the amount of notes of any person, or of any State bank or State banking association, used for circulation and paid out by them.

Tax on notes of towns, cities, etc., used for circulation. *Ibid.*

(Sec. 3413.) Every national banking association, State bank, or banker, or association, shall pay a tax of ten per centum on the amount of notes of any town, city, or municipal corporation, paid out by them.

Monthly returns of notes of persons, cities,

(Sec. 3414.) A true and complete return of the monthly amount of circulation, of deposits, and of capital, as aforesaid, and of the monthly amount of notes of persons, town, city, or municipal corporation, State banks, or State banking associations paid out as aforesaid for the previous six months, shall be made and rendered in duplicate on the first day of December and the first day of June, by each of such banks, associations, corporations, companies, or persons, with a declaration annexed thereto, under the oath of such person, or of the president or cashier of such bank, association, corporation, or company, in such form and manner as may be prescribed by the Commissioner of Internal Revenue, that the same contains a true and faithful statement of the amounts subject to tax, as aforesaid; and one copy shall be transmitted to the collector of the district in which any such bank, association, corporation, or company is situated, or in which such person has his place of business, and one copy to the Commissioner of Internal Revenue.

State banks, etc., paid out. *Ibid.*

(SEC. 3415.) In default of the returns provided in the preceding section, the amount of circulation, deposit, capital, and notes of persons, town, city, and municipal corporations, State banks, and State banking associations paid out, as aforesaid, shall be estimated by the Commissioner of Internal Revenue, upon the best information he can obtain. And for any refusal or neglect to make return and payment, any such bank, association, corporation, company, or person so in default shall pay a penalty of two hundred dollars, besides the additional penalty and forfeitures provided in other cases.

In default of returns, Commissioner to estimate.

(SEC. 3416.) Whenever any State bank or banking association has been converted into a national banking association, and such national banking association has assumed the liabilities of such State bank or banking association, including the redemption of its bills, by any agreement or understanding whatever with the representatives of such State bank or banking association, such national banking association shall be held to make the required return and payment on the circulation outstanding, so long as such circulation shall exceed five per centum of the capital before such conversion of such State bank or banking association.

National bank to make return and payment of tax of converted State bank.

(SEC. 3417.) The provisions of this chapter, relating to the tax on the deposits, capital, and circulation of

Provisions for tax on deposits,

capital and circulation, not to apply to national banks. Act of Feb. 18, 1875, correcting Rev. Stat.

banks, and to their returns, except as contained in sections thirty-four hundred and ten, thirty-four hundred and eleven, thirty-four hundred and twelve, thirty-four hundred and thirteen, and thirty-four hundred and sixteen, and such parts of sections thirty-four hundred and fourteen and thirty-four hundred and fifteen as relate to the tax of ten per centum on certain notes, shall not apply to associations which are taxed under and by virtue of Title "NATIONAL BANKS."

United States securities exempt from local taxation. Bank *vs.* Supervisors, 7 Wall. 26.

(SEC. 3701.) All stocks, bonds, treasury notes, and other obligations of the United States, shall be exempt from taxation by or under State or municipal or local authority.

STAMP-TAX ON BANK-CHECKS.

Tax on bank checks. Act of Feb. 8, 1875, sec. 15.

(SEC. 3418.) There shall be levied, collected, and paid for and in respect of every bank-check, draft, or order for the payment of money, drawn upon any bank, banker, or trust company, at sight or on demand, by any person who makes, signs, or issues the same, or for whose use or benefit the same is made, signed, or issued, two cents.

Official checks exempt from tax.

(SEC. 3420.) All bank-checks, drafts, or orders, as aforesaid, issued by the officers of the United States Government, or by officers of any State, county, town, or other municipal corporation, are exempt from taxation: *Provided*, That it is the intent hereby to exempt from liability to taxation such State, county, town, or other municipal corporations in the exercise only of functions strictly belonging to them in their ordinary governmental and municipal capacity.

Unstamped checks not admissible in evidence.

(SEC. 3421.) No bank-check, draft, or order, required by law to be stamped, which is issued without being duly stamped, nor any copy thereof, shall be admitted or used in evidence in any court until a legal stamp, denoting the amount of tax, is affixed thereto, as prescribed by law.

Penalty for failure to stamp checks.

(SEC. 3422.) Any person or persons who shall make, sign, or issue, or who shall cause to be made, signed, or issued, any instrument, document, or paper of any kind or description whatsoever, or shall accept, negotiate, or pay, or cause to be accepted, negotiated, or paid, any draft, or order, for the payment of money, without the same being duly stamped, or having thereupon an adhesive stamp for denoting the tax chargeable thereon, and canceled in the manner required by law, with intent to evade the provisions of this Title, shall, for every such offense, forfeit the sum of fifty dollars, and such instrument, document or paper, draft, [or] order, not being stamped according to law, shall be deemed invalid and of no effect: *Provided*, That hereafter, in all cases where the party has not affixed to any instrument the stamp required by law thereon, at the time of making or issuing the said instrument, and he or they, or any party having an interest therein, shall be subsequently desirous of affixing such stamp to said instrument, or if said instrument be lost, to a copy thereof, he or they shall appear before the collector of the revenue of the proper district, who shall, upon the payment of the price of the proper stamp required by law, and of a penalty of double the amount of tax remaining unpaid, but in no case less than five dollars, and where the whole amount of the tax denoted by the stamp required shall exceed the sum of fifty dollars, on payment also of interest, at the rate of six per centum on said tax from the day on which such stamp ought to have been affixed, affix the proper stamp to such instrument or copy, and note upon the margin thereof the date of his so doing, and the fact that such penalty has been paid; and the same shall thereupon be deemed and held to be as valid, to all intents and purposes, as if stamped when made or issued. . . . **Stamp may be subsequently affixed by collector.**

(SEC. 3423.) In all cases where an adhesive stamp is used for denoting any tax imposed under this chapter, except as hereinafter provided, the person using or affixing the same shall write thereon the initials of his name and the date on which such stamp is attached or used, so that it may not again be used. **Stamps to be canceled.** And every person who fraudulently makes use of an adhesive stamp to denote any tax imposed by this chapter without so effectually canceling and obliterating such stamp, except as before mentioned, shall forfeit the sum of fifty dollars. . . . **Penalty for fraudulent use.**

Method of cancellation.

(SEC. 3424.) The Commissioner of Internal Revenue is authorized to prescribe such method for the cancellation of stamps as substitute for, or in addition to the method prescribed in this chapter, as he may deem expedient and effectual. . . .

CHAPTER VII.

CRIMES AND MISDEMEANORS.

Penalty for unlawfully countersigning or delivering circulating notes.

(SEC. 5187.) No officer acting under the provisions of this Title shall countersign or deliver to any association, or to any other company or person, any circulating notes contemplated by this Title, except in accordance with the true intent and meaning of its provisions. Every officer who violates this section shall be deemed guilty of a high misdemeanor, and shall be fined not more than double the amount so countersigned and delivered, and imprisoned not less than one year and not more than fifteen years.

Penalty for imitating national-bank notes, etc.

(SEC. 5188.) It shall not be lawful to design, engrave, print, or in any manner make or execute, or to utter, issue, distribute, circulate, or use, any business or professional card, notice, placard, circular, hand-bill, or advertisement, in the likeness or similitude of any circulating note or other obligation or security of any banking association organized or acting under the laws of the United States which has been or may be issued under this Title or any act of Congress, or to write, print, or otherwise impress upon any such note, obligation or security any business or professional card, notice or advertisement, or any notice or advertisement of any matter or thing whatever. Every person who violates this section shall be liable to a penalty of one hundred dollars, recoverable one-half to the use of the informer.

Penalty for mutilating national-bank notes, etc.

(SEC. 5189.) Every person who mutilates, cuts, defaces, disfigures, or perforates with holes, or unites or cements together, or does any other thing to any bank-bill, draft, note, or other evidence of debt, issued by any national banking association, or who causes or procures the same to be done, with intent to render such bank-bill, draft, note, or other evidence of debt unfit to be reissued by said association, shall be liable to a penalty of fifty dollars, recoverable by the association.

Penalty for offering or receiving United States or national-bank notes as security for loan, etc.

(SEC. 5207.) No association shall hereafter offer or receive United States notes or national-bank notes as security or as collateral security for any loan of money, or for a consideration agree to withhold the same from use, or offer or receive the custody or promise of custody of such notes as security, or as collateral security, or consideration for any loan of money. Any association offending against the provisions of this section shall be deemed guilty of a misdemeanor, and shall be fined not more than one thousand dollars and a further sum equal to one third of the money so loaned. The officer or officers of any association who shall make any such loan shall be liable for a further sum equal to one quarter of the money loaned; and any fine or penalty incurred by a violation of this section shall be recoverable for the benefit of the party bringing such suit.

Penalty for embezzlement.

(SEC. 5209.) Every president, director, cashier, teller, clerk, or agent of any association, who embezzles, abstracts, or willfully misapplies any of the moneys, funds, or credits of the association; or who, without authority from the directors, issues or puts in circulation any of the notes of the association; or who, without such authority, issues or puts forth any certificate of deposit, draws any order or bill of exchange, makes any acceptance, assigns any note, bond, draft, bill of exchange, mortgage, judgment, or decree; or who makes any false entry in any book, report, or statement of the association, with intent, in either case, to injure or defraud the association or any other company, body politic or corporate, or any individual person, or to deceive any officer of the association, or any agent appointed to examine the affairs of any such association; and every person who with like intent aids or abets any officer, clerk, or agent in any violation of this section, shall be deemed guilty of a misdemeanor, and shall be imprisoned not less than five years nor more than ten.

Obligations or other securities of the United States defined. Act of Feb. 18, 1875, correcting Rev. Stat.

(SEC. 5413.) The words "obligation or other security of the United States" shall be held to mean all bonds, certificates of indebtedness, national-bank currency, coupons, United States notes, treasury notes, fractional notes, certificates of deposit, bills, checks or drafts for money, drawn by or upon authorized officers of the United States, stamps and other representatives of value, of whatever denomination, which have been or may [be] issued under any act of Congress.

Penalty for counterfeiting national-bank notes.

(SEC. 5415.) Every person who falsely makes, forges, or counterfeits, or causes or procures to be made, forged or counterfeited, or willingly aids or assists in falsely making, forging, or counterfeiting, any note in imitation of, or purporting to be in imitation of, the circulating notes, issued by any banking association now or hereafter authorized and acting under the laws of the United States; or who passes, utters, or publishes, or attempts to pass, utter, or publish, any false, forged, or counterfeited note, purporting to be issued by any such association doing a banking business, knowing the same to be falsely made, forged, or counterfeited, or who falsely alters, or causes or procures to be falsely altered, or willingly aids or assists in falsely altering any such circulating notes, or passes, utters, or publishes, or attempts to pass, utter, or publish as true, any falsely altered or spurious circulating note issued, or purporting to have been issued, by any such banking association, knowing the same to be falsely altered or spurious, shall be imprisoned at hard labor not less than five years nor more than fifteen years, and fined not more than one thousand dollars.

Penalty for using plates to print notes without authority.

(SEC. 5430.) Every person having control, custody, or possession of any plate, or any part thereof, from which has been printed, or which may be prepared by direction of the Secretary of the Treasury for the purpose of printing, any obligation or other security of the United States, who uses such plate, or knowingly suffers the same to be used for the purpose of printing any such or similar obligation, or other security, or any part thereof, except as may be printed for the use of the United States by order of the proper officer thereof; and every person who en-

Engraving false plate.

graves, or causes or procures to be engraved, or assists in

engraving, any plate in the likeness of any plate designed for the printing of such obligation or other security, or who sells any such plate, or who brings into the United States from any foreign place any such plate, except under the direction of the Secretary of the Treasury or other proper officer, or with any other intent, in either case, than that such plate be used for the printing of the obligations or other securities of the United States; or who has in his control, custody, or possession any metallic plate engraved after the similitude of any plate from which any such obligation or other security has been printed, with intent to use such plate, or suffer the same to be used in forging or counterfeiting any such obligation or other security, or any part thereof; or who has in his possession or custody, except under authority from the Secretary of the Treasury or other proper officer, any obligation or other security, engraved and printed after the similitude of any obligation or other security issued under the authority of the United States with intent to sell or otherwise use the same; and every person who prints, photographs, or in any other manner makes or executes, or causes to be printed, photographed, made, or executed, or aids in printing, photographing, making, or executing any engraving, photograph, print, or impression in the likeness of any such obligation or other security, or any part thereof, or who sells any such engraving, photograph, print, or impression, except to the United States, or who brings into the United States from any foreign place any such engraving, photograph, print or impression, except by direction of some proper officer of the United States, or who has or retains in his control or possession, after a distinctive paper has been adopted by the Secretary of the Treasury for the obligations and other securities of the United States, any similar paper adapted to the making of any such obligation or other security, except under the authority of the Secretary of the Treasury or some other proper officer of the United States, shall be punished by a fine of not more than five thousand dollars, or by imprisonment at hard labor not more than fifteen years, or by both.

Having in possession false plate.

Having in possession spurious national-bank notes.

Printing or photographing notes, etc.

Bringing into the United States photographed notes, etc.

Having in possession distinctive bank-note paper.

Penalty for passing, selling, etc., counterfeit or altered notes.

(SEC. 5431.) Every person who, with intent to defraud, passes, utters, publishes, or sells, or attempts to pass, utter, publish, or sell, or brings into the United States with intent to pass, publish, utter, or sell, or keeps in possession or conceals with like intent any falsely made, forged, counterfeited, or altered obligation, or other security of the United States, shall be punished by a fine of not more than five thousand dollars, and by imprisonment at hard labor not more than fifteen years.

Penalty for taking impression of tools, implements, etc.

(SEC. 5432.) Every person who, without authority from the United States, takes, procures, or makes, upon lead, foil, wax, plaster, paper, or any other substance or material, an impression, stamp, or imprint of, from, or by the use of any bed-plate, bed-piece, die, roll, plate, seal, type, or other tool, implement, instrument, or thing used or fitted or intended to be used, in printing, stamping, or impressing, or in making other tools, implements, instruments, or things, to be used, or fitted or intended to be used, in printing, stamping, or impressing any kind or description of obligation or other security of the United States, now authorized or hereafter to be authorized by the United States, or circulating note or evidence of debt of any banking association under the laws thereof, shall be punished by imprisonment at hard labor not more than ten years, or by a fine of not more than five thousand dollars, or both.

Penalty for having in possession impression of tools, implements, etc.

(SEC. 5433.) Every person who, with intent to defraud, has in his possession, keeping, custody or control, without authority from the United States, any imprint, stamp, or impression, taken or made upon any substance or material whatsoever, of any tool, implement, instrument, or thing, used, or fitted or intended to be used, for any of the purposes mentioned in the preceding section; or who, with intent to defraud, sells, gives or delivers any such imprint, stamp, or impression to any other person, shall be punished by imprisonment at hard labor not more than ten years, or by a fine of not more than five thousand dollars.

Penalty for buying, selling or dealing in

(SEC. 5434.) Every person who buys, sells, exchanges, transfers, receives, or delivers, any false, forged, counterfeited, or altered obligation or other security of the

United States, or circulating note of any banking association organized or acting under the laws thereof, which has been or may hereafter be issued by virtue of any act of Congress, with the intent that the same be passed, published, or used as true and genuine, shall be imprisoned at hard labor not more than ten years, or fined not more than five thousand dollars, or both.

forged or altered notes.

(SEC. 5437.) In all cases where the charter of any corporation which has been or may be created by act of Congress has expired or may hereafter expire, if any director, officer, or agent of the corporation, or any trustee thereof, or any agent of such trustee, or any person having in his possession or under his control the property of the corporation for the purpose of paying or redeeming its notes and obligations, knowingly issues, re-issues, or utters as money, or in any other way knowingly puts in circulation any bill, note, check, draft, or other security purporting to have been made by any such corporation whose charter has expired, or by any officer thereof, or purporting to have been made under authority derived therefrom, or if any person knowingly aids in any such act, he shall be punished by a fine of not more than ten thousand dollars, or by imprisonment not less than one year nor more than five years, or by both such fine and imprisonment. But nothing herein shall be construed to make it unlawful for any person, not being such director, officer, or agent of the corporation, or any trustee thereof, or any agent of such trustee, or any person having in his possession or under his control the property of the corporation for the purpose hereinbefore set forth, who has received or may hereafter receive such bill, note, check, draft, or other security, bona fide and in the ordinary transactions of business, to utter as money or otherwise circulate the same.

Penalty for unlawfully putting in circulation the notes, drafts, etc., of closed associations.

Persons not officers or agents of closed associations may circulate the notes of such associations.

THE INTEREST LAWS OF THE STATES.

[Compiled from the *Banker's Almanac and Register* for 1875.]

See page 225 for penalty for usury by national banks.

	State.	Rate per cent. Legal.	Special.	Penalty of Usury.
1	Alabama	8	—	Loss of interest.
2	Arizona	10	§	None.
3	Arkansas	6	§	None.
4	California	10	§	None.
5	Colorado	10	§	None.
6	Connecticut	7	§	Forfeiture of all interest.
7	Dacotah	7	18	Forfeiture of contract.
8	Delaware	6	6	Forfeiture of contract.
9	Dist. of Columbia	6	10	Forfeiture of all interest.
10	Florida	8	§	None.
11	Georgia	7	7	None.
12	Idaho	*10	24	$300, or imprison't 6 mos. or both.
13	Illinois	6	10	Forfeiture of all the interest.
14	Indiana	6	10	Forfeiture of interest and costs.
15	Iowa	6	10	Forfeiture of excess.
16	Kansas	7	12	Forfeiture of excess over 12 per ct.
17	Kentucky	6	10	Forfeiture of all the interest.
18	Louisiana	5	8	Forfeiture of interest.
19	Maine	6	§	Forfeiture of excess.
20	Maryland	6	6	Forfeiture of excess.
21	Massachusetts	6	§	None. (6 per cent on judgments.)
22	Michigan	7	10	Forfeiture of excess.
23	Minnesota	7	12	Forfeiture of excess over 7 per cent.
24	Mississippi	6	§	None.
25	Missouri	6	10	Forfeiture of all interest.
26	Montana	10	—	None.
27	Nebraska	10	12	Forfeiture of all interest, and costs.
28	Nevada	10	§	None.
29	New Hampshire	6	6	Forf. of 3 times the interest rec'd.
30	New Jersey	7	7	Forfeiture of all interest.
31	New Mexico	6	12	None.
32	New York	*7	7	Forfeiture of contract.
33	North Carolina	6	8	Forfeiture of interest.

State.	Rate per cent. Legal.	Special.	Penalty of Usury.
34 Ohio	6..	8..	Forfeiture of excess.
35 Oregon	10..	12..	Forf. of inter't, principal and costs.
36 Pennsylvania	6..	6..	Forf. of excess. *Act May 28, 1858.*
37 Rhode Island	†6..	§..	Forfeiture, unless a greater rate is contracted.
38 South Carolina	7..	§..	None.
39 Tennessee	6..	10..	Forfeiture of excess over 6 per cent, and $100 fine.
40 Texas	8..	§..	None.
41 Utah	10..	§..	None.
42 Vermont	6..	‡7..	Forfeiture of excess.
43 Virginia	6..	12..	Forfeiture of contract.
44 Washington Terr.	10..	§..	None.
45 West Virginia	6..	6..	Forfeiture of excess.
46 Wisconsin	7..	10..	Forfeiture of all the interest.
47 Wyoming	10..	§..	None.

* Usurers liable to arrest for misdemeanor.
† Rate on judgments unless otherwise expressed.
‡ On railroad bonds only.
§ No limit.

TABLE No. 1.—NATIONAL BANKS IN THE UNITED STATES IN OCTOBER OF EACH YEAR.

	No. of Banks.	Capital.	Surplus.	Deposits.	Loans.
1863	66	$7,188,393	$........	$9,478,860	$5,466,088
1864	508	86,782,802	2,010,286	157,028,921	93,238,657
1865	1513	393,157,206	38,713,380	723,281,252	478,170,136
1866	1644	415,278,969	53,359,277	734,394,802	603,247,503
1867	1642	420,073,415	66,695,587	678,426,603	609,675,214
1868	1644	420,634,511	77,995,761	724,965,504	657,668,847
1869	1617	426,399,151	86,165,334	641,946,755	682,883,106
1870	1615	430,399,301	94,705,740	625,889,332	715,928,079
1871	1767	458,255,696	101,112,672	789,716,706	831,552,210
1872	1919	479,629,144	110,257,516	869,544,773	872,500,104
1873	1973	490,678,367	120,314,499	650,304,688	801,067,032
1874	2004	493,765,121	128,958,107	865,119,036	949,870,628
1875	2087	504,829,700	134,356,076	885,087,560	980,222,251
1876 (March)	2090	504,768,666	133,089,012	824,980,049	945,868,248

For comparison with the above amounts the following summary of the condition of banks in the United States about January 1, 1857, is taken from the annual report of Hon. Howell Cobb, then Secretary of the Treasury:

No. of Banks.	Capital.	Deposits.	Loans.
133	$370,834,686	$230,351,352	$684,456,887

TABLE No. 2.—RELATIVE VALUES OF GOLD AND UNITED STATES NOTES.

Showing the gold value of United States notes with gold at any price not exceeding 285 in currency.*

Premium on Gold.	Gold Value Legal T'rs.	Premium on Gold.	Gold Value Legal T'rs.	Premium on Gold.	Gold Value Legal T'rs.	Premium on Gold.	Gold Value Legal T'rs.	Premium on Gold.	Gold Value Legal T'rs.
1	.99	38	.72½	75	.57⅛	112	.47⅛	149	.40⅛
2	.98	39	.72	76	.56¾	113	.47	150	.40
3	.97	40	.71½	77	.56½	114	.46¾	151	.39⅞
4	.96¼	41	.71	78	.56⅛	115	.46½	152	.39⅔
5	.95¼	42	.70½	79	.55¾	116	.46¼	153	.39½
6	.94⅓	43	.70	80	.55½	117	.46	154	.39⅓
7	.93½	44	.69½	81	.55¼	118	.45⅞	155	.39⅛
8	.92½	45	.60	82	.55	119	.45⅔	156	.39
9	.91¾	46	.68½	83	.54⅔	120	.45½	157	.38⅞
10	.91	47	.68	84	.54⅓	121	.45¼	158	.38¾
11	.90⅛	48	.67½	85	.54	122	.45	159	.38⅝
12	.89¼	49	.67⅛	86	.53¾	123	.44⅞	160	.38½
13	.88½	50	.66⅔	87	.53½	124	.44⅔	161	.38⅓
14	.87¾	51	.66¼	88	.53¼	125	.44½	162	.38⅛
15	.87	52	.65¾	89	.53	126	.44¼	163	.38
16	.86¼	53	.65⅜	90	.52⅝	127	.44	164	.37⅞
17	.85½	54	.65	91	.52⅓	128	.43⅞	165	.37¾
18	.84¾	55	.64½	92	.52	129	.43⅔	166	.37⅝
19	.84	56	.64⅛	93	.51¾	130	.43½	167	.37½
20	.83½	57	.63⅔	94	.51½	131	.43¼	168	.37⅓
21	.82⅝	58	.63¼	95	.51¼	132	.43	169	.37⅛
22	.82	59	.62⅞	96	.51	133	.42⅞	170	.37
23	.81½	60	.62½	97	.50¾	134	.42⅔	171	.36⅞
24	.80⅔	61	.62⅛	98	.50½	135	.42½	172	.36¾
25	.80	62	.61¾	99	.50¼	136	.42⅓	173	.36⅝
26	.79⅓	63	.61⅜	100	.50	137	.42⅛	174	.36½
27	.78¾	64	.61	101	.49¾	138	.42	175	.36⅜
28	.78⅛	65	.60⅔	102	.49½	139	.41⅞	176	.36¼
29	.77½	66	.60¼	103	.49¼	140	.41⅔	177	.36⅛
30	.77	67	.59⅞	104	.49	141	.41½	178	.36
31	.76⅜	68	.59½	105	.48¾	142	.41⅓	179	.35⅞
32	.75¼	69	.59⅛	106	.48½	143	.41⅛	180	.35¾
33	.75⅛	70	.58¾	107	.48¼	144	.41	181	.35⅝
34	.74⅝	71	.58½	108	.48	145	.40⅞	182	.35½
35	.74⅛	72	.58⅛	109	.47⅞	146	.40⅔	183	.35⅓
36	.73½	73	.57¾	110	.47⅝	147	.40½	184	.36¼
37	.73	74	.57½	111	.47⅜	148	.40⅓	185	.35⅛

* According to the officially-published quotations of the gold market in New York, the currency price of $100 gold reached its maximum on the 11th day of July, 1864, the quotations for that day ranging from $276 to $285. The average price of $100 gold for the month of July, 1864, was $258.10, and the average price of $100 gold for the quarter-year ending September 30, 1864, was $244.90.

TABLE No. 3.

Showing currency price in dollars of one hundred dollars in gold in the New York market by months, quarter-years, half-years, calendar years and fiscal years, from January 1, 1862, to August 31, 1875, both inclusive.

Periods.	1862.	1863.	1864.	1865.	1866.	1867.	1868.	1869.	1870.	1871.	1872.	1873.	1874.	1875.
January	102.5	145.1	155.5	216.2	140.1	134.6	138.5	135.6	121.3	110.7	109.1	112.7	111.4	112.5
February	103.5	160.5	158.6	205.5	138.4	137.4	141.4	134.4	119.5	111.5	110.3	114.1	112.3	114.5
March	101.8	154.5	162.9	173.8	130.5	135	139.5	131.3	112.6	111	110.1	115.5	112.1	115.5
April	101.5	151.5	172.7	148.5	127.3	135.6	138.7	132.9	113.1	110.6	111.1	117.8	113.4	114.8
May	103.3	148.9	176.3	135.6	131.8	137	139.6	139.2	114.7	111.5	113.7	117.7	112.4	115.8
June	106.5	144.5	210.7	140.1	148.7	137.5	140.1	138.1	112.9	112.4	113.9	116.5	111.3	117
July	115.5	130.6	258.1	142.1	151.6	139.4	142.7	136.1	116.8	112.4	114.3	115.7	110	114.8
August	114.5	125.8	254.1	143.5	148.7	140.8	145.5	134.2	117.9	112.4	114.4	115.4	109.7	113.5
September	118.5	134.2	222.5	143.9	145.5	143.4	143.6	136.8	114.8	114.5	113.5	112.7	109.7	115.8
October	128.5	147.7	207.2	145.5	148.3	143.5	137.1	130.2	112.8	113.2	113.2	108.9	110	.....
November	131.1	148.0	233.5	147	143.8	139.6	134.4	126.2	111.4	111.2	112.9	108.6	110.9	.....
December	132.3	151.1	227.5	146.2	136.7	134.8	135.2	121.5	110.7	109.3	112.2	110	111.7	.....
First quarter-year	102.6	153.4	159	198.5	136.3	135.7	139.8	133.8	117.8	111.1	109.8	114.1	111.9	114.2
Second quarter-year	103.8	148.3	186.6	141.4	135.9	136.7	139.5	136.7	113.6	111.5	112.9	117.3	112.4	115.9
Third quarter-year	116.2	130.2	244.9	143.2	148.6	141.2	143.9	135.7	116.5	113.1	114.1	114.6	109.8	114.7
Fourth quarter-year	130.6	148.9	222.7	146.2	142.9	139.3	135.6	126	111.6	111.2	112.8	109.2	110.9	.....
First half-year	103.2	150.8	172.8	169.9	136.1	136.2	139.6	135.3	115.7	111.3	111.4	115.7	112.2	115.1
Second half-year	123.4	139.6	233.8	144.7	145.8	140.3	139.8	130.8	114	121.1	113.4	111.9	110.3	.....
Calendar year	113.3	145.2	203.3	157.3	140.9	138.2	139.7	133	114.9	111.7	112.4	113.8	111.2	.....
Fiscal year ended June 30.	.....	137.1	156.2	201.9	140.4	141	139.9	137.5	123.3	112.7	111.8	114.6	112	112.7

TABLES Nos. 4 AND 5.

EXHIBITING THE VALUES, IN UNITED STATES MONEY OF ACCOUNT, OF THE PURE GOLD OR SILVER REPRESENTING, RESPECTIVELY, THE MONETARY UNITS OF FOREIGN COUNTRIES, AND THE VALUE OF THE STANDARD COINS IN CIRCULATION OF THE VARIOUS NATIONS OF THE WORLD, JANUARY 1, 1874.

TREASURY DEPARTMENT, WASHINGTON, D. C., *January 1, 1874.*

The first section of the act of March 3, 1873, provides "that the value of foreign coin, as expressed in the money of account of the United States, shall be that of the pure metal of such coin of standard value," and that "the values of the standard coins in circulation of the various nations of the world shall be estimated annually by the Director of the Mint, and be proclaimed on the first day of January by the Secretary of the Treasury." The following tables have been prepared and are published in compliance with the above stated provisions of law:

TABLE 4.—*Values, in United States money of account, of the pure gold or silver representing the monetary units, respectively, of foreign countries.*

Country.	Monetary unit.	Standard.	Value in U. S. money of account.
Argentine Republic	Peso fuerte	Gold	$1.00.00
Austria	Florin	Silver	.47.60
Belgium	Franc	Gold and silver	.19.30
Bolivia	Dollar	Silver	.96.50
Brazil	Millreis of 1,000 reis	Gold	.54.56
Brit'h Possessions in N. America.	Dollar	Gold	1.00.00
Central America	Dollar	Silver	.96.50
Chili	Peso	Gold	.91.23
China	Tael	Pure silver	1.61.00
Cuba	Peso	Gold	.92.58
Denmark	Crown	Gold	.26.80
Ecuador	Dollar	Silver	.96.50
Egypt	Dollar of 20 piasters	Silver	1.00.39
France	Franc	Gold and silver	.19.30
Great Britain	Pound sterling	Gold	4.86 65
Greece	Drachma	Silver	.19.30
German Empire	Mark	Gold	.23.82
Hayti	Dollar	Silver	1.00.00

Country.	Monetary Unit.	Standard.	Value in U. S. money of account.
Jamaica	Pound sterling........	Gold	4.86.65
Japan	Yen	Gold	.99.70
India	Rupee of 16 annas	Silver	.45.84
Italy.............	Lira	Gold and silver	.19.30
Liberia	Dollar	Gold	1.00.00
Mexico...........	Dollar	Silver	1.04.75
Netherlands.......	Florin	Silver	.40.50
Norway...........	Crown	Gold	.26.80
Paraguay	Peso...............	Gold	1.00.00
Peru	Dollar	Silver	.96.50
Porto Rico	Peso...............	Gold	.92.58
Portugal..........	Millreis of 1,000 reis ..	Gold	1.08.47
Russia............	Roubles of 100 copecks	Silver	.77.17
Sandwich Islands..	Dollar	Gold	1.00.00
Spain.............	Peseta of 100 centimes.	Gold and silver	.19.30
Sweden	Crown	Gold	.26.80
Switzerland	Franc...............	Gold and silver	.19.30
Tripoli...........	Mahbub of 20 piasters.	Silver	.87.09
Tunis.............	Piaster of 16 caroubs..	Silver	.12.50
Turkey	Piaster.............	Gold	.04.39
U. S. of Colombia..	Peso...............	Silver	.96.50
Uruguay..........	Patacon	Gold	.94.98
Venezuela.........	Peso...............	Silver	.77.73

NOTE.—Where silver is the legal standard and represents the unit of account, its value is reduced to the basis of gold, on the assumption that the ratio of 15½ to 1 represents the relative values of silver and gold.

TABLE 5.—*Weight, fineness and value of foreign coins, as determined by United States mint assays.*

EXPLANATORY REMARKS.

1. The weight is expressed in fractions of an ounce troy, agreeing with the terms used in the United States mints.

If it is desired to have the weight of any piece in grains, regard the thousandths of an ounce as integers, take their half, from which deduct 4 per cent of that half, and the remainder will be grains.

2. The fineness is expressed in thousandths parts, *i.e.*, so many parts of pure gold or silver in 1,000 parts of the coin. The old carat system is generally abandoned (except for jewelry), but it may be worth while to say that 41⅔ thousandths equal one carat.

3. The valuation of gold is a direct calculation from weight and

fineness, at the legal rate of 25.8 grains, 900 fine, being equal to $1; or $20.672 (nearly) per ounce of fine gold.

Foreign coins, if converted into United States coins, will be subject to a charge of one-fifth of one per cent.

4. For the silver there is no fixed legal valuation as compared with gold. The value of the silver coins is computed at the rate of 120 cents per ounce, 900 fine, payable in subsidiary silver coin, that having been the mint price when the assays were made.

The gold value of silver is to be found in the bullion markets; at present it is about 113 cents per ounce, 900 fine.

5. These tables generally give the one principal coin of each country, from which the other sizes are easily deduced. Thus, when the franc system is used, there are generally gold pieces of 40, 10, 20, and 5 francs, all in due proportion. But in silver the fractional coins are very often of less intrinsic value than the normal coin, proportionately. These are seldom exported.

GOLD COINS.

Country.	Denomination.	Weight.	Fineness.	Value in U. S. gold coin.		
		Ounces.	*1000ths.*	*Dls.*	*cts.*	*ms.*
Austria	Fourfold ducat........	0.448	986	9	13	2
Do	Souverain (not now c'd)	0.363	900	6	75	4
Do	4 florins (new)	0.104	900	1	93	5
Belgium	25 francs	0.254	899	4	72	0
Brazil	20 millreis............	0.575	916.5	10	89	4
Central America	2 escudos.............	0.209	853.5	3	68	8
Do	4 reals	0.027	875	0	48	8
Chili...........	10 pesos (dollars)......	0.492	898	9	13	6
Colombia and S. America generally...	Old doubloon*	0.867	870	15	50	3
Denmark	Old 10 thaler.........	0.427	895	7	90	0
Egypt	Bedidlik (100 piasters).	0.275	875	4	97	4
England	Pound or sov'gn† (new)	0.256.8	916.5	4	86	5
Do	Pound average (worn).	0.256.3	916.5	4	85	6

* The *doubloon* (doblon, or more properly *onza*, though not really an ounce Spanish) is now generally discontinued. These figures answer as well for the doubloon of Peru, Chili, Bolivia, etc., and therefore this item stands for all. Popayan pieces were rather inferior.

† The sovereigns coined at Melbourne and Sydney, in Australia, and distinguished only by the mint marks M and S, are the same as those of the London mint. Sovereigns generally are up to the legal fineness, 916$\frac{2}{3}$ (or 22 carats).

Country.	Denomination.	Weight.	Fineness.	Value in U. S. gold coin.		
		Ounces.	*1000ths.*	*Dls.*	*cts.*	*ms.*
France..........	20 franc (no new issues)	0.207	899	3	84	7
Germany.......	Old 10 thaler (Prussian)	0.427	903	7	97	1
Greece..........	20 drachmas..........	0.185	900	3	44	2
India (British)..	Mohur, or 15 rupees*..	0.375	916.5	7	10	5
Italy	20 lire (francs)........	0.207	899	3	84	7
Japan	Cobang (obsolete)......	0.289	572	3	57	6
Do	New 20 yen...........	1.072	900	19	94	4
Mexico	Old doubloon (average)	0.867	870	15	59	3
Do	20 pesos (empire)......	1.086	875	19	64	3
Do	20 pesos (republic), new	1.081	873	19	51	5
Netherlands.....	10 guilders...........	0.215	899	3	99	7
New Granada ..	10 pesos (dollars)......	0.525	891.5	9	67	5
Peru...........	20 soles..............	1.055	899	19	21	3
Portugal.......	Coroa (crown).........	0.308	912	5	80	7
Russia.........	5 roubles.............	0.210	916	3	97	6
Spain..........	100 reals	0.268	896	4	96	4
Do	80 reals..............	0.215	869.5	3	86	4
Do	10 escudos...........	0.270.8	896	5	01	5
Sweden	Ducat................	0.111	975	2	23	7
Do	Carolin (10 francs).....	0.104	900	1	93	5
Tunis..........	25 piasters...........	0.161	900	2	99	5
Turkey	100 piasters...........	0.231	915	4	37	0

SILVER COINS.

Country.	Denomination.	Weight.	Fineness.	Value in subsidiary silver coin.		
		Ounces.	*1000ths.*	*Dls.*	*cts.*	*ms.*
Austria	Old rix dollar.........	0.902	833	1	00	2
Do	Old scudo (crown)	0.836	902	1	00	5
Do	Florin, before 1858....	0.451	833	0	50	1
Do	New florin	0.397	900	0	47	6
Do	New Union dollar.....	0.596	900	0	71	5
Do	Maria Theresa dol.,1780	0.895	838	1	00	0
Belgium	5 francs..............	0.803	897	0	96	0
Do	2 francs..............	0.320	835	0	35	6
Bolivia	New dollar...........	0.801	900	0	96	1
Brazil	Double millreis	0.820	918.5	1	00	4
Canada	20 cents..............	0.150	925	0	18	5
Do	25 cents..............	0.187.5	925	0	23	1
Central America	Dollar................	0.866	850	0	98	1
Chili...........	Old dollar	0.864	908	1	04	6

* The last coinage of *mohurs* was in 1862.

Country.	Denomination.	Weight.	Fineness.	Value in subsidiary silver coin.		
		Ounces.	*1000ths.*	*Dls.*	*cts.*	*ms.*
Chili	New dollar	0.801	900.5	0	96	2
China	Dollar (English mint)	0.866	901	1	04	0
Do	10 cents	0.087	901	0	10	5
Denmark	2 rigsdaler	0.927	877	1	08	4
Egypt	Piaster (new)	0.040	755	0	04	0
England	Shilling (new)	0.182.5	924.5	0	22	5
Do	Shilling (average)	0.178	925	0	21	9
France	5 franc (average)	0.800	900	0	96	0
Do	2 franc	0.320	835	0	35	6
N. Germ'n States	Thaler (before 1857)	0.712	750	0	71	2
Do Do	Thaler (new)	0.595	900	0	71	4
S. German States	Florin	0.340	900	0	40	8
German Empire	5 marks (new)	0.804	900	0	96	5
Greece	5 drachmas	0.719	900	0	86	3
Hindostan	Rupee	0.374	916.5	0	45	7
Italy	5 lire	0.800	900	0	96	0
Do	Lira	0.160	835	0	17	8
Japan	Itzebu, no longer coined	0.279	890	0	33	1
Do	1 yen	0.866.7	900	1	04	0
Do	50 sen	0.402	800	0	42	8
Mexico	Dollar (average)	0.866	901	1	04	0
Do	Peso of Maximilian	0.861	902.5	1	03	6
Netherlands	2½ guilders	0.804	944	1	01	2
Norway	Specie daler	0.927	877	1	08	4
New Grenada	Dollar of 1857	0.803	896	0	96	0
Peru	Old dollar	0.866	901	1	04	3
Do	Dollar of 1858	0.766	909	0	92	8
Do	Half dollar of 1836–'38	0.433	650	0	37	5
Do	Sol	0.802	900	0	96	0
Portugal	500 reis	0.400	912	0	48	6
Romania	2 lei (francs), new	0.322	835	0	35	8
Russia	Rouble	0.667	875	0	77	8
Spain	5 pesetas (dollar)	0.800	900	0	96	0
Do	Peseta (pistareen)	0.160	835	0	17	8
Sweden	Ricksdaler	0.273	750	0	27	3
Switzerland	2 francs	0.320	835	0	35	6
Tunis	5 piasters	0.511	898.5	0	61	2
Turkey	20 piasters	0.770	830	0	85	2

WM. A. RICHARDSON, *Secretary of the Treasury.*

TABLE No. 6.

Showing the values in United States money of the pure gold or silver representing, respectively, the monetary units and standard coins of foreign countries, January 1, 1876.

TREASURY DEPARTMENT, WASHINGTON, D. C., *January 1, 1876.*

The estimate of values contained in the following table has been made by the Director of the Mint, and is hereby proclaimed in compliance with the provisions of law.

Country.	Monetary Unit.	Standard.	Value in U. S. Money.	Standard Coins.
Austria	Florin	Silver	.45.3	Florin.
Belgium	Franc	Gold and silver	.19.3	5, 10 and 20 francs.
Bolivia	Dollar	Gold and silver	.96.5	Escudo, ½ bolivar and bolivar.
Brazil	Millreis of 1,000 reis	Gold	.54.5	None.
Brit. Possessions in N. America	Dollar	Gold	$1.00	
Bogota	Peso	Gold	.96.5	
Central America	Dollar	Silver	.91.8	Dollar.
Chili	Peso	Gold	.91.2	Condor, doubloon and escudo.
Denmark	Crown	Gold	.26.8	10 and 20 crowns.
Ecuador	Dollar	Silver	.91.8	Dollar.
Egypt	Pound of 100 piasters	Gold	4.97.4	5, 10, 25 and 50 piasters.
France	Franc	Gold and silver	.19.3	5, 10 and 20 francs.
Great Britain	Pound sterling	Gold	4.86.6½	½ sovereign and sovereign.
Greece	Drachma	Gold and silver	.19.3	5, 10, 20, 50 and 100 drachmas.
German Empire	Mark	Gold	.23.8	5, 10 and 20 marks.
Japan	Yen	Gold	.99.7	1, 2, 5, 10 and 20 yen.
India	Rupee of 16 annas	Silver	.43.6	
Italy	Lira	Gold and silver	.19.3	5, 10, 20, 50 and 100 lire.
Liberia	Dollar	Gold	1.00	
Mexico	Dollar	Silver	.99.8	Peso or dollar, 5, 10, 25 and 50 centavo.
Netherlands	Florin	Gold and silver	.38.5	Florin; 10 guldens, gold ($4.01.9).
Norway	Crown	Gold	.26.8	10 and 20 crowns.
Peru	Dollar	Silver	.91.8	
Portugal	Millreis of 1,000 reis	Gold	1.08	2, 5 and 10 millreis.
Russia	Rouble of 100 copecks	Silver	.73.4	¼, ½ and 1 rouble.
Sandwich Islands	Dollar	Gold	1.00	
Spain	Peseta of 100 centimes	Gold and silver	.19.3	5, 10, 20, 50 and 100 pesetas.
Sweden	Crown	Gold	.26.8	10 and 20 crowns.
Switzerland	Franc	Gold and silver	.19.3	5, 10 and 20 francs.
Tripoli	Mahbub of 20 piasters	Silver	.82.9	
Tunis	Piaster of 16 caroubs	Silver	.11.8	
Turkey	Piaster	Gold	.04.3	25, 50, 100, 250 and 500 piasters.
United States of Columbia	Peso	Silver	.91.8	

B. H. BRISTOW, *Secretary of the Treasury.*

TABLE No. 7.—PRICES OF A DOZEN ARTICLES FROM 1821 TO 1874.

In the New York market, on the first day of January in each year.

Year.	Mess Beef, ℔ bbl.	Mess Pork, ℔ bbl.	Cod Fish, ℔ quintal.	S'fine Flour, ℔ bbl.	Southern Y Corn, ℔ bu.	Rice, ℔ 100 lbs.	St. D. Coffee, ℔ lb.	Tea, ℔ lb.	Mus. Sugar, 100 lbs.	B. A. D. salted Hides, ℔ lb.	N. O. mid. f'r Cotton, ℔ lb.	Smyrna wash'd Wool, ℔ lb.
1821	$8 62	$13 12	$2 67	$4 12	$0 40	$3 12	$0 22½	$0 53	$8 55	$0 12½	$0 17¾	$0 18
1822	7 75	13 00	3 25	7 25	65	3 00	20¼	50	6 25	18	17½	14
1823	8 00	12 50	2 75	7 75	72	2 87	18¼	52	6 12	17	14¼	13
1824	8 12	11 87	2 56	6 81	50	3 87	13¾	62	8 63	17¾	17¼	13
1825	9 25	13 00	2 87	5 75	48	3 31	10⅝	55	8 75	16½	17	12
1826	9 50	12 25	1 94	5 87	70	3 37	12	61	9 37	14¼	18	12
1827	9 12	13 25	2 35	5 87	64	3 75	9⅛	49	7 10	15¼	14	11
1828	9 87	14 12	2 87	6 12	46	3 19	8	47	9 62	16¾	12¾	12
1829	10 25	13 25	2 25	9 00	55	3 75	7	49	7 05	12⅛	12⅝	7
1830	9 12	11 75	2 05	5 37	47	2 87	6½	42	7 80	14¾	13⅛	12
1831	8 50	12 25	2 37	5 75	64	2 62	7½	43	5 25	16¼	13	24
1832	10 25	13 75	2 75	6 87	85	3 12	11	68	5 15	15	10¾	25
1833	10 62	14 37	2 56	6 25	73	3 50	12	68	7 25	13¾	12½	17
1834	10 50	12 00	2 25	5 75	61	3 00	12⅛	60	5 00	13⅝	15¼	23
1835	10 75	15 50	2 12	5 25	75	3 25	10	37	6 37	14½	19¼	30
1836	10 75	19 00	2 57	7 75	1 00	3 25	11⅛	47	6 95	13¼	18¼	17
1837	14 50	26 75	3 12	11 25	1 06	3 12	11½	42	7 07	12	19½	21
1838	14 25	20 50	3 19	9 50	88	4 12	8½	45	7 25	14	12	20
1839	16 00	23 50	3 30	8 69	92	4 12	9⅝	38	5 56	15¾	16	20
1840	12 58	14 73	2 37	6 18	70	3 62	10	57	6 05	14¾	11¾	20
1841	10 18	13 21	2 62	5 50	53	3 62	9¾	67	5 87	16¼	10⅛	20
1842	8 25	9 97	2 00	6 37	62	3 25	8⅛	56	3 75	14⅞	10	20
1843	6 78	9 41	1 75	4 50	48	2 87	5¾	47	3 90	12¼	7½	20
1844	7 00	10 25	2 50	4 75	53	2 50	5⅝	47	3 95	12⅛	9⅝	21
1845	7 25	9 25	2 37	4 75	49	3 25	5⅝	55	4 75	11¾	6¼	17
1846	8 40	13 25	2 62	5 75	76	4 75	6⅝	62	6 40	12	8⅛	17
1847	9 00	10 31	3 12	5 50	72	4 00	6⅝	58	7 30	11	11¼	14
1848	8 62	11 75	3 56	6 50	76	3 87	6¼	58	4 50	10¼	9¼	16
1849	11 00	13 75	2 12	5 50	64	3 25	5½	55	4 00	9	7⅛	13
1850	10 00	10 37	2 37	5 25	60	3 25	10⅛	55	5 05	10¾	12⅝	14
1851	10 00	12 25	2 62	5 25	68	3 62	10⅝	38	5 15	14	15	19
1852	10 00	14 75	2 62	4 75	64	3 50	8⅝	38	4 55	11½	9⅞	18
1853	13 25	20 50	3 50	6 25	71	4 62	8¼	38	4 75	14½	11⅝	21
1854	14 25	16 25	3 00	7 62	78	4 50	11¼	38	4 50	21	11⅝	23
1855	15 25	16 00	2 75	9 62	1 05	5 62	9¼	35	5 35	19	10⅝	20
1856	14 25	18 75	3 75	9 50	95	5 37	10¾	35	7 50	26	14⅛	20
1857	15 25	20 50	3 25	7 37	78	4 50	10¾	35	9 75	31	11⅝	21
1858	14 50	15 62	3 25	5 50	70	3 75	9½	37	5 87	19	10	26
1859	11 25	19 00	3 87	4 62	85	3 50	9½	35	7 12	25	12¾	22
1860	10 75	16 25	3 31	5 25	93	3 87	11	36	6 87	24	11½	28
1861	9 00	16 25	2 87	5 50	80	3 81	11	37	5 19	19¼	13¾	22
1862	12 00	12 25	2 91	5 47	72	7 12	15¼	51	5 50	19½	39	35
1863	12 50	11 40	3 50	5 87	90	7 25	27	67	6 25	24½	69	36
1864	13 25	19 37	6 12	6 30	1 31	6 62	26	70	9 00	28½	81	32
1865	20 50	40 00	8 50	9 72	1 94	10 75	38	72	14 50	33	1 18	57
1866	19 00	30 75	6 50	7 60	1 05	5 75	24	61	8 25	17¾	54	30
1867	13 50	20 50	5 75	9 42	1 18	7 18	18	56	6 50	22¾	38	21
1868	15 00	21 20	4 50	8 70	1 40	9 50	16	45	8 37	23	16¼	22
1869	14 00	27 62	6 25	5 70	1 02	8 87	14	62	7 87	27	27	26
1870	14 00	29 75	6 12	4 92	1 08	6 87	12	40	7 75	25	26½	21
1871	12 50	20 90	6 00	5 50	85	6 62	10¼	39	7 50	23	15¼	23
1872	10 00	14 00	4 12	6 00	81	8 41	15¼	29	7 25	26	21⅛	33
1873	11 00	13 12	4 87	5 95	66	8 00	16	34	7 00	31½	20½	25
1874	10 37	16 50	3 62	5 95	85	8 00	24¼	30	4 94	29¾	16½	18
Av.	$11 30	$16 26	$3 35	$6 48	$0 77	$4 61	$0 12½	$0 49	$6 60	$0 18	$0 18½	$0 21

TABLE No. 8.—TABLE OF PRICES FOR FIFTY YEARS.

The following table was prepared by Hon. Jeremiah M. Rusk, of Wisconsin, and used as part of his argument in a speech on the Tariff delivered in Congress August 11, 1876:

Statement of wholesale prices of provisions and other staple goods in the New York market on the 1st day of January in each year from 1825 to 1876, inclusive.

(The quotations are for first qualities of goods, excepting cotton middlings.)

Year.	Wheat, per bushel.	Flour, per barrel.	Corn, per bushel.	Corn meal, per barrel.	Coal, per chaldron.	Cotton middlings, per pound.	Iron, pig, per ton.	Lead, pig, per hundred pounds.	Leather, sole, per p'nd.	Molasses, New Orleans, per gallon.	Molasses, foreign, per gallon.	Pork, mess, per barrel.	Beef, mess, per barrel.	Hams, smoked, per p'd.	Lard, per pound.	Butter, per pound.	Cheese, per pound.	Rice, per hundred p'ds.	Salt, per bushel.	Sugar, New Orleans, per pound.	Sugar, foreign, per p'd.	Wool, per pound.
									Cts.		Cts.			Cts.	Cts.	Cts.	Cts.		Cts.	Cts.	Cts.	Cts.
1825..	$1 00	$5 12	$0 42	$2 50	$9 00	$0 13	$35 00	$7 50	22	$0 30	24	$13 25	$7 75	8	9	8	5	$3 00	48	8	8	30
1826..	85	5 12	73	3 75	12 00	13	60 00	7 00	21	33	26	11 50	8 00	9	7	15	6	2 00	50	8	9	30
1827..	1 00	5 37	67	3 50	12 00	9	50 00	6 00	18	33	27	11 75	8 75	10	9	15	6	3 50	50	7	8	20
1828..	1 04	5 37	56	3 00	11 00	8	50 00	6 00	18	34	30	14 00	8 50	9	8	14	6	3 00	53	7	9	20
1829..	1 75	8 00	58	3 25	11 00	9	50 00	5 00	18	31	25	12 00	8 75	9	5	13	4	3 50	47	7	8	18
1830..	1 03	4 87	52	2 75	12 00	9	40 00	3 00	18	28	20	11 00	8 00	9	5	12	5	2 50	45	7	7	18
1831..	1 25	5 75	54	3 25	7 00	9	40 00	3 00	19	33	26	13 50	8 50	10	8	12	5	2 50	42	5	6	20
1832..	1 25	6 37	75	3 50	10 00	7	40 00	5 00	20	26	26	13 00	9 00	9	9	15	5	3 25	45	5	5	25
1833..	1 28	6 00	75	3 75	8 50	10	40 00	6 00	17	32	25	12 50	8 50	9	8	14	6	3 25	45	7	6	30
1834..	1 05	5 37	55	3 62	5 50	10	38 00	5 00	16	30	25	14 00	8 50	9	9	13	7	2 25	38	7	7	30
1835..	1 04	5 00	73	3 62	5 50	15	38 00	5 00	15	27	21	13 50	8 75	8	7	14	6	3 00	32	6	7	25
1836..	1 37	7 25	90	4 75	7 00	14	38 00	6 00	14	32	28	18 00	9 50	9	11	22	7	3 00	34	9	8	35
1837..	1 55	10 00	1 00	4 75	10 00	15	60 00	7 00	18	42	40	23 00	12 00	13	13	20	8	3 50	40	7	6	40
1838..	1 85	8 62	85	4 50	8 50	11	50 00	......	16	40	35	21 50	14 00	10	10	18	7	3 50	35	6	6	28

1839..	1 37	8 75	90	3 87	7 50	14	37 50	......	23	32	26	23 00	15 75	14	13	22	8	4 00	35	6	7	37
1840..	1 00	5 87	57	3 87	6 50	9	37 50	......	17	26	22	14 00	12 00	....	7	18	8	2 75	32	5	5	30
1841..	1 00	4 94	50	2 87	7 00	9	35 00	......	22	27	20	13 00	9 75	....	8	9	6	3 18	30	5	5	25
1842..	1 25	6 00	66	3 00	8 00	8	34 00	4 00	18	25	16	9 00	7 50	....	5	10	6	2 75	...	5	4	18
1843..	87	4 69	57	2 56	5 00	7	27 00	......	16	19	16	8 25	6 00	....	6	9	5	2 50	28	3	4	18
1844..	1 00	4 62	43	2 56	5 00	8	31 00	......	16	29	21	10 00	6 12	....	5	8	4	2 25	...	6	6	25
1845..	1 00	4 68	56	2 50	5 00	5	30 00	3 00	14	24	25	9 25	5 50	5	6	9	5	2 87	24	3	5	28
1846..	1 27	5 87	73	4 00	5 00	6	36 00	4 75	13	23	20	13 25	8 00	10	5	14	6	4 25	28	5	6	26
1847..	1 00	5 50	78	3 87	6 00	10	33 00	4 37	11	34	15	10 25	8 25	6	6	13	6	3 25	25	6	6	22
1848..	1 20	6 37	76	3 25	5 50	7	35 00	4 25	14	28	23	11 00	8 25	9	6	14	6	3 00	26	4	4	28
1849..	1 20	5 87	70	2 93	7 00	6	25 00	4 25	13	28	18	14 12	10 25	9	7	15	6	2 87	21	4	4	25
1850..	1 24	5 37	60	2 93	5 50	11	23 00	4 25	15	26	21	11 75	8 50	10	6	15	5	2 25	23	4	4	30
1851..	1 18	5 06	64	2 93	6 50	13	22 00	4 80	14	29	22	12 12	8 75	8	7	16	5	3 00	22	5	4	33
1852..	1 03	5 00	70	3 00	5 00	8	19 50	4 42	12	27	18	14 62	8 25	....	9	15	6	2 75	20	4	4	30
1853..	1 30	5 75	68	3 81	5 00	9	30 00	6 00	17	29	20	19 50	9 50	....	12	20	8	3 75	27	4	4	38
1854..	2 00	7 87	82	3 75	6 50	10	37 50	6 00	23	27	23	13 37	8 50	....	10	15	8	4 12	45	4	4	38
1855..	2 35	9 12	1 00	4 25	7 00	7	27 50	6 25	19	24	22	12 62	8 25	....	10	20	10	2 50	50	4	4	24
1856..	2 12	8 25	92	4 12	5 90	9	32 00	7 00	24	48	42	17 25	10 50	....	12	23	9	4 25	27	8	7	30
1857..	1 70	6 10	73	3 25	6 50	13	30 00	6 75	31	80	38	19 37	10 50	....	12	20	9	3 27	22	9	8	33
1858..	1 35	4 20	58	3 20	5 00	9	26 00	5 00	22	34	18	15 50	9 00	....	8	14	6	2 75	16	5	5	27
1859..	1 35	4 20	76	3 40	5 25	11	25 00	5 55	25	36	19	17 25	7 75	....	11	16	8	3 00	17	6	5	36
1860..	1 40	5 25	88	3 75	5 50	11	24 00	5 70	21	53	23	16 12	5 00	....	10	15	9	3 50	19	7	6	38
1861..	1 40	5 20	72	3 10	5 50	12	20 00	5 25	20	32	15	16 00	5 75	....	10	14	9	3 25	17	4	4	30
1862..	1 34	5 40	66	3 00	4 25	36	21 00	7 00	20	50	20	12 00	5 00	....	8	13	5	7 37	20	8	6	47
1863..	1 58	5 85	70	3 90	8 50	66	23 00	8 00	29	50	24	14 00	7 00	....	9	18	10	3 75	30	8	8	62
1864..	1 53	8 00	1 27	5 30	8 75	81	42 00	10 50	31	50	38	19 75	5 80	....	12	27	12	8 50	47	....	13	80
1865..	2 55	10 75	1 86	7 75	9 50	1 20	38 00	14 75	38	1 35	53	36 00	20 00	....	20	46	15	12 00	70	....	24	95
1866..	2 30	8 25	90	4 25	13 00	51	50 00	9 75	35	1 00	35	27 75	11 00	....	15	44	17	12 60	45	....	11	70
1867..	3 05	11 40	1 15	5 00	8 00	35	49 00	6 75	32	65	40	20 00	12 00	....	12	38	14	9 00	55	....	9	50
1868..	2 80	10 75	1 38	6 15	6 50	15	38 00	6 45	27	70	37	20 90	12 00	....	12	40	11	8 50	48	....	11	55
1869..	2 00	7 00	1 06	4 25	9 00	26	40 00	6 50	28	60	35	26 50	9 00	...	16	43	15	8 00	48	....	14	60
1870..	1 35	5 60	1 09	4 75	7 50	26	38 00	6 25	30	70	30	29 50	8 00	....	16	39	15	6 75	43	....	10	55
1871..	1 47	6 25	76	4 00	6 50	15	31 00	6 30	29	65	20	20 00	10 00	....	12	25	10	6 75	45	...	9	53
1872..	1 68	8 25	76	3 65	4 50	21	36 00	5 90	28	48	23	14 00	8 00	....	9	25	9	8 25	45	....	9	60
1873..	1 85	9 50	60	3 28	5 00	21	45 00	6 50	28	60	32	14 75	11 00	....	8	25	14	7 50	35	....	8	65
1874..	1 65	6 80	78	4 00	5 25	18	35 00	6 87	27	71	40	14 50	10 00	....	8	24	10	7 50	30	....	8	55
1875..	1 17	5 25	93	4 60	6 00	15	26 00	6 15	28	......	37	20 00	12 00	11	14	40	13	8 00	28	....	8	50
1876..	1 26	5 40	74	3 65	6 50	14	23 00	6 00	27	.....	...	21 00	12 50	13	13	36	14	7 00	30	....	....	52

Where the leaders (....) are inserted no quotations were given in the New York markets.

POPULATION OF THE GLOBE.

THE population of various countries of the globe, but particularly of the countries of Europe, is a question that is constantly coming up in connection with the amounts of the precious metals available for use as money. In regard to Asia, containing more than half the entire population of the world, there is even yet comparatively little definite information, but on the whole the knowledge of the distribution of the world's inhabitants has been greatly improved in the last quarter of a century. Twenty-five years ago the commonly accepted estimate was one thousand millions, but a recent estimate by Dr. Wagner (of which a synopsis was printed in the *Bankers' Magazine* for May, 1875,) places the estimate for the total at 1,391,032,000. The population of each of the countries in the period from 1874 to 1876 may be stated as in the following table, in which I have also given the populations of some of the most important countries at various previous dates to show the increase — though it is possible that a part of the apparent increase may be due to more accurate enumeration.

EUROPE.

	Prior to 1874.	1873–5.
Russian Empire, in Europe and Asia	65,200,000 (1855)	87,700,000 (1875)
German Empire	....	41,060,695
France	35,780,000 (1851)	36,102,921
Austria-Hungary	....	35,912,755
Great Britain and Ireland, including Gibraltar, Malta and Heligoland	29,293,300 (1861)	31,977,128
Italy, Monaco and San Marino	21,728,500 (1861)	26,811,584
Spain	15,464,340 (1857)	16,551,647

Turkey, including Servia, Romania and Montenegro	....	15,737,019
Belgium	4,671,187 (1861)	5,087,105
Portugal and Azores	....	4,249,503
Sweden	....	4,250,402
Netherlands	....	3,674,402
Switzerland	....	2,669,147
Denmark, with the islands of Iceland and Faroe	....	1,864,496
Norway	....	1,741,621
Greece	....	1,457,849
Luxemburg	....	197,528
Andorra	....	12,000
Population of Europe and European islands, and Russia in Asia......		316,500,000

NORTH AMERICA.

		1874-6.
Greenland	....	10,500
Canada	....	4,000,000 (1875)
Newfoundland	....	146,536
St. Pierre and Miquelon.......	....	4,383
United States and Alaska	23,191,876 (1850)	42,000,000 (1875)
Mexico (census 1869)..........	....	9,000,000 (1875)
Bermudas	....	12,686
Total North America		56,169,000

SOUTH AMERICA.

Venezuela	....	1,400,000
States of Colombia	....	2,774,000
Guiana	....	282,300
Brazil	7,677,800 (1850)	10,000,000
Ecuador	....	1,300,000
Peru	....	4,500,000
Chili	....	2,043,000
Argentine Republic...........	....	1,812,500
Uruguay....................	....	400,000
Patagonia and Fireland.......	....	24,000
Paraguay....................	....	1,000,000
Falkland Islands	....	800
Total of South America		25,500,000

CENTRAL AMERICA.

Guatemala..................................	1,194,000
Honduras..................................	351,800
British Honduras..........................	24,700
San Salvador	600,000
Nicaragua	250,000
Costa Rica	165,000
Panama	236,000
Total of Central America........................	2,891,500

WEST INDIES.

Spanish possessions, Havana, 202,488 (census 1867)....	2,068,870
British possessions	1,042,585
French possessions	306,244
Dutch possessions	35,482
Danish possessions	37,821
Swedish possessions	2,898
Hayti	572,000
San Domingo	136,500
Total of West Indies	4,202,400

ASIA (EXCLUSIVE OF RUSSIA).

	1874-6.
Turkey in Asia	13,686,315
Arabia	3,700,000
Persia	5,000,000
Toorkistan, Toorkomania, Khokand, Bokhara and Chiva	4,556,000
Afghanistan, with Beluchistan and Kalfiristan	5,300,000
China	425,392,937
Japan	33,110,503
Hindoostan, with British Possessions and Ceylon	240,112,001
Burmah, Siam and Cochin-China	25,935,082
East India Islands	30,465,030
Total of Asia and Asiatic islands	787,200,000

AUSTRALIA AND POLYNESIA.

Australian Continent	1,674,500
Polynesian Islands	2,763,500
Population of Australia, etc	4,438,000

AFRICA.

Egypt	8,442,000
Morocco	6,000,000
Tunis	2,000,000
Algiers	2,414,000
Tripoli, Barka and Fezan	1,150,000
Sahara	3,700,000
Abyssinia	3,000,000
Samauli	8,000,000
Galla-country and country east of White Nile	15,058,000
Mohammedan States of Central Soudan	38,800,000
West Soudan, Upper Guinea and Equatorial Region...	89,100,000
South Africa	20,285,000
Islands	5,351,000
Population of Africa	203,300,000

www.ingramcontent.com/pod-product-compliance
Lightning Source LLC
Chambersburg PA
CBHW032116230426
43672CB00009B/1755
* 9 7 8 3 7 4 4 7 4 1 4 2 2 *